KANTIAN CONSEQUENTIALISM

Kantian Consequentialism

David Cummiskey

New York   Oxford
OXFORD UNIVERSITY PRESS
1996

Oxford University Press

Oxford   New York
Athens   Auckland   Bangkok   Bombay
Calcutta   Cape Town   Dar es Salaam   Delhi
Florence   Hong Kong   Istanbul   Karachi
Kuala Lumpur   Madras   Madrid   Melbourne
Mexico City   Nairobi   Paris   Singapore
Taipei   Tokyo   Toronto

and associated companies in
Berlin   Ibadan

Published by Oxford University Press, Inc.
198 Madison Avenue, New York, New York 10016

Oxford is a registered trademark of Oxford University Press

Library of Congress Cataloging-in-Publication Data
Cummiskey, David.
Kantian consequentialism / David Cummiskey.
p.   cm.
Includes bibliographical references and index.
ISBN 0-19-509453-0
1. Consequentialism. 2. Kant, Immanuel, 1724–1804—Ethics.
I. Title.
BJ1031.C69   1996
171'.5—dc20   95-11811

1 3 5 7 9 8 6 4 2

Printed in the United States of America
on acid-free paper.

For
Sarah, Luke, and Owen

PREFACE

When I started this project, I shared the common belief that Kantian ethics stands in stark opposition to all forms of consequentialism. My initial goal was to clearly articulate Kant's objection to utilitarianism, and to consequentialism in general. In pursuing this goal, I have found many interesting arguments and insights in Kant's texts, but consequentialism always seemed stubbornly compatible and consistent with Kant's main argument. Over time, and with the help of many others, I have become convinced that although Kant himself was not a consequentialist, Kant's main argument is consistent with consequentialism and provides a compelling justification for a new form of Kantian consequentialism.

In graduate school at the University of Michigan, when I first began working on these issues, I learned a tremendous amount from my teachers, Stephen Darwall, Allan Gibbard, Peter Railton, and, in political science, Joel Schwartz. I took my first Kant seminar, which focused on Kant's political theory and philosophy of history, with Joel. I also studied Rousseau with Joel and, through his example, learned of the pleasures and rewards of a close study of historical texts. Peter is a wonderful teacher. As his student and teaching assistant, I have learned much about Mill, Rawls, Nozick, and others who developed theories of justice. I took my first normative ethics class from Allan, and he first made me realize how difficult it is to articulate, in a convincing manner, the Kantian objection to consequentialism. Steve, on the other hand, helped me to see the point and importance of the Kantian approach to the foundation of ethics. He has also provided a steady source of support and encouragement. In different ways, each has shaped the way I think about the central issues of moral theory.

While writing this book, I have discussed these issues and received comments from many people. I would like to thank Judith Baker, Simon Blackburn, Hilary Bok, Richard Dean, Laura Ekstrom, Stephen Engstrom, Ralph Geiger, Paul Hurley, Robert Johnson, Joel Kidder, David Kolb, Don Loeb, Thomas McCarty, Jay Rosenberg, Geoffrey Sayre-McCord, Dion Scott-Kakures, Ed Sherline, Larry Simon, Walter Sinnott-Armstrong, John Taylor, Larry Temkin, and Tom Tracy for their helpful comments and questions. I would also like to thank Barbara Herman, Christine Korsgaard, Mark Okrent, Ken Westphal, and Susan Wolf for their comments on the first draft of the manuscript, and Charlotte Witt for her comments on the final draft.

Christine Korsgaard and Thomas Hill have had a special influence on my interpretation of Kantian ethics. Chris's criticism of a paper of mine on Kant and consequentialism led me to approach some of the central issues in this book in a new and more promising way. I have also learned a great deal from her remarkably clear reconstructions of Kant's arguments. While I was writing this book, I visited the University of North Carolina at Chapel Hill for a semester. As a result, I have benefited a great deal from many long and wonderful discussions with Tom about consequentialism and Kantian ethics. In addition, Tom's papers on Kant have provided much insight into the subtlety and richness of Kant's moral theory. Since I agree with both Chris and Tom about so many issues, their work has especially helped me identify the issues that separate Kantian deontology from Kantian consequentialism. Although they have not yet, they may someday turn me into a *real* Kantian.

Special thanks go to Andrews Reath, Shelly Kagan, and Sarah Conly. Andy Reath has read many drafts of chapters and two drafts of the whole manuscript. Some of the most central arguments have been shaped by his suggestions and objections, and he has helped clarify and revise countless smaller points. This book has been greatly improved by Andy's efforts.

Shelly Kagan read an early draft of the book and responded with a dazzling array of suggestions and objections. I have spent many months working through his detailed commentary and rewriting the book from cover to cover as a result. In addition, his professional support and enthusiastic encouragement have been invaluable. Thank you, Shelly.

Sarah Conly has read every draft of every chapter. In addition to her countless objections to specific points and her general skepticism about Kantian ethics, she has steadily insisted that I present my thesis and argument more clearly and simply. Without her companionship, encouragement, and constant assistance, I simply never would have written this book.

For financial support, I would like to thank Bates College; the Woodrow Wilson National Fellowship Foundation for a Charlotte W. Newcombe Fellowship during 1985–86, when I did much of the initial research for this project and wrote my dissertation on utilitarianism and autonomy; and the National Endowment for the Humanities for fellowship support during 1991–92, when I wrote the first draft of this book.

Two of my articles have been reworked into the book: "Kantian Consequentialism," *Ethics* 100, no. 3, April 1990: 586–615 (Copyright © 1990 by The University of Chicago) and "Consequentialism, Egoism, and the Moral Law,"

Philosophical Studies 57, Fall 1989: 111–34 (Copyright © 1989 by Kluwer Academic Publishers). I gratefully acknowledge the permission of the publishers to use material from these pieces.

Lewiston, Maine   D. C.
June 1995

CONTENTS

ABBREVIATIONS FOR KANT'S WORKS

CPrR   *Critique of Practical Reason* (1788), translated by Lewis White Beck. Bobbs Merrill, 1965.

GMM   *Grounding for the Metaphysics of Morals* (1785), translated by James W. Ellington. Hackett, 1983.

LE   *Lectures on Ethics* (1775–80), translated by Louis Infield. Harper & Row, 1963. Reprinted by Hackett, 1980.

MM   *The Metaphysics of Morals* (1798), translated by Mary Gregor. Cambridge University Press, 1991.

PPE   *Perpetual Peace and Other Essays* (1784–95), translated by Ted Humphrey. Hackett, 1983.

REL   *Religion within the Limits of Reason Alone* (1792), translated by Green Hudson. Harper & Row, 1960.

SRL   "On the Supposed Right to Lie from Altruistic Motives," in *Immanuel Kant: Critique of Pure Reason and Other Writings in Moral Philosophy*, edited by L. Beck. Garland, 1976.

Page number citations refer to the Prussian Academy edition. See *Kant's gesammelte Schriften*, Preussische Academie der Wissenschaften, 1900–1942.

KANTIAN CONSEQUENTIALISM

1

INTRODUCTION

The central problem for normative ethics is the conflict between two extremely reasonable beliefs: that we should do what is necessary to bring about the best possible consequences and that we should respect the rights of the individual. The apex and epitome of rights theory is Kantianism. Kantians and non-Kantians alike assume that Kantianism, with its resonant insistence on the dignity of the individual, and consequentialism, with its plausible claim that we should do as much good as possible, are incompatible. In fact, however, Kant's theory and consequentialism are compatible. Indeed, Kantian moral theory, properly understood, generates an extremely compelling consequentialist normative theory. I call this theory "Kantian consequentialism."

Kant's moral theory is primarily a theory about the justification of normative principles and the nature of moral motivation (GMM 389–92).[1] Not only are these aspects of Kant's theory consistent with a consequentialist principle of right action; in fact, they entail such a principle. Kantian consequentialism, however, is radically different from other consequentialisms. Indeed, it captures most of the intuitive appeal of both Kantianism and consequentialism. This synthesis is the source of a solution both novel and convincing.

The familiar account of Kant's normative ethics is that Kant explicitly rejected utilitarianism and all forms of consequentialism; that is, roughly, he rejected any moral principle that justifies actions by appealing to the consequences of the actions. Unlike Bentham, Mill, and other utilitarians, Kant defends a theory, it is argued, that is fundamentally duty-based and agent-centered. Certain actions, like sacrificing the innocent, are categorically forbidden—let the consequences be what they may. This familiar account, despite its pedagogical virtues, is philosophically inadequate.

First, as we shall see, Kant does not present an argument against normative consequentialism, nor does he present an explicit argument for deontological or agent-centered constraints on the maximization of the good. These were not his concerns. I will explain this rather bald and jargon-laden claim more fully below. Second, and more controversially, Kant's approach to the justification of normative principles actually generates a complicated form of consequentialism. Third, Kantian consequentialism resolves traditional difficulties many have had with consequentialism and its apparent failure to respect the individual, because Kantian consequentialism insists that respect for persons is more important than maximizing happiness. The Kantian theory of the good has a two-tiered structure. According to this theory, the capacity of rational agency is prior to the value of happiness. For most practical purposes, this means that one cannot sacrifice persons or the conditions necessary for autonomous rational agency simply in order to maximize happiness.

Following John Rawls, we will refer to this concept as a lexical priority of rational nature over happiness.

> A serial or lexical order . . . is an order which requires us to satisfy the first principle in the ordering before we can move on to the second, the second before we consider the third, and so on. A principle does not come into play until those previous to it are fully met or do not apply. A serial [or lexical] ordering avoids, then, having to balance principles at all; those earlier in the ordering have an absolute weight, so to speak, with respect to later ones, and hold without exception. We can regard such a ranking as analogous to a sequence of constrained maximum principles. For we can suppose that any principle in the order is to be maximized subject to the condition that the preceding principles are fully satisfied.[2]

Kantian consequentialism picks up this suggestion; that is, it constrains the maximization of happiness with a principle that requires one to maximally promote the conditions necessary for autonomous rational agency. This version of consequentialism thus provides a justification for the common view—or at least the Kantian view—that preserving, developing, and exercising our rational capacities is more important than maximizing happiness. It is simply not acceptable to sacrifice the life or liberty of some in order to produce a net increase in the overall happiness. As a result, many standard objections to utilitarian consequentialism are avoided in a straightforward and theoretically motivated fashion.

The possibility of Kantian consequentialism undermines the familiar sweeping contrasts between Kantian and consequentialist approaches to ethics. Of course, Kant did not actually defend consequentialism, and some of his particular examples are thoroughly anti-consequentialist. My thesis, however, is not about the position Kant set out to defend: it is about the conclusion that follows from his arguments. Kant's moral theory justifies a form of consequentialism whether he thought so or not. Kantian consequentialism is thus a *rational reconstruction* of the most central and influential aspects of Kant's moral theory.

I.   THE CONSEQUENTIALIST CATEGORICAL IMPERATIVE

Most contemporary Kantians seem to think it is obvious that Kant has provided a justification for deontological or agent-centered constraints—forbidding the killing of one person, for example, to save two others. After all, they argue, a principle that demands respect for the unique value of the individual is the heart and essence of Kant's moral theory. This principle is Kant's formula of humanity (or of the end-in-itself): "Act in such a way that you treat humanity whether in your own person or in the person of any other never simply as a means but always at the same time as an end" (GMM 429). The moral law cannot require us to sacrifice others, or ourselves, because to do so would be to treat persons as a means only: it would not treat all persons as free and equal members of a shared moral community—what Kant calls a "kingdom of ends." Since consequentialism may sometimes require us to harm some persons in order to aid others, it does not treat persons as ends-in-themselves, and it is thus unfit for the supreme principle of morality. In short, consequentialism does not acknowledge the special value of each person because it may allow sacrifices that fail to treat persons as ends-in-themselves. Kantians thus reject consequentialism and appeal to Kant for a justification of a deontological moral theory.

Despite its Kantian tone, and despite widespread philosophical opinion, there is no defensible Kantian basis for this type of objection to consequentialism. Indeed, the central Kantian principle requiring that all persons be treated as ends rather than means only is a principle that generates a consequentialist conclusion. The reason Kant does not draw the consequentialist conclusion involves other aspects of his view that are not nearly as central to his overall theory and that do not follow from his more influential arguments.[3] Indeed, we shall see that a conscientious Kantian moral agent should be a consequentialist and thus may be required to "sacrifice the innocent" in order to promote the good of others. More specifically, one may be required to sacrifice oneself to save others or one may be required to save as many other persons as possible. As with any consequentialist principle, when it comes to acting in the real world, a conscientious agent will be moved more indirectly to promote the good by virtuous character traits and secondary principles or decision-making procedures. The important point for now, however, is that a conscientious Kantian agent should recognize that the basic principle of right action has a consequentialist structure.

Given that so much of Kant's moral theory is clearly non-consequentialist, this contention needs clarification. I am of course aware of the deontological emphasis of some of Kant's specific examples, and, thus, *I am not suggesting that Kant intended to defend consequentialism.* Most obviously, Kant's defense of capital punishment seems to be thoroughly and uncompromisingly retributivist.[4] Kant says that even if a community is going to dissolve and never mutually interact again, "the last murderer remaining in prison must first be executed, so that each has done to him what his deeds deserve and blood guilt does not cling to the people for not having insisted upon this punishment; for otherwise the people can be regarded as collaborators in this public violation of legal justice" (MM 333). Kant also argues that it is impermissible to lie in order to help save a friend from a murderer.[5] These cases, and others, show Kant's uncompromising insistence that some actions are forbidden even if performing the forbidden act may seem likely to cause more overall good.[6]

Kant's discussion of moral problems and his account of moral deliberation clearly is not consequentialist. The point, though, is that Kant's rejection of consequentialism rests primarily on an intuitive reliance on commonsense morality, rather than on any argument he provides. I do not deny that deontological intuitions have their appeal. Surely, however, when contemporary Kantians appeal to Kant in arguments against consequentialism, they do so in the belief that Kant has provided a justification for the specific deontological intuitions. They appeal to the force of Kant's arguments, not just the authority of Kant's intuitions. Whether those intuitions are supported by explicit, or even implicit, argument of truly justificatory force is, thus, a crucial issue. Just as one cannot assume that utilitarianism generates a practically indefeasible right to liberty simply because Mill argues that it does, one cannot take it for granted that Kant's theory generates deontological constraints on the maximization of the good.

Many Kantian deontologists seem to think that the concept of a categorical imperative conflicts with consequentialism. They argue that the unconstrained pursuit of the good can justify all sorts of wicked deeds and that thus, for a consequentialist, there is no action that is categorically forbidden. Clearly there is nothing that Kant is more explicit about than the illegitimacy of doing evil so that good might come of it. If Kantianism *stands for* anything, these Kantian deontologists insist, it is a recognition that the ends do not always justify the means.

Since so many Kantian deontologists consider this to be a conclusive objection, I will briefly sketch an initial response. (The full response, of course, is the main argument of the book.) First, Kantian consequentialism does not require doing anything *wrong* in order to promote the good. If lying, for example, is the best means of promoting the good, then it is not wrong. It is simply question-begging to designate certain actions as always wrong and then to point out that one of the designated actions might promote the good. Second, the objection is confused when it states that, for a consequentialist, no action is categorically required or forbidden. According to Kantian consequentialism, we are categorically required to adopt the set of ends, or of principles, that is most likely to promote the good. The duty to promote the good is a categorical imperative. Finally, as we have just seen, Kantianism does not simply "stand for" deontological constraints. Kantianism is a distinctive and complicated view about the foundation or grounding of morals, and a view that allegedly supports a deontological normative theory. A normative theory that simply stands for normative deontology should be dubbed "groundless deontology."

Nonetheless, this type of objection has considerable appeal. The central normative demand of Kant's ethics is that we treat persons as ends-in-themselves. Kantian deontologists typically redescribe this principle as a principle of "respect for persons." If respect for persons requires anything, they argue, it requires that we do not sacrifice the innocent simply to maximize the good. In chapters 7 and 8, after I have set out the main argument for Kantian consequentialism, I will return to this issue and consider more fully the problem of the sacrifice of the innocent.

II.   FOUNDATIONAL THEORY AND NORMATIVE PRINCIPLES

Many Kantian deontologists will grant that there is much more to Kant's theory than a commitment to deontological constraints and also that Kant's particular examples are inadequately developed and unconvincing, but they will still insist that Kant argues at great length against consequentialism. In addition to his particular examples, the major theme of Kant's ethical writings is nothing less than a rejection of consequentialist *justifications* of normative principles. As we shall see this issue is really quite complex. Clearly, however, when it comes to the justification of normative principles, Kant's views are not consequentialist in any familiar sense.

In order to clarify the Kantian consequentialist position, we need to differentiate two distinct tasks of moral theory. The first task involves determining *what* I am required or permitted to do; what is the basic normative principle that governs conduct? The second task involves the justification of the basic normative principle: *Why* am I required to do that kind of thing? What justifies the rule of action that I have adopted as my practical norm? This second task requires a more meta-ethical investigation of the foundations of normative theory. The distinction between meta-ethics and normative ethics is by no means a sharp distinction, and therefore, this talk of two tasks is somewhat misleading. Indeed, the task of justifying normative principles exhibits the continuum between the levels of ethical theory. Nonetheless, we can roughly distinguish the foundational task of justifying basic normative principles and the normative principles that we believe are justified.

Utilitarian theories are the most familiar consequentialist theories. These theories can be distinguished from Kant's theory both by their accounts of the justification of normative principles and by the normative principle defended. It is commonplace to think of these theories as being consequentialist about both the justification of a normative principle and the principle of right action justified. After all, for classical utilitarians the justificatory enterprise begins with a theory of the good (rather than, say, a theory of obligation or rights). For example, such a foundational consequentialist might be a utilitarian who insists that the most basic ethical consideration is the value of happiness (or individual well-being) and that a rational or justified action is one that maximally promotes this value. If one takes the good to be basic, as, for example, Jeremy Bentham and G. E. Moore claimed to, then one may plausibly be described as a foundational consequentialist. Within such a view, in the final analysis, the goodness of ends justifies the normative principle.

It is worth noting, however, that even Bentham's utilitarian consequentialism is supported by other justificatory considerations: namely, his hedonist moral psychology, his naturalism about the good, and his account of rationality. And similarly, Moore's consequentialism is supported by his non-naturalism, his intuitionism, his method of isolation, and his theory of organic unities. The appeal to the good is importantly basic or "bedrock" for such theorists, but we shall see, the important foundational contrast between Kant and the utilitarians actually involves the more meta-ethical considerations about the nature of justification. Indeed, the emphasis on the priority of the theory of value is really more misleading than it is helpful.[7]

Normative consequentialism, on the other hand, involves the structure of the basic normative principle, not the arguments used to justify the principle. For our purposes, a normative theory has a consequentialist structure if the basic normative principle, whatever its justification, is a requirement to promote the good, and if it does not include basic agent-centered constraints on the maximization of the good. So understood, egoism and act utilitarianism are consequentialist normative theories. Such theories can include a recognition of the significance of secondary principles, decision procedures, character traits, and personal projects that do not directly aim at the good. Since I am not concerned with generating a complete topology, I leave aside the question of how one should classify various rules or indirect versions of consequentialism. Although I will defend maximization, a theory without constraints that does not require the maximization of the good is still consequentialist. The point of interpreting normative consequentialism in this particular way is to emphasize the main difference between Kantian deontologists and typical consequentialists. As we shall see in the next section, the central difference is over the role and significance of agent-centered constraints.

There are many possible foundational paths to a consequentialist normative principle. The logic of moral language (R. M. Hare), a Rawlsian contractual agreement (John Harsanyi), a rational intuition (Henry Sidgwick), a divine command, and many other possibilities might justify a consequentialist normative principle. As these many paths to consequentialism indicate, the distinction between foundational questions about the justification of norms and normative consequentialism is not itself controversial. Indeed, Kantian deontologists agree that one can be a normative consequentialist without being a classical foundational consequentialist about the justification of normative principles.[8] What is controversial about Kantian consequentialism is its claim that Kant's foundational theory is consistent with and supports a consequentialist normative principle.

Central to Kant's foundational theory is the thesis that the concept of rational action generates substantial normative principles; that is, as a rational agent willing an action, one must accept specific normative principles as action-guiding. As we shall see, Kant does not begin with a theory of the goodness of ends and move to a conception of the right or of obligation. On the contrary, he begins with a conception of obligation and moves to a conception of value. Kant's view is thus strikingly different from classical and contemporary utilitarian views. The widespread view that Kant's theory is incompatible with consequentialism seems to assume that these foundational aspects of his theory undermine all versions of consequentialism. Since Kant simply did not consider, and thus did not reject, a consequentialist interpretation of his normative theory, we must see whether Kant's arguments do indeed undermine consequentialism.

Contrary to the clearly widespread assumption, an evaluation of Kant's concept of obligation or duty, his distinction between formal and material principles, his theory of the good, and his derivations of the categorical imperative demonstrate the compatibility of Kantian foundations and consequentialism. Kant's arguments, which purport to establish the purely "formal" categorical imperative of duty, do not rule out a consequentialist principle of right conduct. This claim requires much explanation and defense, but, as a first approximation, here is why it is correct. According to Kant's foundational arguments, a moral agent does not do her duty because of self-interest, natural inclinations, or even sympathetic or affectionate desires. A person's desires are a product of natural and social contingencies and vary from person to person. Duty, however, applies equally to us all; it does not depend on an inclination or a desire to do as one ought. Thus, the personal desire-based goals of actions (which Kant calls the "matter" of a principle of conduct), whether self-regarding or other-regarding, cannot provide the basis or foundation of duty. Kant concludes that since duty is not based on the matter (or goals) of action, it must be based on the "formal" features of the principles of duty; namely, that they are unconditional and universal, action-guiding principles, or, as he succinctly puts it, categorical imperatives. We thus get Kant's supreme principle of duty: Act only on the basis of principles that you can also will to be universal laws.

Since all actions, including moral actions, have an end, Kant then goes on to derive an end suitable as a basis, or determining ground, of such a categorical imperative. He argues that the end of moral action must be rational nature itself, first, because it provides an objective and thus universal end, and, second, because rational choice is the source of all possible value and is thus, in a sense to be explained, an end that is presupposed by all rational agents.

Kant's foundational theory clearly conflicts with some versions of utilitarianism. His arguments can also be extended to reject some other types of consequentialism. But there is no basis for the assumption that Kantian foundational theory is inconsistent with a consequentialist normative principle. A conscientious moral agent acts from a sense of duty, not from self-interest or inclination, but for all that Kant says, she nonetheless may strive to maximally promote the good. More specifically, even if a formal principle determines the normative content (or end) of moral principles, it may nonetheless be the case that the right action maximally promotes that content (or end). Or, to put the same point differently, even if categorical imperatives constrain the pursuit of self-interested ends, these constraints on self-interest may be consequentialist constraints, rather than agent-centered constraints on the maximization of the good. Of course, as stated above, I shall defend a much stronger conclusion: In addition to the consistency of consequentialism and Kant's arguments, we shall see that Kantianism properly understood entails a new and compelling form of consequentialism.

This thesis is a far cry from the familiar utilitarian and consequentialist responses to Kantianism. Consequentialists from Mill through Hare have maintained that universalizability, which they take to be the essence of Kantianism, is a purely formal principle that is compatible with virtually any normative principle, including principles that require the sacrifice of the innocent. Thus, they say, their theories satisfy the Kantian requirement of universalizability, so they are not open to criticism by Kantians. My arguments are distinct in at least four important ways from this time-honored approach, however, for the good reason that this time-honored approach does not do the work it sets out to do.

First, on my interpretation of Kant, his deontological foundational theory *generates* normative consequentialism. In addition to its obvious historical importance, this rational reconstruction of Kant's normative theory is significant for at least two reasons: It provides a foundation other than naturalism or intuitionism for consequentialism, and the resulting normative principle is categorically binding but has all the contextual flexibility of consequentialism. Some of the most telling objections both to consequentialism and to Kantianism are thus avoided. With regard to the sacrifice of the innocent, the intuitive objection to normative consequentialism remains, but it has no Kantian basis. If one rejects deontological intuitionism, then an indirect consequentialist account of our deontological intuitions is the only worthwhile game in town.

Second, I show that Kantianism entails consequentialism by a thorough exploration of Kant's most influential normative principle—the formula of humanity, with its emphasis on treating persons as ends and not using them as means only, not the often-criticized formula of universalizability. Even those sympathetic to Kant have wondered if the formula of universalizability alone may not be trivial and thus compatible with consequentialism. They have insisted, however, that the formula of humanity, which requires that all persons be treated as ends-in-themselves and not as means only, is the most central expression of Kant's thought, and they have argued that it categorically refutes consequentialism. I agree that the formula of humanity is most central to Kant's thought, but I will show that far from refuting consequentialism it, actually entails it.

Third, as I already mentioned, the consequentialism that follows from Kant's foundational theory has a distinctly Kantian, two-tiered theory of the good. More specifically, the capacity of rational agency is lexically prior to the value of happiness. Kantians have not considered the possibility of a Kantian two-tiered consequentialist normative theory. So, in addition to providing an alternative justification of consequentialism, Kantian consequentialism can also capture much of the intuitive appeal of the standard deontological approach. As a result, Kantian consequentialism should prove to be a welcome alternative to the false dichotomy of Kantianism or consequentialism.

Fourth, critics, like proponents, must consider the overall development of Kant's normative theory, not just the formulations of the categorical imperative. In addition to the well-known arguments in Kant's *Groundwork*, one needs to consider Kant's later development of his theory in the *Metaphysics of Morals*. To this end, I consider not just the formula of humanity but also the relevance of Kant's distinctions between duties of justice and duties of virtue, between external and internal legislation, between maxims of action and maxims of ends, and between perfect and imperfect duties. The point is not to provide a survey of Kant's distinctions but to see whether Kant's later articulation of his normative theory provides any reason for rejecting consequentialism.

The claim that Kant's normative theory naturally lends itself to a consequentialist interpretation is quite controversial. On reflection, however, it should be clear that Kant was primarily concerned with questions of moral psychology and the a priori basis of morals. Kant never even considered the now familiar problem of the justification of deontological, or agent-centered, constraints.

III.   AGENT-CENTERED CONSTRAINTS

I said previously that a normative theory has a consequentialist structure if the basic normative principle, whatever its justification, requires the agent to promote certain ends and does not involve any agent-centered constraints that limit how one is to promote the good. From this it should be clear that I take the justification of *basic, agent-centered constraints* to be the issue of dispute between Kantian deontologists and consequentialists.

The thesis that there are agent-centered constraints is a refinement of the more familiar thesis that negative duties—roughly, duties of non-interference—are more stringent than positive duties—roughly, duties to aid.[9] It is a commonplace objection to consequentialism that it cannot adequately account for the intuition that our negative duties are more stringent than our positive duties; for example, a consequentialist might have to hang an innocent person to calm an angry mob and thereby prevent much mayhem. The consequentialist response is equally familiar. There are good consequentialist reasons for moral codes, or secondary principles, and for moral dispositions to include some sort of priority of negative over positive duties; that is, one can argue that developing moral dispositions and following moral principles (not to mention a legal system) that include some type of priority of negative duties (or agent-centered constraints) is the best way to maximize the good.[10]

Thus, what the Kantian must claim is that consequentialist accounts fail to capture the correct motivation or justification behind our intuitive moral judgments. The usual reason for this claim is that consequentialist accounts provide an indirect and, in principle, defeasible justification of the intuitions in question.[11] Thus the assumption behind the Kantian criticism of consequentialism is that there is a more direct and, in principle, indefeasible Kantian justification for our intuitive moral judgments. Kantianism thus must justify *basic* constraints on the promotion of the good.

Agent-centered constraints are limits on the acceptable means that may be used in the pursuit of goals; such constraints are typically duties not to use others in certain ways. These constraints or duties are "agent-centered" because they take the perspective of a particular agent rather than an impartial or neutral perspective.

The basic idea is to articulate and motivate an account of rights that does not *collapse* into a consequentialist normative theory—a "utilitarianism of rights." A utilitarianism of rights builds into its conception of a good consequence the positive value of not having rights violated. Moral agents are to minimize the violation of rights (and promote the non-violation of rights). Respect for rights becomes another moral goal. A utilitarianism of rights would still fall prey to standard objections to utilitarianism: Since it builds the non-violation of rights into its desirable end state, it could allow the (allegedly) unacceptable use of persons as a means only. For example, "someone might try to justify his punishing another *he* knows to be innocent of a crime that enraged a mob, on the grounds that punishing this innocent person would help to avoid even greater violations of rights by others, and so would lead to a minimum weighted score for rights violations in the society." In contrast, the *agent-centered* perspective views the non-violation of rights as a constraint on action and thereby "forbids you to violate these moral constraints in the pursuit of your goals."[12]

Of course, consequentialists do not advocate public policies that violate rights; Hume and Mill are part of a long tradition that defends agent-centered constraints because they in fact reliably promote the good. The deontologist, however, is not satisfied with the consequentialist rationale and thus searches for a more direct, and thus secure, foundation, one that will justify our deeply felt intuitions about rights and duties.

Nonetheless, despite the intuitive appeal of the constraint view, it is not at all clear how one can *justify* basic agent-centered constraints. "If nonviolation of [a constraint] C is so important, shouldn't that be the goal? How can a concern for the nonviolation of C lead to the refusal to violate C even when this would prevent other more extensive violation of C?" The Kantian answer should not be surprising: "the Kantian principle that individuals are ends and not merely means [provides] a rationale for placing the nonviolation of rights as a side-constraint upon action instead of including it solely as a goal of one's action."[13]

The problem here is *not* the possible disastrous consequences of honoring a constraint. One can be committed to constraints without being committed to the view that constraints are always morally overriding; that is, one can hold the view that there are (prima facie) constraints on the acceptable means to a goal and still recognize that serious consequences can override the constraints. Indeed, Stephen Darwall has argued that as a minimal claim a constraint view of rights only entails that "it [is] wrong to violate [a constraint] to prevent one exactly similar violation by someone else."[14] The key point is that in deciding what one should do, it makes a difference whether it will be oneself or someone else violating the constraint (independent of any consequentialist considerations).

The problem is that the rationale for agent-centered constraints cannot be the objective disvalue of the constraint being violated. If the only consideration is one of value, then it would make no basic difference whether oneself or someone else violated the constraint; either way, the constraint would be violated and there would be the same loss of value. Thus, as Kantians have recognized, the basic question becomes: What is the rationale for a constraint upon the means to ends other than the disvalue of the constraint being violated? The Kantian rejection of consequentialism thus seems to presuppose that there is a *non- value-based rationale* for agent-centered constraints.[15] In short, although Kant emphasizes the deontological aspect of common sense morality, it is necessary to demonstrate that basic agent-centered constraints are indeed justified by Kantian moral theory.[16]

One last point of clarification: both agent-centeredness and constraints are necessary parts of a typical Kantian, non-consequentialist, normative theory. As I have defined it, a moral theory can have an agent-centered theory of value and still be consequentialist in structure; rational egoism is such a theory. To avoid the consequentialist challenge, Kantianism must generate basic agent-centered constraints that limit the acceptable means of promoting the good. Egoism, however, is a rogue case, and thus it is best to distinguish it from the forms of consequentialism that have agent-neutral theories of value. Thus I will typically limit my use of 'consequentialism' to refer only to these types of theories.

It may appear that agent-centered prerogatives, permissions, or options provide an alternative to consequentialism that does not necessitate the justification of constraints.[17] Agent-centered prerogatives are options not to promote the good; that is, it is always permissible, although not required, to maximally promote the good. The motivation for this moderate alternative seems to be roughly as follows: Consequentialism can be an extremely demanding moral theory. It may require us to be vegetarians, or to give away a lot of money to combat world hunger, or to work hard for social and political transformation. My personal projects and commitments, however, may do little to advance the good, so consequentialism may demand that I change my priorities and reorient my commitments in fundamental ways.

The appeal of options is that they provide a conception of morality that meshes with the typical not-so-saintly behavior of human beings. It is thus a more moderate position—a compromise, if you will, between the excessive demands of consequentialism and the excessive permissiveness of egoism. Although this is an uncharitable way of putting the point, the moderate, much like the rational egoist, is looking for a rationale for an option to do whatever the moderate most wants to do. The moderate, however, is not inclined to trample on others even if doing so is necessary to advance his or her own ends. The moderate believes that there are both limits on what can be demanded of us and limits on what we can do to others. Indeed, many moderates even grant that one *ought* to aid the needy *provided* the costs of doing so are small enough and the costs of not aiding are large enough.

This brings us to the crucial point. The defenders of options accept constraints—not necessarily constraints on the maximization of *the* good, but constraints on the maximization of *their own* good. Indeed, the most intuitively plausible position includes an option to *allow harm* (or to foresee it) but not an option to *do harm*. Without constraints, the comfortable moderate view rapidly evaporates into rational egoism.[18] The Kantian deontologist is clearly not an egoist and thus must justify basic agent-centered constraints.

So, although Kant often emphasizes the deontological aspects of common-sense morality, it is necessary to demonstrate that agent-centered constraints follow from his normative theory. We shall see, first, that Kant's moral theory is compatible with consequentialism; second, that it justifies a duty to maximally promote the good; and, third, that it does not justify basic agent-centered constraints. Of course, it is widely assumed that there is indeed a Kantian justification for constraints.[19] Indeed, even most consequentialists view Kant as an enemy rather than an ally. Kantian consequentialism challenges this common faith.

IV.   A COMMENT ON INTERPRETATION

The best interpretation of Kant's normative theory is consequentialist. By best, of course, I mean most consistent and philosophically most defensible; not best in a strictly textual or historical sense. The book's method is rational reconstruction, not scholarly interpretation. Of course, this is simply a point of emphasis. Although I discuss Kant's arguments at length and in great detail, I do not pursue the countless interesting textual questions, and I do not focus on the many brilliant, although conflicting, interpretations of Kant's intentions.[20] Rather than pursuing original intentions, a rational reconstruction of Kant's argument requires a more activist approach. The analogy with Ronald Dworkin's account of judicial review is apt. In interpreting the text we must determine which are the most important underlying principles and then decide particulars in light of these principles. Just as the original intentions of the authors of the Constitution do not determine the constitutionality of particular laws, for example, the Fugitive Slave Act or abortion rights, so, too, Kant does not have the last word on the interpretation and application of his theory.

The issue, to my mind, is simply to present a reasonable reconstruction of a rich and difficult set of texts. We should also be aware that Kant himself might have changed his thinking and developed it further if he were a living participant in our current debates. After all, great philosophers do not finish; they die. With this in mind, I construct an argument that moves from the most central ideas in Kant's ethics to a new form of consequentialism. In short, the primary goal of this book is to advance the current state of the philosophical debate by presenting an interesting and compelling moral theory that uses Kantian foundations to justify a consequentialist normative principle.

V.   AN OVERVIEW OF THE ARGUMENT

Like Kant, the Kantian consequentialist maintains that moral principles necessarily provide any rational agent with reasons for action; however, unlike Kant, the Kantian consequentialist maintains that the fundamental normative principle has a consequentialist structure. All rational agents are rationally required to maximally promote a two-tiered conception of the good.

The structure of the main argument for this conclusion is quite simple. In chapters 2 and 3, we see that Kant's analysis of the concept of a categorical imperative, his account of the motive of duty, and his argument that moral principles must be universalizable are consistent with a consequentialist normative principle. We also see that Kant's conception of the end-in-itself and the formula of humanity must provide the substantive normative content of Kantian ethics. Chapter 4 presents Kant's argument that rational nature must be an end-in-itself, and chapters 5 through 8 defend the thesis that Kantian ethics justifies a new form of consequentialism.

In the end we see that even though Kant seems to accept basic agent-centered (or deontological) constraints, his normative theory fails to justify these constraints. The fundamental equality of all rational beings dictates that the interests of others may sometimes override my own interests and that morality thus requires the dutiful sacrifice of my life or my liberty. In such cases, if I am "sacrificed," I am not treated as a means only. On the contrary, my sacrifice is required by a principle that, as a free and conscientious rational agent, I must endorse. Of course, I may not be inclined to accept my lot or do as I ought; but, nonetheless, my sacrifice is not a violation of my autonomy or my rights.

As a first approximation, we are duty-bound to strive, as much as possible, first, to promote the conditions necessary for rational agency, and, second, to promote happiness.[21] Of course, the advancement of these moral goals may require that the interests of some give way to the stronger interests of others. On the other hand, the maintenance of the conditions necessary for rational agency takes priority over the mere satisfaction of desire. As a consequence of the priority of rational agency over happiness, many of the typical intuitive objections to utilitarianism simply do not apply to Kantian consequentialism. For example, the mild headaches of the many, even in principle, can not be relieved at the expense of the life or liberty of the few. The two-tiered theory of the good also justifies an intuitively plausible and distribution-sensitive consequentialism. Indeed, in the end we shall see that Kantian consequentialism is an improvement over both utilitarianism and Rawls's theory of justice.[22] In short, Kant's rationalist two-tiered theory of the good is more plausible than utilitarianism; it justifies distribution-sensitive public policies, much like Rawls's theory of justice does, but it does not generate the desired agent-centered constraints.

Kantian consequentialism, in addition to being the best rational reconstruction of Kantian moral theory, captures most of the appeal of both Kantianism and consequentialism; a resolution and synthesis which I assume has hitherto been desired by all but universally conceded to be impossible.

So what explains the widespread assumption that there is a fundamental opposition between Kantian and consequentialist ethics? There are many possible explanations for the opposition. First, the more familiar classical arguments for consequentialism are strikingly different from Kant's arguments. Second, there is also the simplifying division of moral theories into deontological or teleological. This simplifying division is part of a more general failure to distinguish foundational issues from normative principles. Third, the explanation surely also involves Rawls's rejection of utilitarianism and presentation of Kantian ethics as the deontological alternative. Although Rawls emphasized that his Kantian contract approach could be used to justify a form of utilitarianism, the significance of this possibility has been somewhat neglected by Rawls's Kantian followers. (Indeed, given that Rawls does not defend Kantian internalism or derive his principles of justice from it,[23] Kantian consequentialism is in this important respect more Kantian than Rawls's "deontological" alternative.)

Of course, most important, we teach and read Kant as if he had set out to refute contemporary utilitarianism. As will become clear, we read much into Kant's argument that is not there and simply does not follow. As a result, the all-too-familiar reading of Kant presents many familiar objections to the very idea of Kantian consequentialism.

First, there is Kant's conception of the good will and the motive of duty. Kant's ethics focuses on the agent's will, not the independent goodness of states of affairs. It starts from inside a rational agent, not from a detached God's-eye view of the universe. The consequentialist typically starts with a theory of the goodness of states of affairs and then defines rational action as that which maximizes the good. Kant turns this approach on its head and insists that the good is simply the object of a good will. Many consequentialists are thus mystified by Kant's approach, and many Kantians conclude that the consequentialist approach is practically irrelevant.

Second, since there is no independent good to be maximized, Kant claims that duty must involve the "form" of the principle of action rather than the purpose, or "matter," of the principle. As we shall see, this conclusion is supposed to follow from Kantian internalism itself. The supreme principle of morality, the categorical imperative, is thus the formula of universal law, which certainly does not seem to be a consequentialist principle. Kantian internalism thus seems to rule out consequentialism.

These first two points accurately reflect the Kantian rejection of both foundational consequentialist and externalist, impartial-spectator approaches to the justification of normative principles. The assumption behind these two rejections of consequentialism seems to be that the arguments against these types of foundational consequentialist approaches also rule out normative consequentialism. The idea would be that Kantian internalism generates the formula of universal law, which in turn provides a direct justification of deontological constraints on the maximization of the good. Kantian internalism would thus provide a refutation of all forms of consequentialism.

Third, there is Kant's influential formula of the end-in-itself. This formula seems to imply that there are deontological constraints on the acceptable means to moral ends. We must treat each person as an end, not simply as a means to promote the good of others. As Rawls declares, "Each person has an inviolability founded on justice that even the welfare of society as a whole cannot override." This formula is the inspiration for the idea that rights are "trumps" (Ronald Dworkin) or "side-constraints" (Robert Nozick) on the maximization of the good. It is thus the Kantian inspiration for recent rights-based theories.[24] So interpreted, the formula of humanity expresses quite clearly the most disturbing and controversial aspect of consequentialism. Kantian ethics thus appears to rule out the consequentialist sacrifice of the innocent, and it thereby reflects Kant's conviction that individuals have a dignity that is above all price.

Fourth, although Kant recognizes duties of mutual aid and beneficence, he also recognizes, it is argued, that these are not duties to maximize the good of others. These are only "imperfect" duties, thus they are compatible with an option, permission, or prerogative to pursue one's own projects and goals even when doing so is not optimific. On this interpretation, Kantian duties would not be overly demanding. Here again is an alleged fundamental difference, and advantage of Kantian ethics over consequentialism.

Kantian ethics starts from the perspective of an individual agent and concludes that one should sometimes help others but must always respect individual rights. Consequentialism starts with the goodness of states of affairs and concludes that one should always maximize the good. One could not really hope for a clearer distinction and difference than that—it is claimed. We shall consider and reject each of these points of contrast between Kantian ethics and consequentialism. If we are successful, then this comfortable way of thinking about Kantian and consequentialist ethics must be reconsidered and recast in different terms. The goal is thus a fundamental paradigm shift in how we see and understand the foundations of ethics.

NOTES

1. Abbreviations for Kant's works are listed in the front matter of this book.

2. John Rawls (1971): 42–43.

3. For example, Kant's principle of justifiable coercion and his account of perfect and imperfect duties both play a crucial role in Kant's particular applications of his theory, but, as we shall see, the principle and the account do not follow from the categorical imperative.

4. Kant's overall theory of punishment is less clearly retributivist. Indeed, he seems to give a deterrence-based justification of a retributivist system of punishment. This idea is suggested by Tom Hill, in (1978) and defended by Sharon Byrd, in (1989). See also Don Scheid, (1983). For an excellent discussion of the complexities and difficulties of attributing a unified theory of punishment to Kant, see Jeffrie Murphy, (1987).

5. See Kant, SRL.

6. Of course, a consequentialist can attempt to build retributivist considerations into the theory of value. Similarly, a consequentialist could claim that any lie is worse than allowing a murder. It thus may be possible to account for Kant's views within a consequentialist approach. Clearly, however, these consequentialist justifications do not capture the normative structure of Kant's reasoning.

7. I am here backing away from the contrast between normative and foundational consequentialism that I have defended elsewhere. In thinking about this issue, I have benefited from Shelly Kagan's (1992). One might also compare the discussion of philosophical utilitarianism, in Thomas Scanlon (1982).

8. Thomas Scanlon (1982); John Rawls (1971): 15, 161–66; Christine Korsgaard, comments on a section of my "Consequentialism, Egoism, and the Moral Law," at the Central Division meeting of the American Philosophical Association, April 1988; also Korsgaard (1989a) and (1996) and Stephen Darwall, personal correspondence, 1988.

9. The terminology 'positive' and 'negative' can be misleading. Although it is still an approximation, the distinction I have in mind is as follows. 'Negative duties' refers to all obligations (1) not to interfere coercively with another's legitimate pursuit of his or her interests; (2) not to interfere coercively with the property rights or legitimate claims, whatever they may be, of others; (3) to honor (or not to omit) chosen obligations, like promises and contracts; and (4) to tell the truth (or not to lie). Negative duties thus include such acts as promise-keeping, which often require positive action. Duties involving promising, and perhaps truth-telling, are typically considered negative because one must voluntarily take on the obligation. One can avoid violating any such duties by simply not entering a promise (or not speaking?). 'Positive duties' refers to all unchosen or noncontractual obligations to further the interests of others. (I leave aside questions involving positive and negative duties to oneself.) Although the terminology can be misleading, it is familiar enough that one might as well use it. Thus it is claimed that, provided one does not choose to become obligated, all negative duties can be satisfied by simply doing nothing. Positive duties, one the other hand, require that one actually do something.

There are, of course, many problematic cases. The duties of parents toward their children, e.g., are often classified as chosen positive obligations. More generally, the positive/negative distinction presupposes a clear distinction between chosen and unchosen obligations. The positive/negative distinction also presupposes a further distinction between illegitimate coercive interference and legitimate conflict or competition in the pursuit of goals. Finally, the positive/negative distinction presupposes a justification and specification of property rights or legitimate claims. For our present purposes, however, these questions and difficulties are not important. As a consequentialist, one draws the distinction in such a way as to further the good. For now, I leave it to the Kantian nonconsequentialist who objects to the arguments below to clarify the distinction she defends. The above formulation is an approximation sufficient for our purposes.

10. On the role of rights and duties in a consequentialist theory, see, e.g., Thomas Hobbes (*Leviathan*, 1651), Francis Hutcheson, (*Inquiry into the Original of our Ideas of Beauty and Virtue*, 1725), David Hume (*Treatise on Human Nature*, 1739), and J.S. Mill ([1861] 1962) and ([1859, 1869] 1989). For recent discussions, see, e.g., John Rawls (1955): 3–32, David Lyons (1976a): 101–20 and (1977): 113–29, R. M. Hare (1981): esp. 25–64, and Allan Gibbard (1984): 92–102 and (1982): 71–85.

11. For two clear cases, see A. J. Simmons's (1982: esp. 97–98) criticism of Gibbard (1982) and James Fishkin's criticism (1984: 103–7)(1984). See also The references in n. 19 below.

12. Robert Nozick, (1974): 28–29. Nozick refers to these moral constraints as "side-constraints." Following Thomas Nagel, Samuel Scheffler, Derek Parfit, and Stephen Darwall, I call these constraints "agent-centered."

13. This and previous quotes are in Nozick (1974): 30–31. Nozick goes on to argue that the Kantian principle also provides a basis for his libertarian constraints upon action, which form the cornerstone of his historical entitlement conception of justice: no force, no theft, and no fraud. The constraint view of rights, however, is not linked to the rest of Nozick's theory. For example, despite his rather different normative theory of rights, Ronald Dworkin's thesis that we should conceive of rights as trumps is equivalent to Nozick's thesis that rights are constraints (see Ronald Dworkin, [1978]: 90–94, 364–68). For an argument that these views are equivalent, see Philip Pettit (1987). For the Kantian foundations of Dworkin's view of rights, see Dworkin (1978): 180–93 (though also see p. xi).

More recently Samuel Scheffler has emphasized the problem of justifying such constraints; see Scheffler (1982a) and (1988).

14. Stephen Darwall (1986): 291–319, esp. 301.

15. I do not here distinguish between agent-neutral and agent-relative accounts of value. Of course, the problem is especially clear if value assessments are made from an objective, impersonal, or agent-neutral point of view. From an objective or neutral point of view, if the same loss of value occurs, it does not matter which person violates the constraint. This has suggested to some that the key to justifying constraints involves focusing on the personal, agent-relative perspective. Ed Sherline and Shelly Kagan (in conversation) have suggested that only an agent-neutral value-based rationale is incompatible with constraints.

Whatever the general promise of this approach, as we shall see in chapter 5, it is hard to see how agent-relative or subjective *values*, in particular, can justify the deontological constraints of commonsense morality. Agent-relative theories of value generate various forms of egoism, but they do not justify deontological constraints. Indeed, a concern for the personal, or subjective, may require that one violate commonsense deontological constraints. So if one focuses on agent-relative value, the personal perspective seems to lead to a more Hobbesian perspective.

Furthermore, even if this difficulty is overcome, the original problem remains in a new form. It would still be unclear why I should not lie or kill, say, in order to prevent myself from lying or killing more in the future. The personal perspective may provide the key to the justification of constraints, but agent-relative value alone is not the key.

16. Darwall (1986) has suggested that responsibility for one's moral integrity requires that one give priority to what one does rather than what one allows others to do. But why would a Kantian perspective require a preoccupation with one's own actions even at the expense of the integrity of others? Why is it morally irresponsible to do something that is prima facie wrong in order to preserve the moral integrity of others? Intuitively, I should not lead others into temptation. Furthermore, it is a good thing to help lead others to virtue and to direct others away from vice. So a morally good person is concerned with the virtue of others. The claim is thus simply that I should not do something wrong in order to prevent someone else from doing something wrong. But this claim is unhelpful—the issue is whether it is in fact wrong to lie, say, in order to stop others from lying. If it is not wrong but indeed required than a concern for my moral integrity, for what I do, would require that I lie. In short, if lying in such a circumstance is the right thing to do, then there is no loss of moral integrity. The appeal to integrity thus cannot account for the wrongness of such a lie.

17. Samuel Scheffler (1982a) suggests that even if there is no good argument against the permissibility of always maximally promoting the good, we may still be able to avoid the demands of a consequentialist moral theory if we can just justify an agent centered prerogative to not do what is best. I am not here discussing Scheffler's own view, because it is clearly not a Kantian view. In chapter 5 and 6, however, we see that Kantianism generates a requirement to promote the good, not simply an option or permission.

The general type of argument I have in mind is exemplified by Bernard Williams's objections to both Kantian and consequentialist approaches, see, e.g., Williams (1976, 1981a). Another example would be Susan Wolf's argument in (1982): 419–39). Although I am not here concerned with the details of such positions, these issues are discussed in chapter 2, section V.

18. As Shelly Kagan (1989) has pointed out, the moderate optionist must present a rationale for an option to allow harm that is not also a rationale for an option to do harm. Kagan, I believe, demonstrates that the typical appeals to "the personal point of view" do not meet this challenge.

19. Stephen Darwall, Ronald Dworkin, Alan Donagan, Joel Feinberg, Charles Fried, Christine Korsgaard, Jeffrie Murphy, Robert Nozick, John Rawls, David Richards, and Michael Walzer, despite their important differences, have all assumed that there is a Kantian rationale for rejecting consequentialist normative theories and accepting agent-centered constraints.

These theorists are, of course, a diverse lot. The positions of Murphy, Rawls, Dworkin, and Richards are less extreme than the positions of Nozick and Fried. Donagan, Feinberg, and Walzer's positions are not easy to classify. But whatever the differences, the consequentialist analysis of Kant's normative and political theory is relevant to any allegedly Kantian theory.

See Jeffrie Murphy (1970); John Rawls (1971): 26–27, 29–30, 158–61, 178–90; Joel Feinberg (1973): 87–90; Alan Donagan (1977); Charles Fried (1978): 8–13, 28–29, 160–63; Michael Walzer (1980): 209–29, 222 n.24, 223–27; and David A. J. Richards (1981): 3–20, esp. 5, 17–20.

20. On the other hand, I follow quite closely Christine Korsgaard's reconstruction of Kant's foundational arguments, especially in chapters 2 and 4. I have two reasons for

this strategy. First, Korsgaard's interpretation of Kant's overall argument and of the nature of his theory of the good is the clearest and most convincing textual reconstruction of Kant's position. Second, by following Korsgaard's interpretation, I hope to make it especially clear where the Kantian deontologist and the Kantian consequentialist part company. My presentation of Kant's view also draws heavily on Thomas Hill's work, and his more deontological account of Kant's normative theory is considered in chapters 6 and 7.

21. For a full statement of the basic normative principle(s), see chapter 5, section V.
22. See chapter 9. On Rawls's theory, see also chapter 7, section III.
23. See Rawls (1971), (1980), and (1985).
24. See Rawls (1971): 3; Dworkin (1978): 90–94; Nozick (1974): 28–29.

2

THE MOTIVE OF DUTY

I.   THE PLACE OF UNIVERSALIZABILITY

The most familiar aspect of Kant's theory is the universal law formula of the categorical imperative; that is, roughly, an action is right if one can will that the principle of the action could also be a law that was universally obeyed.[1] If the principle, which provides the reason for the action, is inconsistent with also willing that everyone follow the principle, then the action cannot be based on a moral principle (in part, because a moral principle necessarily applies equally to all). Kant thus claims that we may test the rightness of an action with the following procedural test: "I should never act except in such a way that I can also will that my maxim [the principle upon which I act] should become a universal law" (GMM 402). Although the interpretation of this thesis may be controversial, it is part of the idea of a moral principle that it must be universalizable in some sense.

There are two main controversies about the universalizability of moral judgments. First, there is the question of what this formula actually says and whether it succeeds in demonstrating that any action is wrong. This controversy is over the formula's "fertility," as Onora O'Neill has called it. Here we have the familiar claims, on the one hand, that Kant's specific applications of the formula in the *Groundwork* fail to generate the desired conclusions. Hegel and countless others have objected that mere universalizability is either a trivial or an empty or insufficient requirement. And, consequentialists have claimed that their theories satisfy the universalizability requirement. On the other hand, Kantians have responded with many creative interpretations of the formula that claim to demonstrate its qualified success. These contemporary Kantians suggest that even though Kant's application of the universalizability procedure was at times misguided, the procedure nonetheless justifies many of our most important moral judgments. We thus have the logical interpretation, the teleological interpretation, the pragmatic interpretation, the modal interpretation, and the value-salience interpretation of the categorical imperative procedure.[2]

The second controversy involves the justification of the formula itself: Has it been shown that the supreme normative principle of morality is in fact the formula of universal law? What is noteworthy at this point, however, is that for a Kantian the logic of justification demands that the controversy over the fertility of the universalizability formula depends on this second controversy. The controversy over fertility should not even arise except on the basis of some resolution to the second controversy. First we must show that the formula of universal law can be derived as the supreme principle of morality. That derivation presumably has some bearing on how one should interpret the universalizability procedure.

So the fertility of the formula depends on what exactly universalizability is, and that in turn depends on what principle of universalizability we can in fact justify. Of course, it may turn out that the universalizability formula is not even the basic normative principle (what Kant called the "supreme principle of morality"). Indeed, we shall see that the formula of humanity is essential for the derivation of duties.

The Kantian key to the correct formulation of the supreme principle of morality should be settled by discovering which principle of action we are rationally required to adopt. Thus, the correct interpretation of the universalizability formula, and even the alleged supremacy of the formula, are logically dependent on the adequacy of the derivation of the formula.

So the derivation of the formula of universal law will determine the formula's substantive normative implications and, thus, whether or not it is compatible with consequentialism. Although this point about the logic of justification may seem obvious, it is routinely neglected by those who construct and evaluate interpretations of universalizability using only their own particular moral judgments or intuitions as a guide. Since Kantianism is not intuitionism, we should not assume our own particular moral judgments (or Kant's) and try to come up with a formula for generating the "rightness" of our willings. Kant clearly did assume that his "common-sense" morality would be validated by a metaphysics of morals. Still, Kant does not derive the supreme principle of morality by presupposing particular practical conclusions and then searching about for a principle that will generate them. Many contemporary Kantians, following Rawls, approach ethical justification in this more intuitionist fashion. Kant, however, was concerned with the *rational* foundation of ethics, which he insisted required an a priori justification of a supreme principle of morality.

This is not to deny the centrality of the sense of duty or the concept of moral judgments in the argument for first principles. We must use our sense of what a moral judgment is when searching for the basic normative principle. Moral judgment in the abstract, however, must not be confused with particular moral judgments. Particular moral judgments and duties do provide examples by means of which we may isolate the concept and nature of duty; as Kant emphasizes, however, we cannot derive the supreme principle of morality from the particular examples. On the contrary, "every example . . . must itself first be judged according to principles of morality in order to see if it is fit to serve as an original example, i.e., model. But in no way can it authoritatively furnish the concept of morality" (GMM 408).[3]

Of course, since it is reasonable to expect that many of our more considered intuitions are at least partially justified, intuitions can even provide a helpful guide in thinking about justification. The point is that from a Kantian perspective, intuitive support alone does not constitute an argument. In a complete account of morality, pre-critical particular judgments ultimately must be accounted for (either justified or explained), but they do not provide the foundational material for the construction of a Kantian moral theory.[4]

So once we have considered the justification of the basic normative principle, or supreme principle of morality, we can judge the title and adequacy of the universalizability procedure.

II.   THE KANTIAN INTERNALIST STRATEGY

The key to the rejection of consequentialism, and the vindication of Kantian deontology, is the justification of basic agent-centered constraints on the maximization of the good. If one starts with the perspective of a free and rational deliberating agent, rather than the value of states of affairs, it has seemed to many that one may be able to justify basic deontological constraints.[5] For this reason, we will start with Kant's basic approach to ethics and then look at the details of his account in order to see if it does indeed conflict with consequentialism and justify the desired constraints.

Kant's basic approach to ethics is an internalist approach. He held that there is a necessary connection between morality and reasons for action. This means, first, that moral principles provide an agent with conclusive reasons for action. In addition, if an agent concludes that an action is morally required, then the agent will have a motive for doing the action. The motive may or may not be sufficient for action. The strength of the moral motive depends both on the significance of reason in the deliberation of the agent and on competing influences on the agent's will (GMM 412–13). For the Kantian, it is important that the agent not simply believe that the action is justified and thus required but also *see why* the action is required. The motivation is the result of the person's practical reasoning; it is not a passive belief. The thesis that obligation entails motivation is thus a substantial claim that is based on a particular account of the nature of practical reason. (For a more complete explanation of Kantian internalism and a discussion of recent controversies about the nature of the connection between morality, rationality, and motivation, see the appendix.)

'Kantian internalism' and 'internalism,' unless otherwise indicated, will refer to this complex position. 'Reason,' unless otherwise indicated, will stand for the following: overriding justificatory reason, the awareness of which would provide some corresponding motivation to act accordingly; the reason would provide overriding motivation, if the agent were decisively moved by practical reason.

Internalism clearly implies that an adequate moral theory must take as its starting point the perspective of the deliberating moral agent. If morality is not centered on the deliberating agent, it cannot fulfill its essential action-guiding role and provide the agent with an overriding reason for action. In this very important sense, moral principles must be agent-centered.

Now, to look ahead, as I reconstruct and interpret Kant's internalist argument, we are *required* to promote two tiers of Kantian value (chapters 4 and 5). Consequentialism, so interpreted, is indeed an agent-centered constraint on all subjective and "arbitrary" ends. Since a moral principle must be universal and unconditional, morality is clearly a constraint on subjective and contingent desires (chapter 3). Nonetheless, consequentialism can also be a constraint in this sense. So although impartial morality does constrain one's inclinations and other personal projects, it need not include agent-centered constraints on the maximization of the good. Indeed, as we shall see, it is not even clear that agent-centered constraints on the maximization of the good are universalizable (chapter 3, section IV).

The requirement to promote Kantian value is an agent-centered requirement, and it is even an agent-centered constraint on the maximization of one's *own good.* What distinguishes Kantian consequentialism from standard deontology is simply that it does not recognize any *additional* agent-centered constraints on the maximization of *the good.*[6]

Although Kantian internalism does reflect an agent-centered view of morality, consequentialism can be agent-centered in the sense required by internalism. If Kantian internalism and consequentialism are incompatible, this must be the result of some specific feature of the derivation of the categorical imperative. We thus must focus on the details of Kant's argument for the formula of universal law and see if it does indeed conflict with consequentialism.

The Kantian strategy for justifying the formula of universal law starts with the concept of morality and its special action-guiding role in our practical deliberation and moves to "the supreme principle of morality" (GMM 392). By analyzing the concept of a moral principle and a moral judgment, we uncover the necessary conditions presupposed by morality and then also the basic normative principle of morality. As Kant puts it, "we want first to inquire whether perhaps the mere concept of a categorical imperative may not also supply us with the formula containing the proposition that can alone be a categorical imperative" (GMM 420).

Although this sounds innocuous enough, Kant does start with a fairly thick conception of morality.[7] The Kantian goal is to uncover the nature and content of an *unconditional* moral requirement where the requirement is also a justifying and motivating reason for action for *all* rational agents. More specifically, if we assume that there is such a thing as being motivated by duty (by the recognition of an unconditional and universal requirement), then we can use the motive of duty to discover the type of reason that would have to motivate a morally good agent.

Let me explain: According to Kant, if there is a requirement, then there is a reason for action. If an agent recognizes a requirement and is thus motivated to act as she is required, then the reason for action is also the agent's motive.[8] Indeed, a good person is motivated to conform to moral requirements *because* she sees that the requirement is a valid reason for action. The good person does the right action because it is right. So if we can see why a good person conforms to moral requirements, we will discover both her reason for action and the nature of moral reasons in general.[9] In addition, we may discover the *nature* of the unconditional reasons, which are presupposed by moral requirements, and perhaps even discover *how* they are able to motivate a rational agent.[10] This is why Kant starts his quest for the supreme principle of morality by examining the motive of duty.

Again, as we shall see, Kant's argument shows that a moral agent acts from a sense of duty and not from inclination; and that, thus, moral principles must be "formal" and not "material" principles. It follows that the justification of moral principles cannot be a simple natural inclination, or desire to promote the good. Nonetheless, Kant's argument does not rule out a "duty-based" justification of a consequentialist normative principle. Indeed, Kant's argument is fully consistent with the conclusion that the supreme principle of morality is a consequentialist categorical imperative. Since so many ethical theorists, both Kantians and non-Kantians, consider Kant's argument straightforwardly incompatible with consequentialism, it is important to correct this misconception.[11]

The *Groundwork* is Kant's most familiar work, and it will provide our point of departure for evaluating Kant's account of the motive of duty. Specifically, I focus on the significance of his emphasis on the good will and the motive of duty in chapter 1 of the *Groundwork*. The next chapter will focus on Kant's argument, in chapter 2 of the *Groundwork* and *The Critique of Practical Reason*, that moral principles must be formal principles. Together these two chapters show that Kant's derivation of morality is consistent with consequentialism. In light of this conclusion, we will return to Kant's famous formula of universalizability and see that consequentialism is indeed compatible with it. In subsequent chapters, Kant's argument for the formula of the end-in-itself (or formula of humanity) will be presented, and I shall then argue that Kant's moral theory provides the groundwork for a derivation of consequentialism.

One might also roughly parse the overall argument by saying that chapters 2 and 3 demonstrate the compatibility of consequentialism and the derivation of the formula of universal law and chapters 4 through 8 show that the derivation of the formula of humanity, and of the principle that persons should be treated as ends and not means only, supports a new form of consequentialism.[12]

III.   THE GOOD WILL

"There is no possibility of thinking of anything at all in the world, or even out of it, which can be regarded as good without qualification, except a *good will*" (GMM 393). According to Kant, a "good will" is "good without qualification"; it is also the "indispensable condition" of the goodness of all other goods, and as such it is "unconditionally good." The concept of unconditional goodness will be developed in due course, and in the process we shall clarify and justify the proper interpretation of Kant's striking opening claim.

For now, however, we shall interpret this controversial passage as expressing nothing more than a fundamental commitment to do what one conscientiously believes is the right thing to do. One might say that a person with a good will does what is right at any cost. Of course, costs may count in determining what is right; but once a person with a good will has determined what is right, that person is committed to doing what is right. In this sense, the goodness of a good will, the choice-worthiness of doing what is right, is prior to and independent of all other goods.[13]

Although we do not always do the right thing, it is difficult to understand, except perhaps in a paradoxical way, how one could reasonably reject a higher-order commitment to act according to one's best judgment.[14] The "higher vocation" of reason, to use Kant's phrase, is to reveal the principles of right action and thereby enable one to act according to one's best judgment. All other goods are subordinate to and conditional on the good will, because a reasonable and conscientious person must consider the reasons for acting and decide when an action is justified and when an end is worth pursuing.

The discussion of the good will is thus really a fleshing out of the very idea of a free, rational, and reasonable agent. One simply can never be *justified* in placing any particular good in front of a commitment to doing what reason requires one to do. This says nothing about *what* we are rationally required to do. Since we do not yet have a principle of right action, the priority of the good will is not a substantive claim about the ranking and ordering of particular goods or principles. In short, the idea of a good will is really a "formal," not a substantive, ideal.[15]

It does, however, set the stage by distinguishing justification from inclination. In the order of nature, it is a distinguishing feature of human beings that they are moved by reason and not by instinct alone. Kant also insists that the purpose of reason is not simply to promote the end of happiness, for an implanted natural instinct could have more certainly achieved this end (GMM 395–96). Now even though Kant is wrong about the utility of higher-order desires and socially transmitted practical wisdom, the point again is really that reason itself, in some sense, must judge the value of self-preservation and desire-satisfaction. We can decide whether to preserve ourselves or kill ourselves. We can decide whether to buy a new coat or help someone in need. We can decide whether to simply pursue personal pleasure or whether to structure our lives so that they reflect a recognition of the equal value of others. Even if one desperately wants to be happy, one may still ask whether pursuing happiness is indeed justified. Kant believes that this question is the basis of the rational desire to be worthy of happiness. More modestly, it follows that even the rational pursuit of happiness presupposes that one believes that the end of happiness justifies action.

So one of Kant's initial goals is to uncover the difference between being moved by natural impulse and being motivated by a principle; and to show that moral motivation involves the latter. According to Kant, the idea of the unconditional value of a good will "already dwells in the natural sound understanding and needs not so much to be taught as to be elucidated." In particular, it is already contained in the ordinary "concept of *duty*, which includes that of a good will, though with certain subjective restrictions and hindrances" (GMM 397). So by examining the concept of duty, we hope to discover the supreme principle of morality (GMM 392).

It should be clear, however, that the primacy of the good will, which involves a commitment to justified action, in no way conflicts with the thesis that the supreme principle of morality has a consequentialist structure. If consequentialism is incompatible with a fundamental commitment to always conform to the principles that justify action, we have not yet seen why this would be so.[16]

IV.   THE DETERMINING GROUND OF THE WILL

Kant starts his search for the supreme principle of morality by examining the motive of duty. Kant's most famous example of the motive of duty is his contrast between natural sympathy and principled beneficence (GMM 398). Since the duty to aid is recognized by both Kantians and consequentialists, this example provides a particularly apt starting point for our effort to see whether consequentialism could be the supreme principle of morality.

It is generally agreed that it is morally good to promote the happiness of others. There are, however, many reasons why one might promote happiness.

First, one might act beneficently for the sake of some ulterior motive. For example, one might give a yacht to a worthy charity in order to receive a substantial tax break. Assuming that it is permissible to take advantage of tax deductions, we may say that this action is in accordance with duty but is not done for the sake of duty. Second, one might act beneficently for its own sake. For example, one might give a yacht to a charity for no other reason then to benefit the inner-city children whom the charity helps. Now, this second case needs to be fleshed out, because the example leaves open the question of why we have the goal of helping needy children.

This second case presents two (inclusive) possibilities: either one is naturally (or because of social conditioning) a sympathetic person who finds an inner pleasure in helping others, or one is a principled person who sees helping as something one ought to do—as a duty or requirement.[17] The naturally sympathetic person has the purpose of helping others because *it is pleasant*. The other person has the exact same purpose because *it is a duty*. Unlike the sympathetic person, the person motivated by duty has a principled commitment to help the needy. The point here is that principled beneficence, unlike natural sympathy, results from recognizing a moral requirement to adopt the end of helping the needy.

This point presupposes an important distinction between *purposes* and *reasons for adopting purposes*. The distinction between the purpose and the reason why we have a purpose is not the ordinary distinction between an immediate purpose and an ulterior purpose. The sympathetic person does not help others as a means to pleasure any more than the principled person helps others as a means of doing her duty. Kant refers to the *reason why we have a purpose* as the "determining ground of the will" (GMM 401).[18] Pleasure and duty are not additional purposes; they are determining grounds or *reasons why* the agent has the purposes.[19]

There are at least three notions of 'reason' that we should distinguish: justificatory reasons; a person's motivating reasons; and explanatory reasons.[20] Some reasons justify actions; these reasons are normative in the sense that they provide rational guidance or advice and a basis for rational choice. Such justificatory reasons are distinct from both explanatory reasons and a person's reason for action. A person's reason often reflects what the person believes to be a justificatory reason, but, of course, such a belief may or may not be accurate. A person's reason also provides a possible causal explanation of the "reason why" the action happened. The three kinds of reasons are thus related.[21]

The concept of the determining ground of an act of choice is ambiguous between a person's conception of a justificatory reason and the idea of an explanatory reason. Although the notion of reason at work may conflict with Kant's philosophy of action, in Kant's discussion of the "determining ground" of an action motivated by a naturally sympathetic constitution, this notion seems to be that of an explanatory reason. The principled person believes that the other's need provides a justification for helping. Clearly, the explanation, or the determining ground, of the principled person's decision to help is the *recognition of a justificatory reason*. The naturally sympathetic person, on the other hand, has the end of helping the needy because doing so is pleasant. The explanation of the helping action in this case is the *force of an inclination*—the contingent desire that moves the person to have the end of helping the needy. The explanation is a causal explanation that does not presuppose that the agent has consciously adopted the end of helping for a reason. The person just happens to take pleasure in helping because of a natural, implanted, inclination.[22]

In contrast, the principled person has set herself the end of helping, and this is the determining ground of her choice. Again, the reason why she has set herself this end is because it is required; it is an end a person ought to have. She recognizes that she ought to help whether she happens to want to help or not. Indeed, she sees that she ought to help even if she happens to find helping unpleasant.

Now, it might be objected that the determining ground of the ends that motivate choices—the reason why an agent has an end—must always be a person's reason, not simply an explanatory reason.[23] Nonetheless, even if the sympathetic person has also chosen or *set herself the end* of helping the needy *because it is pleasant* (rather than simply having the end and being moved by it), her justification is still strikingly different from that of the principled person. If the reason for the end is its pleasantness, then it is really contingent that the agent has the particular end of helping at all. It is not that the end itself is worth having; it is simply that given the agent's contingent constitution, she happens to take pleasure in this end. If she stopped taking pleasure in helping, then she would have no reason to help the needy. We need to be clear about the structure of this type of person's motivation. On this interpretation, the sympathetic person takes her *susceptibility to pleasure* to be a sufficient basis for choice. But if that is the source of her motivation, we are likely to feel much less sympathy for the "sympathetic" person. What is attractive is the end that this person happens to take pleasure in; the person's motivational structure is now seen to be rather unattractive.[24]

As I have already claimed, it is misleading to interpret the sympathetically "constituted" person in this overly reflective way. Surely a person may simply be sympathetic and act accordingly without having adopted a principle of acting on the basis of contingent susceptibility to pleasure. However, the more reflective case is still instructive. The sympathetic person may not have engaged in adequate self-reflection, but nonetheless, the *reason why* she has her contingent ends is simply her susceptibility to pleasure, not her judgment that the beneficent end is justified because one ought to help the needy.

In contrast, as Christine Korsgaard has pointed out, the dutiful or principled person really does want to help people in need. Helping others is something the principled person is fundamentally committed to doing. Indeed, we should think of the principled person as having a deeper commitment to *helping* than the sympathetic person. To quote Korsgaard, "Kant's idea here is captured by saying that the sympathetic person's motive is *shallower* than the morally worthy person's."[25]

In addition, Korsgaard argues that once a purpose has been adopted because it is right, one will naturally take pleasure in its realization. Principled beneficence becomes genuine benevolence. The Kantian point is simply that the determining ground of a good will must be a sense of duty. Of course, one might recognize that beneficence is required and yet still not be adequately motivated by the beneficent end. But the good person is motivated by her sense of what is right, and thus she has actually come to have as an end the helping of others. When a person succeeds in making helping an end, then such a person will experience pleasure in pursuing the end. Kant explicitly recognizes this point in *The Critique of Practical Reason* "I am far from denying that frequent practice in accordance with [the moral law] can itself finally cause a subjective feeling of satisfaction. Indeed, it is a duty to establish and cultivate this feeling, which alone deserves to be called the moral feeling" (CPrR: 38).[26]

The standard objection to the Kantian motive of duty is thus doubly mistaken. First, duty for duty's sake is not the *purpose* of moral action. And, second, helping is not an unpleasant or indifferent *means* to the end of dutiful action. The standard objection confuses the determining ground of the will with the purposes embraced by the moral agent. The morally worthy person really and deeply wants to help those in need, and thus, when helping others, such a person typically will experience the full range of sympathetic pleasures and emotions. She too will find an inner joy in helping others; it will simply have a different source.

Moral motivation does not emerge fully formed; it is the result of years of moral education and reflection. Over time, certain aspects of one's character are developed and other aspects are restrained, redirected, or eliminated. Of course one does not grow alone—we are embedded in communities—but the point of moral education is not simply to tame; it is also to understand the basis of the norms that regulate one's conduct. The morally good agent understands and embraces the norms that regulate her conduct. In this sense, her concern for the good of others is a reflection of her values and the result of her agency. In contrast, if a susceptibility to pleasure alone leads one to help others, then the agent is comparatively passive and the motive is shallow and superficial.[27]

So the difference between the principled person and the sympathetic person is to be found in the different reasons why each has the beneficent end and regards it as good. The former takes the end itself to be justified. In contrast, the sympathetically constituted person does not take the end to be good because it is itself justified; such an agent simply has this end, perhaps because of the pleasure it happens to bring.

Recall that we had hoped to discover the reason behind moral requirements by discovering the motive of a good person. We have seen that it is not simply the end of good action that motivates the good person; it is also the recognition that the end is required. The good-willed person does the right action because it is right or required. But now we want to know what it is about an end that makes it right or what it is to recognize that an end is required.

Kant equates acting on principle and acting according to one's *conception of a law*. If one recognizes a moral requirement, then one recognizes an unconditional principle of action that applies equally to all persons. Since the principle of action is unconditional and universal, we can say (perhaps somewhat unnaturally) that one takes it to be a *law*, or a command, that one should adopt the purpose. Moral principles are universal laws. Kant, of course, describes such an unconditional command, or universal law, as a categorical imperative.

Now, according to the Kantian internalist approach, if there is a moral requirement, there is a reason for action. If the agent sees that she has a reason, then she will be motivated to do the action. Clearly, however, the only way that reasons can necessarily motivate is by having a source in the agent's motivational capacities. So, in this sense, a moral requirement must have a *source* internal to the agent. What does this mean? Well, an unconditional requirement must be derivable from any agent's otherwise contingent motivational capacities. Since moral requirements are reasons for action, the agent's particular principles of action must somehow also be the source of the requirement; the requirement must be a principle that the agent must accept, if any of the agent's subjective principles are supposed to justify her actions.

According to Kant, this entails that the source and validity of a moral requirement must involve an intrinsic feature of the morally good agent's principle of action.[28] For if the source of the requirement were "external" to the principle of action, then this external source is what would make the action right. But an external source cannot in itself give the agent a motivating *reason* for action. So the final source of the requirement must be an intrinsic feature of the principle of action. If the agent recognizes a justificatory reason for action, then the agent will have a motive for doing the action. The good person's reasons motivate her right action. If a good person does the right action because it is right (if her motivating reason is its rightness), and since motivating reasons must be derived from an agent's motivational capacities, what makes the action right cannot be external to the principle of action; it must be an intrinsic feature of the principle itself.

Consider classical utilitarianism:[29] Assume there is an external law (that is, a law that is not derived from one's subjective motivational set) stating that happiness should be maximized and that you are thus "required" to do whatever actions are prescribed by the principle of utility. Now, the question is how this *external* requirement can provide a *reason for you* to do the "required" action. As Philippa Foot has pointed out, it is not sufficient for the law to simply address itself to you, for then you would be morally required to obey the laws of etiquette (or any other set of silly rules that apply to you).[30] The principle of utility can give all rational agents a reason for action if and only if each must recognize and accept the utilitarian requirement. Furthermore, if it is the supreme principle of morality, the reason why it is required and the reason why it motivates you must be the same. It cannot be the case, as the structure of Mill's *Utilitarianism* suggests, that the internal sanction and the proof of the principle of utility are distinct.[31] It cannot be both an external law and a moral principle, because only a recognition of the rightness of the principle can constitute the requisite motivating and justifying reason for action.

To put the point rather simply, as long as the rightness of the principle of utility (or any other consequentialist principle) is supposed to be based on an external source, it cannot satisfy the Kantian internalist conception of obligation. Of course, without further argument, this is question-begging against the externalist. The point at issue, however, is not whether externalism or internalism is true. The question is over the nature of Kantian internalism and whether it is incompatible with consequentialism, and thus far, Kant's argument has simply pointed out that it is incompatible with what we might call externalist justifications of consequentialism.

As Kant recognized, but Kantian deontologists have apparently failed to notice, the Kantian account of the motive of duty as the determining ground of the good will is compatible with a wide range of normative principles; it is even compatible with a utilitarian normative principle. Kant writes,

> The happiness of others may be the object of the will of a rational being, but if it were the determining ground of the maxim, not only would one have to presuppose that we find in the welfare of others a natural satisfaction but also one would have to find a want such as that which is occasioned in some men by a sympathetic disposition. . . . *The material of the maxim can indeed remain but cannot be its condition, for then it would not be fit for a law.* The mere form of a law, which limits its material, must be a condition for adding this material to the will but not presuppose it as the condition of the will. (CPrR: 34, emphasis added)

Kant is quite clear here. As long as the principle of utility has an appropriate determining ground, it could turn out to be the basic normative principle. As long as the reason for adopting the principle of utility is that it is right (or has the form of law), and not simply that we are naturally inclined to do so, then Kant has not yet presented any objection to the position.

In the final analysis, Kant will reject the utilitarian account of the good. The argument thus far, however, does not rule out (or rule in) any particular normative principle. This is not a criticism of Kant, because his point is to emphasize the essential features of a normative principle and to argue that the "mere concept of a categorical imperative" (that is, a moral reason) may be sufficient for determining the supreme principle of morality. Here is the basic idea: A moral agent is moved by a principle that is unconditional and universal (that is, it is a reason that is independent of her specific desires, and that applies equally to all rational agents). In this sense, she takes her principle of action to be a law. As we have just seen, according to Kant, only an intrinsic feature of the subject's principle of action (or maxim) can provide the requisite reason (or determining ground) for adopting the principle. Since the requisite feature is not the end or purpose of the principle of action, the only remaining intrinsic feature is the principle's *lawlike form;* and lawlike form is simply unconditionality and universality.

Since moral principles are reasons for action, Kant concludes that he has uncovered a test or procedure for determining the morality of any proposed principle of action: If a proposed principle of action cannot also serve as a universal law, then it cannot have the form of a law, thus it is not an acceptable moral principle. More specifically, a morally good agent will never act on a principle unless she can *also will* that a generalized version of her own principle of action could serve *at the same time* as a law for all other rational agents. In short, Kant concludes that the supreme moral principle is simply the requirement that any principle of action be universalizable.

Of course, this conclusion is far from simple, and its basis is really not as clear as Kant implies. I will discuss these complications in the next chapter. In particular, we will look much more closely at Kant's distinction between the form and the matter of a principle and the relevance of this distinction to the alleged refutation, or at least rejection, of consequentialism.

V.   THE REGULATIVE ROLE OF DUTY

Before proceeding further, however, we need to pause and address an important objection to the very idea of a consequentialist interpretation of Kantian internalism. The objection goes as follows: According to Kantian internalism, the reason why a morally good agent does an action and the reason why the action is the right action are the same. This internalist requirement seems to rule out a distinction between day-to-day virtues and decision-making procedures and the right-making characteristics of an action. Now, it follows from the structural features of consequentialism that the best way to promote the good does not necessarily involve directly promoting the good. Most obviously, the best way to promote the good surely does not involve always being preoccupied with doing the best possible act. Since, in principle, any consequentialist theory must recognize some distinction between decision-making procedures and right-making characteristics, consequentialism *appears* to be inconsistent with the internalist requirement.[32]

A full answer to this objection would be quite involved.[33] Nonetheless, the main idea can be stated quite briefly. The key to answering this objection is to focus on the reasons—the internal reasons—for making the distinction. As long as the subjective decision-procedure is itself adopted because it is right, the Kantian internalist requirement is satisfied. Let me explain.

Kantian internalism can recognize a *hierarchy* of maxims:[34] Most immediately, we have the various purposes or ends that we aim to bring about. But there are also reasons why each agent has one purpose rather than some other purpose. As we have seen, the reason for adopting a purpose is what Kant calls the determining ground of the will. Kant's argument requires only that the determining ground, or reason for adopting the purpose, must essentially involve a judgment that it is right.

An analogous point holds for the decision-making procedures adopted by a morally good agent. As long as the agent adopts the decision procedure in question because it is right, the Kantian internalist should have no objection. We have here exactly the same sort of hierarchy of maxims that the Kantian emphasizes in other contexts. When the internalist principle is properly understood, consequentialism is not inconsistent with the internalist requirement. The exact relationship between right-making characteristics, virtues, and decision procedures is a complex and important topic. Kantian internalism, however, is logically compatible with a simple rule-consequentialist decision-making procedure, or R. M. Hare's distinction between critical and intuitive levels of moral thinking, or a more complex account of the place of character and commitments in a consequentialist theory. The correct Kantian account ultimately must be determined by more substantive considerations.

It might be objected that even if consequentialism is consistent with some version of Kantian internalism, Kant's own account of the motive of duty clearly states that an action has moral worth only if the agent acts out of respect for duty. Doesn't this entail that a moral agent is directly motivated by her sense of duty?

The idea of being constantly preoccupied by duty is not at all attractive because it conflicts with the clear importance of our individual commitments and deep friendships. Clearly, Kant's presentation of his position invites such unflattering interpretations. Kant presents his view by means of the contrast between duty and the "powerful counterweight" of the inclinations. His examples of duty often do not suggest the existence of an inviting place for friendships or personal commitments. Kant appears to reject the warmth of the emotions for the cold demands of duty. As we have already seen, and as Kant's other writings clearly indicate, this is not Kant's view. More important, the idea of acting on principles, which provide sufficient reason for action, simply does not require this overly dualistic and oppositional picture.

Despite the fact that Kantian deontologists cannot so easily dodge the consequentialist challenge, all Kantians should happily distinguish day-to-day decision-making procedures and higher-order right-making characteristics. Consequentialists have used this distinction to convincingly respond to Bernard Williams–type integrity objections to all impersonal (or impartial, or universal, or agent-neutral) moral theories. Kantian deontologists can replicate many of the consequentialist responses to these misleading objections.[35]

The Kantian motive of duty is best described as a higher-order *regulative* principle.[36] Kant's most influential discussion of the motive of duty focuses on moral worth and the value of dutiful action. Kant proceeds by way of a contrast with actions based on inclinations. Duty, not inclinations or qualities of temperament, generates moral worth. Although Kant often emphasizes the greater reliability of the motive of duty in producing right actions, the central point is that the agent's own judgment is reflected only by dutiful actions.[37] Inclinations and temperament are contingently given to us by natural (and social) chance. In contrast, in the case of dutiful actions, the agent determines his or her own actions.[38] For the Kantian internalist, the justification of an action involves a recognition that the action is right. When an agent sets herself an end, and acts for this reason, the action is a reflection of the agent's judgment and self-determination. In this sense, such actions reflect the moral worth of the agent.

There is nothing in this Kantian picture that entails that the agent must be focused on, or preoccupied with, the dutiful aspects of her actions. All that follows is that an action must have *as its determining ground* the recognition that it is right. The immediate motive of the action will typically be some particular goal or purpose. Typically, the constraints of duty have been internalized and function as background conditions. To quote Barbara Herman,

> In acting from the motive of duty the agent sets himself to abide by the moral assessment of his proposed action. . . . This aspect of the motive of duty fits a general pattern of motives that do not themselves have an object (in the normal way), but rather set limits to the ways (and whether) *other motives* may be acted upon. . . . Let us say that such motives provide *limiting conditions* on what may be done from other motives.[39]

This is not to deny that the motive of duty can also directly motivate an action in the sense that one is only moved to do the action because it is a duty. Rather, the point here is that duty can function either as a primary motive or as a secondary regulative constraint.

In addition—and this is important—one's sense of duty (that is, one's sense of what is justified and right) also shapes one's character and commitments. The central role that our reflective judgment plays in shaping our character should not be overlooked. Marcia Baron has provided an excellent description of this aspect of the regulative role of duty:

> One should (ideally) always act from duty, but this is only to say that all of one's conduct should be governed by one's unconditional commitment to doing what one morally ought to do. To say that one should always act from duty is not to say that one should always act from duty as a primary motive. One's sense of duty will serve generally as a limiting condition and at the same time as an impetus to think about one's conduct, to appraise one's goals, to be conscious of oneself as a self-determining being, and sometimes to give one the strength one needs to do what one sees one really should do.[40]

The point is not that one should be preoccupied by some abstract and distant conception of duty. The point is that one's judgment of what is right and what is wrong should govern one's life and thus shape one's character. Although morality will indeed conflict with some projects, commitments, and relationships, it need not weaken or undermine responsible commitments and relationships.

Although Kant is less explicit about this point, he does at times endorse such a point of view. He writes, "*Beneficence* is a duty. If someone practices it often and succeeds in realizing his beneficent intention, he eventually comes to actually love the person he has helped. . . . *do good* to your fellow man and your beneficence will produce love of man in you" (MM 402). The motive of duty both regulates one's conduct and provides a reason for adopting certain ends; when one adopts and advances an end, one comes to genuinely care for the end. In such a case, the motive of duty is the source of genuine benevolence.

Clearly, the best decision-making procedures and character traits will not involve a single-minded focus on duty. It is equally clear, however, that Kantian morality does not require a compulsive fixation on abstract duty. As long as the procedures we follow and the character traits we nurture are themselves governed and shaped by our sense of duty, we have satisfied the internalist demand of Kantian morality.

Of course, the nature of the decision-making procedures and the best character traits must be determined by the basic normative principle of morality. If, as I shall argue, Kantian internalism generates normative consequentialism, the basic normative principle will have a consequentialist structure, and thus the familiar consequentialist accounts of these issues will come into play.[41] The important point for now is that a consequentialist normative principle is compatible with the regulative role that Kantian ethics, properly understood, assigns to the motive of duty.

Let us review the argument of this chapter. First, Kant distinguishes between actions determined by duty and actions determined by inclination, and he argues that dutiful actions have moral worth. Since a consequentialist can aim to promote the good because of a conception of its rightness or a sense of duty, and not because of a natural inclination, that distinction provides no reason for denying moral worth to actions based on a consequentialist normative principle. Second, Kant argues that the moral worth of actions done from duty depends not on the purpose of the action, but rather on the maxim of the action, which includes the reason for adopting the purpose. Kant's example of the dutiful philanthropist, who acts in accordance with the duty of making the happiness of others his or her end, shows that, *in this passage*, Kant is not arguing against a consequentialist account of the content of the moral law. On the contrary, his argument would allow that as long as it has an appropriate determining ground, a consequentialist principle is a moral principle.

Kant's conclusion—his "second proposition," which states that the moral worth of an action cannot lie in the "purpose that is to be attained" or "the reliazation of the object of the action" (GMM 399–400)—does appear to conflict with consequentialism. We have seen, however, that this proposition expresses Kant's rejection of externalism and the refutation of inclination-based derivations of morality. In the first section of the *Groundwork*, Kant simply has not argued against the view that a moral agent strives to promote the greatest good (because it is right). Indeed, his discussion clearly suggests that he believes that this is one moral principle among several. Kant's thesis is that if an action is to have moral worth, the determining ground of the will cannot be the inner pleasure we experience in performing the action or any other contingent desire for an object. As a consequence, the purpose of the action, considered independently from its determining ground, cannot be the source of its moral worth. We have seen, however, that consequentialism is compatible with this conclusion.

Throughout this chapter we have been focusing on the motive of duty and, more generally, on Kant's internalist conception of moral judgment. In the next chapter we will look more closely at Kant's argument that a moral principle must be a purely formal principle of action and that the only purely formal principle of action is the formula of universalizability. In the process, we will see much more clearly why Kant's argument, properly understood, does not conflict with consequentialism. In chapter 4, we shall see why the full justification of an action requires a final determining ground that is determined by nothing else; such a determining ground is the "end-in-itself," or the unconditioned objective end of action.

NOTES

1. We evaluate actions by evaluating the maxim or principle that provides the basis of the action. Voluntary actions, unlike mere behaviors or acts that are produced by

immediate impulse, always presuppose a principle—that is, a perhaps unselfconscious and inchoate conception of what one is doing. If an action is voluntary, it is directed at some end and is somehow attempting to bring about that end. In this sense, it presupposes a principle that connects the means taken with the end to be achieved. Of course, much human behavior does not reflect our capacity to act on principle. Still it is this human capacity to form, revise, and pursue a goal that makes human beings moral subjects. As Kant puts it, "everything in nature works in accordance with laws. Only a rational being has the power to act *in accordance with his idea* of laws—that is, in accordance with principles—and only so has he a *will*" (GMM 412). The moral evaluation of actions thus focuses on the justification of the principle of the action.

2. For the most widely accepted general interpretation of the categorical imperative as a procedure for evaluating maxims, see Onora Nell (now O'Neill) *Acting on Principle* (1975), esp. ch. 5. Her distinction between the "fertility" and "formality" problems is in chapter 1. For examples and criticisms of the logical and teleological views and a defense of the pragmatic view, see Christine Korsgaard (1985): 24–47. For the modal interpretation, see Onora O'Neill (1989a). The details of O'Neill's version are not clear to me, so I am not sure if or how it is distinct from Korsgaard's interpretation. For the value-salience view, see Barbara Herman (1989): 411–20 and (1985): 414–36. It is not clear that any of these interpretations rule out consequentialism—even if they do undermine rational egoism. Furthermore, none of the above Kantians even discusses the question of whether deontological or agent-centered constraints follow from the interpretation. The universalizability of consequentialism is discussed more fully in chapter 3 section IV.

3. Paton translates this last clause, "it can in no way supply the prime source for the concept of morality." Kant goes on to emphasize this point: "Even the Holy One of the gospel must first be compared with our ideal of moral perfection before he is recognizable as such. Even he says of himself, 'Why do you call me (whom you see) good? None is good (the archetype of the good) except God only (whom you do not see).' But whence have we the concept of God as the highest good? Solely from the idea of moral perfection, which reason frames a priori and connects inseparably with the concept of a free will . . . examples can never justify us in setting aside their true original, which lies in reason, and letting ourselves be guided by them" (GMM 408–9).

4. On this issue, compare Thomas Hill (1994).

5. Stephen Darwall (1986) has stated this position quite clearly.

6. These ideas are more fully developed in chapter 5.

7. For a brief defense of this thick Kantian conception of rationality and morality, see the appendix.

8. The idea here does not presuppose that any and every reflective agent will in fact be motivated by moral requirements. Kant's position only presupposes that reason can motivate and that it will motivate *if reason has (decisive) influence on the will.* So an agent may not be moved by the "recognition" of a moral requirement; but this just shows that the agent is not influenced by the available reasons. For additional discussion of this point, see the appendix.

9. On this part of Kant's argument, see Christine Korsgaard (1989a). Since "a good person does the right thing because it is the right thing," Korsgaard argues, if we can

discover why the good person does an action we will also discover why the action is right (P. 311).

10. There is an important sense in which Kant thinks that we cannot explain moral motivation, because it rests on freedom, and to "explain" a free choice is simply not to view it as free. Kant thus simply assumes moral motivation. At this point, his goal is to extract the supreme principle of morality from this assumption. At other times, however, Kant does provide an account of moral motivation and the feeling of respect for the law that provides the moral incentive that moves one to perform morally worthy actions. In particular, see Kant's *Critique of Practical Reason*, ch.3.

11. One of the more striking examples is Paton's declaration (1947: 58) that chapter 1 of the *Groundwork* "refutes all forms of utilitarianism." Recently Barbara Herman presented a more subtle account of Kant's arguments; see Herman (1989, 1993b). In her view Kant is neither a deontologist nor a consequentialist. I am somewhat sympathetic to this interpretation of Kant's own normative view (which is not the same as what I believe follows from the Kantian approach). Korsgaard has also recently emphasized the inadequacies in the various dichotomies that are used to classify all moral theories; see Korsgaard (1996): esp. note 16. Nonetheless, even if some Kant scholars have gotten more sophisticated, Paton's view is still the more commonly accepted interpretation.

12. It is worth noting that even if the derivation of consequentialism fails to convince, the argument of this chapter and the next chapter would still show that the formula of universalizability should be interpreted in light of the formula of humanity. It would also follow that the rejection of consequentialism would turn on highly controversial claims about the interpretation of the formula of humanity and not on Kant's conception of the foundation (or metaphysics) of morals. Again, there is a parallel here with the current controversy about the derivation of Rawls' principles of justice and the rationality of the maximin strategy in the original position. In both cases what was to be a fundamental opposition is transformed into a narrow and somewhat obscure technical problem.

13. See Thomas Hill (1992b), esp. pp. 288–89, for this interpretation of the unconditional value of the good will.

14. Kant writes, "A man who had been bitten by a mad dog already felt hydrophobia coming on. He explained, in a letter he left, that, since as far as he knew the disease was incurable, he was taking his life lest he harm others as well in his madness. . . . Did he do wrong?" Although the man kills himself, which is usually contrary to duty, he does not place some other good above his reason. On the contrary, he has honored reason above all else by doing the act that he believes is most justified.

Similarly, if it would be rational to stop being rational or even to be irrational, then it is rational to do so. For a thorough discussion of rational irrationality, see Derek Parfit (1984).

15. I follow Hill here as well; see Hill (1992b): 289.

16. Shelly Kagan has pointed out that there is another argument against consequentialism that is inspired by Kant's discussion of the good will: A consequentialist theory cannot tell us to aim at things of mere conditional value, like happiness, for those things are sometimes good and sometimes not. So consequentialism must direct us to promote

things that are always good. But only a good will is unconditionally good. So consequentialism would have to tell us to aim at good willing. But what is that? Good wills aim at doing what is right—that is, obeying the consequentialist theory, which tells us to aim at good willing, which is obeying the consequentialist theory, which tells us to aim at good willing . . . Kantian consequentialism thus involves a vicious circularity, and that is why we must reject consequentialism.

This is a version of the "empty formalism" objection, which goes back to Hegel and is clearly stated by W. D. Ross (1930). Indeed, Hume's discussion of the artificial virtue of justice in the *Treatise* first recognizes this type of problem with the primacy of the motive of duty. More recently, Korsgaard (1989a) does an excellent job explaining the problem and Kant's solution to it.

The consequentialist should respond as follows: First, consequentialism can tell us to aim at conditional goods whenever the condition of their goodness is met (or whenever they are not positively bad), so there is no problem here. As for the unconditional goodness of the good will, first (as we shall see) it is not an independent good type of thing to be promoted, like conditional goods. Second, Kant tries to provide an account of unconditional value that goes beyond the initial purely formal conception of the good will. This is the conception and derivation of rational nature as an end-in-itself. The Kantian consequentialist uses that account to provide the substance for the consequentialist normative principle. Therefore, if circularity and emptiness can be avoided by Kantians in general, it can also be avoided by the Kantian consequentialist in particular. Of course, chapters 3 through 6 will fill in the details of this little sketch.

17. There is really nothing surprising about the thought that we ought to help the needy, yet many people recoil from the thought that it is a duty. Perhaps this is because the concept of imperfect duty has fallen by the wayside. For Kant the imperfect duty to aid is simply a duty to have helping the needy as one of your ends, one of the things you try to do. This duty is imperfect because there are many ways that one might promote this end and also because this end competes with other legitimate ends. For a defense of the Kantian position, see Marcia Baron (1984): 197–220.

18. Henry Allison also interprets the concept of the "determining ground of the will" roughly in this way. See Allison (1990): 124.

19. As we shall see in chapter 4, moral requirements presuppose that there is a determining ground of the will that is unconditionally valuable (or an end-in-itself). Since a determining ground is not necessarily an additional purpose, an end-in-itself does not have to be an actual end or purpose that all people share. For a Kantian, it must be an end that all rational beings have a reason to adopt, but it does not have to be an end that they in fact all do pursue.

20. See Stephen Darwall (1983): ch. 2 for a good discussion of these three kinds of reasons.

21. For a discussion of these distinctions, see the appendix, section II.

22. In the *Metaphysics of Morals*, Kant states that "an *end* is an object of free choice, the representation of which determines it to an action (by which the action is brought about). Every action, therefore, has its end; and since no one can have an end without *himself* making the object of his choice an end, to have any end of action whatsoever is an act of freedom on the part of the acting subject, not an effect of *nature*"

(MM 385). As an analysis of what it is to have an end, this just seems wrong. Of course, I cannot set myself an end, which is the distinguishing characteristic of rational nature, without making the object of my choice an end; and thus, because I am a rational being, my ends are the objects of free choice. I am also, however, a subject of nature, and I thus have some ends as a result of my nature. One may rightly insists that these ends alone cannot justify my actions, but from this it does not follow that they do not explain my action. Although I do have the end of helping, and this end is thus my reason for helping, if I have not also adopted the end of helping, then it is hard to see how I have made helping (the object of my choice) into an end. Should we say that this is what I am doing whether I know it or not? Perhaps the idea is that if I freely act on ends that are simply given by my nature, I must be taking these ends as justifying action. So I am indeed freely adopting these ends. The problem then is not that I consciously take my inclinations to be the source of my reasons but that I am not adequately reflective about my reason.

23. Andrews Reath has emphasized this point; see Reath (1989a): esp. 50–55 and (1989b): 284–302. See also Henry Allison (1990): 125–28.

Although Reath is probably right about Kant's theory of action, I am not convinced that this is the best reading of this passage. As I am choosing, the basic principle determining my choices may be my susceptibility to pleasure without my ever having adopted the principle of promoting ends because they are pleasant. In an important sense, the naturally sympathetic person may have the end of helping without ever having set herself this end. Nonetheless, the agent's choice of actions is still influenced by this end that the agent just passively happens to have. Notice that in Kant's example, the naturally sympathetic person loses the inclination to help because his mind becomes "clouded over with his own sorrow so that all sympathy with the lot of others is extinguished" (GMM 398). The imagery here is clearly passive; there is no decision to abandon the end. Kant goes on to say, "if nature has put little sympathy in this or that man's heart . . . "—a phrase in which there is no suggestion of an act of the will. Similarly, the naturally sympathetic person has been "constituted" with a sympathetic nature and thus "find[s] an inner pleasure in spreading joy" (GMM 398). Now, if the point is to show that both the sympathetic person and the principled person have the same end, so that the difference between them must be the reason why they have the end and not the end itself, as Korsgaard has argued, then we must recognize a sense in which they both have the same end. Since it is clear that the sympathetic person helps because of the influence of inclination, we need to be able to talk about ends given by inclination. We are getting off track, however. According to either interpretation, as we shall see, Kant's point is still consistent with consequentialism.

24. Kant's psychological thesis—that the explanation for the agent having the end must involve her susceptibility to pleasure—is not necessary to make this point. One might also say that the agent has the end of helping *because it is an end that she simply happens to have*. This is still an unattractive motivational structure. Again, it is the end that the agent happens to have that is attractive, and not the motivation to promote any ends that one happens to have.

25. Korsgaard (1989a): 325–26.

26. Unfortunately, Kant usually emphasized his view that inclinations, and thus apparently personal happiness, were an obstacle to virtue. He believed that his readers

would easily recognize the motive of duty as a motive that often must combat the inclinations. In addition, Kant's philosophical opponents were the moral sense theorists, for example, Hutcheson and Hume. He is thus arguing against the view that natural sympathy alone can be the determining ground of duty. Kant thus did not emphasize the happiness that results from virtue. Nonetheless, the Kantian point is simply that the inclinations cannot provide the determining ground of principled or dutiful action. For additional discussion of the regulative role of the motive of duty, see section V of this chapter.

27. This rough picture of moral development is one that is shared by Kant, Mill, Rawls, and Hare, to name just a few Kantians and consequentialists.

28. Although some of the details of the argument that follows may be different, the argument parallels Korsgaard's account of Kant's argument (1989a) quite closely.

29. Korsgaard (1989a) uses the example of divine command theory to exhibit this point.

30. Philippa Foot (1978). Foot's objections to Kantian categorical imperatives are discussed in the appendix.

31. Incidentally, I interpret Mill's "proof" in chapter 4 of *Utilitariansim* as presupposing the conclusions established in chapter 3. So interpreted, Mill's conclusion that the general happiness is a collective end makes a good deal more sense. The motive and the proof would thus be related in the manner required by internalism.

32. This objection was first raised by Stephen Darwall. This type of objection has also been raised by Paul Hurley, Judith Butler, and Christine Korsgaard. Korsgaard's version of the objection helped clarify the problem and thereby inspired much of the main argument of this chapter. For more on the internalist requirement, see Korsgaard (1989a); Darwall (1983); and Hill (1986).

33. A full response would involve a discussion similar to Derek Parfit's treatment (1984) of these issues.

34. Onora O'Neill (1989b) develops this aspect of Kantianism. Korsgaard (1989a) also incorporates this point into her position.

35. Marcia Baron (1984: 197–220). develops this type of Kantian strategy. She discusses Bernard Williams's integrity objections (1973, 1981a, 1981b,); Michael Stocker's objections (1976): 453–66; and Susan Wolf's arguments (1982): 419–39. I refer the readers to Baron's arguments for a more detailed and specific Kantian response to these types of objections.

For the consequentialist responses to these types of objections, see R. E. Bales (1971): 257–65; R. M. Hare (1981): chs. 2–3 and 8–9; Sarah Conly (1983): 298–311, and (1985): 275–86 Peter Railton (1984): 134–71; Samuel Scheffler (1982a) and a review of Scheffler by Conly (1986): 147–50; David Brink (1986): 417–38; Paul Gomberg (1989); and Frank Jackson (1991). For an extremely thorough and rather uncompromising response, see Shelly Kagan (1989): chs. 7–9.

It is sometimes argued that integrity objections are more serious for consequentialism than for Kantianism; but this is only true if Kantianism requires a weaker doctrine of negative responsibility than consequentialism. I argue in chapters 5 and 9 that Kantianism may require a strong doctrine of negative responsibility. In chapter 6, I argue against the all-too-common view that Kantian morality is committed only to an anemic and undemanding duty of beneficence—that is, that the Kantian duty to aid does not require, or even recommend, any significant sacrifice for the sake of others.

36. The account of the motive of duty that follows is based on the ground-breaking work of Barbara Herman (1981): 359–82. I have also been influenced by Paul Benson (1987): 365–82.

37. Paul Benson emphasizes the connection between these two aspects of Kant's view, which he calls "the nonaccidental rightness condition" and "the moral concern condition": "Satisfaction of the moral concern condition explains satisfaction of the nonaccidental rightness condition. The performance of an act of moral worth must accord with duty *because* it issues (at least in part) from the agent's appropriate concern with doing what duty demands" (1987: 367).

38. Allen Wood emphasizes this point in his article "The Emptiness of the Moral Will" (1989): 474–75. As I have explained and will explain further, I do not think that Kantian moral theory entails total self-alienation, as Wood claims. As always, I am concerned with Kantian theory and not the specific problems with Kant's theory. Kant's quasidivine moral worth may be a relic of some forms of Christian commonsense morality. Its status in the final analysis, however, depends on familiar questions involving transcendental freedom and determinism. These are not my topic. Henry Allison (1990) is the best account of Kant's views on these issues.

39. Herman (1981): 372–73. Herman also maintains, however, that for an action to have moral worth, the primary motive must be the motive of duty. I do not see why this point follows from her account. Clearly, as Kant emphasizes, the moral worth of an action shines through when its primary motive is the motive of duty. But even in the case of permissible actions, where some other motive must move one to perform a particular action, the agent's commitment to perform only permissible actions is a source of moral worth. Similarly, when the sympathetic friend of man is in sunny spirits, his actions still have moral worth, if his commitment to duty would provide him the strength to help others even when his spirit suffered from a deadly insensibility that extinguished all sympathy (GMM 398). For a more detailed account of this modification of Herman's view, see Paul Benson (1987) esp. 378–80.

40. Marcia Baron (1984): 209. This is not a new interpretation; Paton emphasizes the same idea (1947: 51), and so does Schroeder (1940). The resilience of the less flattering "misinterpretation" is noteworthy. As anyone who has ever taught Kant surely knows, the text invites it, and Kant thus must bear some of the blame.

41. See note 35.

3

FORMAL PRINCIPLES AND OBJECTIVE ENDS

At the heart of the controversy over the justification of Kant's formula of universalizability is the issue of the "formality" of the moral law. Kant claims to show that moral principle cannot presuppose any substantive content (or "matter"); only the intrinsic or conceptual features of a law as such—e.g., prescriptivity, universalizability, unconditionality, non-contradiction—can provide the basis of moral principles. We must of course flesh out what this talk of form and matter means and what it proves. Clearly, however, Kant argued at length against the idea that the moral law could be a "material" principle, and consequentialist principles *appear* to be material principles. After all, a consequentialist principle requires a substantive theory of the good to guide action; thus consequentialism is not, in any ordinary sense of the word, purely formal. So, the objection goes, the conclusion that the categorical imperative must be a purely formal principle is indeed incompatible with consequentialism.

By focusing on Kant's distinction between form and matter, especially as it is developed and defended in *The Critique of Practical Reason*, we will uncover the rather simple confusion that leads to this objection. In discussing this objection, we will also come to a clearer understanding of the central role of Kant's theory of the good in his overall argument for the categorical imperative.

I. FORMAL AND MATERIAL PRINCIPLES

If we are to understand Kant's position and thereby evaluate this objection, we must first clarify the distinction between the "form" and the "matter" of a principle of action: "all practical principles which presuppose an object (material) of the faculty of desire as the determining ground of the will are without exception empirical (material). . . . by the term 'material of the faculty of desire,' I understand an object whose reality is desired" (CPrR 21). Kant intends to prove that moral principles must be formal principles in the sense that the reason for adopting the principle ("the determining ground of the will") cannot be a desired object ("the material of the faculty of desire") but must be something else instead. In some sense to be determined, the reason for the adoption of the principle must lie in the "form" of the principle. The concept of the "form" of a principle is much more obscure than it at first appears.[1] Nonetheless, it is quite clear that Kant's point must, and does, concern the reason for adopting a principle rather than the structure of the normative principle adopted.

The formal/material distinction simply does not apply to the content, end, or purpose of moral principles; it applies only to the reason why the principle is adopted. Apparently it is easy to conflate these two possibilities. H. J. Paton, for example, states that "the moral maxim is not based on any mere inclination to produce certain results: it holds irrespective of the ends which the action is intended to produce." Now, if the maxim of my action is to promote the greatest good whatever the consequences to my self-interest, then the maxim does not hold "irrespective of the ends which the action is intended to produce." Nonetheless, we need not presuppose that the determining ground of the action is a "mere inclination" or any other object whose reality is desired.[2]

Since consequentialist principles presuppose, in a *structural sense*, a conception of the good (object), it is assumed that they are "material principles." The issue, however, is whether the principle "presupposes as its determining ground" a desire for an object, not whether the structure of the principle itself presupposes a conception of the good in order to guide action. Indeed, as we shall see in the next chapter, Kant goes on to argue that the categorical imperative presupposes that there is something (namely, rational nature as such) that is unconditionally good and thus an end-in-itself. So the categorical imperative itself presupposes a conception of the good. Kant's point is thus clear: Although all principles must have an end, in the case of moral principles, the source of the end cannot be the faculty of desire alone. Hence, the question is not about whether a moral principle must presuppose a conception of the good; rather, the question is about one's reason for adopting that conception of the good.

Kant is objecting to a particular type of alleged justification of normative principles. Although his objection to desire-based principles is simple enough, its implications are far-reaching. Indeed, Kant's novel approach to justification involves nothing short of a "Copernican revolution" in ethics, a revolution that culminates in his conception of the "autonomy of the will" as the authoritative source of the moral law.[3] Kant summarizes his "paradoxical" Copernican revolution in ethics as follows: "The paradox is that the concept of good and evil is not defined prior to the moral law, to which, it would seem the former would have to serve as foundation; rather the concept of good and evil must be defined after and by means of the law" (CPrR 64). In a sense that will be explored in the next chapter, the concept of the moral law (in particular, the "formal" characteristics of universality and necessity) will define and determine the concept of the good. And the concept of the good then determines the particular conception of the end-in-itself, which is the basis of the morally good agent's reason for adopting moral principles. This revolutionary approach to the order of justification satisfies (perhaps uniquely) the Kantian internalist conception of moral principles, because it locates the right-making characteristic and the moral motive in the intrinsic form of any moral principle. As we will see in the next chapter, this approach does indeed lead to a particular conception of the content of a moral principle.

At this point, however, Kant has concluded only that the reason for adopting moral principles is not inclination or the subjective and contingent ends (or objects) of the "faculty of desire." All principles that have this source are "material" principles. Since consequentialist principles need not presuppose that all rational beings, independent from their sense of duty, in fact desire the good ends that they ought to promote, consequentialist principles need not be "material" principles. A dutiful consequentialist may strive to promote the good not because of a natural inclination to do so but because it is the right thing to do. Of course, if this is so, then the reason for adopting the conception of the good must in some sense involve the "formal features" of that conception of the good. Again, at this point it is not clear what this means, but whatever it means, there is no reason to think that it excludes consequentialist normative principles.

Since the formal/material distinction involves the reason or determining ground for adopting a principle of action, not the structure of the principle adopted, consequentialist principles are not necessarily material principles. Kantian deontologists are thus faced with a problem: Given that the formal/material distinction has to do with the justification, and not the content, of the principle of right, how can Kant's arguments for the formality of the moral law rule out consequentialist principles of right?

Since it may not be obvious, let me emphasize why this is important. If consequentialist maxims can be formal principles, then they "conform to law as such" and are thus principles of action that are, at the least, permissible. In addition, given that the *only constraint* on any principle is simply that it can have the form of a law (GMM 421, 402–3), how can the purely formal characteristics of a law justify deontological constraints on a consequentialist principle? Of course, the formula of universal law is more complex than the comparatively *thin* requirement that a principle conform to law as such. Does the *thicker* universalizability procedure show that consequentialist principles are impermissible? But why would this be so? What additional feature does the formula of universal law add to the requirement that a principle have the form of law? And how does this additional feature rule out consequentialism, if the thinner principle does not? We will return to these questions in sections III and IV. Let us first conclude this section by reviewing what has been established thus far, and then, in section II, we will complete our reconstruction of Kant's argument for the formality of the moral law.

First, Kant's examples of the motive of duty in the *Groundwork* clearly demonstrate that even if duty is not "grounded" in the goodness of consequences, duty may still require us to promote good consequences (GMM 397–400). As Kant explicitly states, "to be beneficent [to help others] where one can is a duty" (GMM 398), and "[one should] strive, as much as one can, to further the ends of others" (GMM 430). As we saw in the last chapter, both the sympathetic person and the dutiful person act directly, without any further goal, so as to promote the happiness of others. The difference is that "the determining ground of the will" of the naturally sympathetic person is inclination, not duty.

Furthermore, given that, as Kant often states, all maxims have an end or content (GMM 436), his point is to emphasize that the determining ground or motive of a moral agent cannot be a mere inclination to bring about some state of affairs. Indeed, Kant's doctrine that if there is a categorical imperative, then something must exist as an end-in-itself—as an "objective end" valid for all rational beings—demonstrates that not all ends of a subject are "subjective ends."

According to Kant, practical laws involve

> the relation of a will to itself insofar as it is determined solely by reason. . . . Hence there arises the distinction between subjective ends, which are based on impulsions, and objective ends, which depend on motives valid for every rational being. Practical principles are *formal* when they abstract from all subjective ends. . . . If then there is to be a supreme practical principle and, as far as the human will is concerned, a categorical imperative, then it must be such that from the conception of what is necessarily an end for everyone because this end is an end in itself it constitutes an *objective* principle of the will and can hence serve as a practical law. (GMM 427–28, emphasis added)

There is much that calls for explanation here, and in the next chapter we shall reconstruct the argument for the end-in-itself, but the structure of the argument is clear: First, we subtract (or abstract from) the matter, which leaves us with the formal characteristics of unconditional necessity and universality; next, we seek out something with these formal characteristics that can serve as the end of a practical principle.

It is a unique feature of Kant's conception of the good that the idea of a practical law, the formal character of law as such, determines the nature of the good. Specifically, it must be an end-in-itself—an end that is valid for every rational being, because it is the end of universal and unconditional practical principles; and for this to be so, "it must already be connected (entirely *a priori*) with the concept of the will of a rational being in general" (GMM 426).

It may be quite natural to conclude from this that a consequentialist principle is out of place in the Kantian scheme. What is actually out of place, however, are particular ways of *justifying* consequentialist principles. Specifically, Kant is arguing against all desire-based justifications of morality. The revolutionary idea that the determining ground of the moral will must be in some sense formal rather than material, however, does not have anything to do with the structure of the resulting normative principle.

It follows that there are two different but related conceptions of a formal principle, which correspond with Kant's first two major formulations of the categorical imperative. First, a formal principle is a principle based exclusively on the conceptual features of a moral principle, like necessity and universalizability. Let us call this a "purely formal" principle. Second, a formal principle is a principle that has as its end an objectively justified and necessary end—an end that provides justifying and motivating reason for all rational agents. This second conception will be developed in the next chapter. In the rest of this chapter, I will finish setting the stage for my argument by showing that Kant's arguments for the formality of the moral law do not conflict with the more substantial conception of a formal principle.

Kant thinks we can move rather directly from the idea that the determining ground must be formal to the famous formula of universalizability (act only on maxims that you can will at the same time to be universal laws). I am not convinced that this follows so directly, and I am also unsure of exactly how to interpret this formula. Indeed, I believe we must complete the derivation of the end-in-itself, and arrive at the formula of humanity, in order to get clear content out of the categorical imperative. I would add, however, that I fail to see how recent attempts to make the formula of universalizability work are incompatible with consequentialism. In the final section of this chapter I will explain why. Before we turn to these other issues, though, let us look more closely at Kant's argument for the categorical imperative in the *Critique of Practical Reason*.

II.   SELF-LOVE AND THE MORAL LAW

I have been arguing that Kantian internalism, including Kant's concept of a formal principle of action, is compatible with a duty-based consequentialism. In the *Critique of Practical Reason*, Kant rejected rational egoism and all sympathy-based accounts of morality. His arguments also seem to challenge all broadly empiricist views, including moral sense views. And it has been argued that Kant's arguments can also be generalized to cover all forms of consequentialism. In response to this suggestion, let us look more closely at Kant's arguments.

One line of argument in Kant's writings emphasizes the immediate authority of morality (it is a "fact of reason"). According to Kant, we have direct access in our experience of moral motivation to a capacity of the will that is at odds with the demands of self-love. When confronted with the self-evident demands of duty, we know that we can act contrary to our interest and in conformity with the moral law. Kant claims that we all know that the principle of happiness (or self-love) is the direct opposite of the principle of morality. Only those in "the schools," who have an axe to grind in support of some theory, "are audacious enough to close their ears to that heavenly voice" of morality within us (CPrR 35). Even the "commonest intelligence" can easily and immediately see that the principle of morality is not the principle of self-love (CPrR 36). Even "a child of say eight or nine years old" can without doubt distinguish the requirements of morality and the incentives of self-interest (PPE 286). In the *Groundwork* Kant emphasizes that immorality results from the "powerful counterweight to all the commands of duty. . . . this counterweight consists of his needs and inclinations, whose total satisfaction is summed up under the name of happiness" (GMM 403–5). As a result of the counterweight of feelings and inclinations, there is "a propensity to quibble with these strict laws of duty, to cast doubt upon their validity, or at least their purity and strictness, and to make them, where possible, more compatible with our wishes and inclinations" (GMM 405). Kant also believes that the moral motive is corrupted by the practice of mixing moral and non-moral incentives, which causes the mind to "waver between motives" (GMM 410–11). The problem is not that we are ignorant of the moral law. On the contrary, the problem is that our knowledge of the moral law is weakened and undermined by the natural influence of the inclinations. In short, according to Kant, knowledge of a moral law, which is not the law of self-love or individual happiness, is indeed available to all rational beings. Kant even seems to believe that the particulars of duty are really quite clear.[4]

Kant also appeals to the moral emotions to show that the moral law is not based on self-love. At many places Kant draws attention to the fact that when we act on the basis of self-love, we "cannot silence the accuser" within us (CPrR 98). Even those who seem to have been born villains find the reproaches of their behavior well-grounded (CPrR 61, 99). Similarly, the feeling of respect for moral persons, Kant argues, is something that a rational being necessarily feels. He writes, "To a humble plain man, in whom I perceive righteousness in a higher degree than I am conscious of in myself, *my mind bows* whether I choose or not. . . . Respect is a tribute we cannot refuse to pay to merit whether we will or not; we can indeed outwardly withhold it, but we cannot help feeling it inwardly" (CPrR 77). Similarly, Kant argues that no matter what we may have gained in the way of fortune or the means to happiness, when we compare ourselves with the moral law we feel shame. Since we reproach ourselves even when we otherwise gain, this moral reproach must come from a "different criterion of judgment."

> He who has lost at play may be vexed at himself and his imprudence; but when he is conscious of having cheated at play, even though he has won, he must

> despise himself as soon as he compares himself with the moral law. This must therefore be something else than one's own happiness. For to have to say to himself, "I am a worthless man, though I've filled my purse," he must have a different criterion of judgment than if he approves of himself and says, "I am a prudent man, for I've enriched my treasure." (CPrR 37)

The standard of self-love, of prudence, is one thing, and the standard of morality is another. That this is so, Kant thinks, is brought out if we reflect on our experiences of the moral emotions.

Indeed, according to Kant, it is only because of this capacity to act contrary to our empirical desire for happiness and in conformity with the moral law that we experience the moral emotions (CPrR 98–100). And it is only because of this capacity of the will that transgressions of the moral law are culpable (CPrR 37–38, 97–98, 100).

If we act morally, we are motivated by something other than the strength of our empirical desires (GMM 397–400). But reason, in its normal means-ends capacity, presupposes some antecedent desire of the agent (CPrR 21–25). The principles of empirical means-ends reason are hypothetical imperatives rather than the categorical imperatives of morality. Thus, our experience of the moral ought shows us that reason also has a "higher purpose" (CPrR 61–62); it proves that pure reason can be practical; that is, it can guide us independently of our empirical (self-interested) desires (CPrR 121).

Furthermore, the imperatives of morality are not based on a survey of our empirical desires, because moral imperatives apply to all rational beings whatever their empirical desires happen to be. The character of the will that makes a priori categorical imperatives possible is thus, according to Kant, noumenal freedom (a free will); and, conversely, that we experience being motivated by categorical imperatives is evidence that we in fact possess noumenal freedom (a free will) (CPrR 29, 120–121). As a corollary, through moral motivation we have access to (practical knowledge of) our intelligible selves and "the otherwise transcendent concept of freedom" (CPrR 94).

Although this is not our topic, one need not be concerned about the metaphysics of freedom that is presupposed by this account. The Kantian does need a conception of freedom sufficient for "autonomy of the will." Leaving aside the details, practical reasoning must involve more than judging the strength of one's desires and calculating the most efficient means of satisfying those desires. In addition, practical deliberation may require that one reject particular ends and adopt other ends. Kantian practical reason attempts to account for the rational evaluation of both ends and means. Although this is a deep topic worthy of the detailed explorations it has received, it should be clear that we need not follow Kant on every detail of his theory of freedom in order to embrace his moral theory.

Although we have provided only a brief summary of Kant's overall view, it should be sufficient for our main purpose. Does any part of his argument establish that the moral law must be a non-consequentialist formal principle?

As I have been emphasizing, Kant maintains that if universal happiness were the "determining ground" of the will, then we would have to presuppose were the "determining ground" of the will, then we would have to presuppose that the agent finds a natural satisfaction in helping others. Kant writes,

> the happiness of others may be the object of the will of a rational being, but if it were the determining ground of the maxim, not only would one have to presuppose that we find in the welfare of others a natural satisfaction but also one would have to find a want such as that which is occasioned in some men by a sympathetic disposition. . . . The material of the maxim can indeed remain but cannot be its condition, for then it would not be fit for a law. The mere form of a law, which limits its material, must be a condition for adding this material to the will but not presuppose it as the condition of the will. (CPrR 34)

The happiness of others cannot be the determining ground of the will because it would then be based on our desire for pleasure and would thus be a principle of self-love. Kant's account of sympathy shows that he does not endorse a simple-minded psychological egoism.[5] He insists, rather, that natural sympathy is on a par with self-interested desires, because both are generated by our susceptibility and responsiveness to pleasure. It is simply a contingent fact that some people are moved by sympathy and others are not.

In this sense, both sympathetic and selfish desires are equally, if perhaps misleadingly, described by Kant as principles of self-love. It would be more accurate to emphasize that they are both empirical principles and thereby avoid the appearance of simple-minded psychological egoism. Kant's idea, of course, is that both have pleasure as the determining ground, not that both have the agent's pleasure as the end or purpose of the maxim.

In justifying this point, Kant argues that when the object of the will of a rational being is the happiness of others, "the determining ground of the will" is that "we find in the welfare of others a natural satisfaction . . . a want such as that which is occasioned in some men by a sympathetic disposition. This want, however, I cannot presuppose in every rational being" (CPrR 34). Since such a determining ground of the will lacks universality, Kant concludes that it is an unfit moral motive. It is our capacity to determine our will only by the form of our maxims that provides the universality that defines moral motivation (CPrR 29).

It follows from Kant's views about the psychology of motivation that any empirical condition (material determining ground) of the will must be contingently based on pleasure: If the material of the maxim directly determines the will, it does so because its reality brings pleasure to the subject and it is thus a principle of self-love. Kant writes,

> The determining ground of choice consists in the conception of an object and its relation to the subject, whereby the faculty of desire is determined to seek its realization. Such a relation to the subject is called pleasure in the reality of an object, and it must be presupposed as the condition of the possibility of the determination of choice. (CPrR 21)

According to Kant, we cannot make sense of an agent's motivation to seek an object without assuming that the agent is determined (caused) to seek the object because it will give pleasure. This is so "whether the pleasures have their origin in the sense or in the understanding" (CPrR 22–23).

This empirical psychological claim—that only the susceptibility to pleasure and thus the faculty of desire can provide the reason why we seek an object—is distinct from the mere definition of material principles as principles grounded in contingently given desires. Indeed, Kant's additional psychological claim seems to conflict with his considered view that categorical imperatives presuppose that there are ends that we are moved to promote by reason alone. Kant here seems to fall prey to and invite the conflation of the two distinct interpretations of material principles that were presented in the previous section. However, we might charitably assume that here Kant has set aside the possibility of necessary ends derived from reasons alone (and the true moral pleasures that result from the successful adoption, internalization, and realization of moral ends).[6]

Since any desire for an object or experience (even the desire for knowledge or simple contemplation) is grounded in the agent's susceptibility to pleasure and pain, and since as finite beings we are moved by desires, Kant asserts that "to be happy is necessarily the desire of any rational but finite beings, and thus an unavoidable determinant of its faculty of desire" (CPrR 25). All desire-based action is psychologically grounded in the desire for happiness—that is, "the principle of self-love." Since the moral law is not a principle of self-love, Kant concludes that the moral law cannot have a desire-based determining ground. Therefore, the form of the moral law must in some sense determine the content or end of moral action.

Now, as I argued above, Kant explicitly allows for the compatibility of the categorical imperative and a principle of universal happiness. Kant's objection is very subtle: The material of the maxim can be the happiness of others, but the determining ground (the reason why the person adopts the end) must be solely the legislative form of the maxim. Only then, he argues, do we avoid maxims of self-love. We may reconstruct Kant's argument as follows:

1. There is such a thing as acting on moral principles.
2. Moral principles are universally and unconditionally binding; they apply to all rational beings (CPrR 20–21).
3. Principles of self-love (of one's own happiness) are not unconditionally and universally binding (CPrR 21–26).

Thus from (1), (2) and (3),

4. Moral principles are not based on self-love.
5. "All material principles are, as such, of one and the same kind and belong under the general principle of self love or one's own happiness," because they all presuppose contingently given desires (CPrR 22).

Thus, from (4) and (5),

6. All material principles are unfit for the moral law; all such principles "are without exception empirical and can furnish no practical law" (CPrR 21).
7. "If all the material of a law, i.e., every object of the will considered as a ground of its determination, is abstracted from it, nothing remains except the mere form of giving universal law"—all that is left is its legislative form or law as such (CPrR 26–29).

Thus, from (6) and (7),

8. The moral will is determined by the legislative form of its maxims alone.

Thus, from (2) and (8),

9. Moral principles determine the will because of their universal legislative form; the fundamental law of pure practical reason is "so act that the maxim of your will could always hold at the same time as a principle establishing universal law" (CPrR 30).

I believe that this argument provides a reasonable picture of the structure of Kant's argument. It is also makes it quite clear that conclusion 8 does not conflict with consequentialism. (I will discuss conclusion 9 in section IV.)

As I emphasized in section I, we need to distinguish between two readings of the formal/material distinction: in these readings, material principles are distinguished either by their consequentialist content or by their determining ground. Kant's subsequent arguments establish that he must mean the latter. His own argument clearly states that "the happiness of others may be the object of the will of a rational being" (CPrR 34). Kant's argument only shows that the determining ground of the will in adopting a moral principle cannot be mere subjective desire for an end. The end or purpose must be adopted because of a determining ground that is equally valid for all rational agents as such. In this sense, the end must be objective, not merely subjective

Kant has argued that moral principles cannot be based on any subjective ends or on contingent desires; in this sense, the moral law must abstract from any material content. Kant concludes that the determining ground of the will must be its universal legislative form. Principles have a matter and a form, Kant claims; so if the determining ground is not the matter, then it must be the form. Nonetheless, Kant's explanation of his concept of formal and material principles makes it clear that formal principles can have (and, as we shall see, must have) a necessary and objective end, which must be an end-in-itself. So if there is an internalist justification of a necessary and objective end, then the requirement to advance this end would provide the requisite unconditionally binding practical law—the categorical imperative.[7]

Kant's argument thus far establishes a constraint on the end of the supreme principle of morality: Its determining ground must be necessary, not contingent, thus the end of the supreme moral principle must be an objective end of rational action, not simply a subjective end. If a categorical imperative is possible, there must be an end that has the requisite lawlike form— necessity and universality. So the argument for the categorical imperative is not yet complete.

In short, from a Kantian consequentialist perspective, the question is simply whether or not a consequentialist normative principle can have the appropriate determining ground. Kant believes that the answer to this question turns on whether or not the normative principle can have "the mere form of a law." We have seen that consequentialism could have the requisite lawlike form. But we have not yet seen an argument demonstrating that there is an end that is necessary and universal. Of course, we have also not yet seen an argument that consequentialism does indeed follow from Kant's argument. So there is much work still to be done. Kant's argument that rational nature is an objective end, an end-in-itself, must fill these gaps and thereby establish the supreme principle of morality.

It will surely be objected that this interpretation, which emphasizes the importance of objective ends, seems to conflict with Kant's stated position: Kant's idea that the "determining ground of the will" is the form of law alone implies that "there is nothing left to serve the will as principle except the *universal conformity of its actions to law as such*, i.e., I should never act except in such a way that I can also will *that my maxim should become a universal law*" (GMM 402, emphasis added).[8] This is Kant's stated position, and he seems to think that you can derive commonsense morality from the formula of universal law. This claim, however, has not proved convincing. One can agree that "conformity to universal law as such" is an essential feature of a categorical imperative. But the role of this idea in the practical reasoning of a morally good agent is far from clear. Indeed, if in the *Groundwork* Kant had simply gone on to his explanation of the conceptual need for an objective end and his derivation of the end-in-itself without including the four controversial examples of the formula of universal law procedure, his argument would have flowed quite smoothly (and we would have avoided the apparently endless discussion about the correct interpretation and application of the formula of universal law). Before we continue with the natural flow of the argument, let us briefly consider the important gaps in Kant's derivation of the universalizability procedure and also whether the formula of universal law undermines consequentialism and supports basic deontological constraints.

III. THE DERIVATION OF THE FORMULA
OF UNIVERSAL LAW

There is a clear gap in Kant's derivation of the categorical imperative that was pointed out by Bruce Aune (1979). The gap is in Kant's move, in the *Groundwork*, from "conform your actions to universal law as such" to the canonical universal law formulation of the categorical imperative—that is, "act only according to that maxim whereby you can at the same time will that it should become a universal law" (GMM 421). The first requirement is consistent even with rational egoism; but, suitably interpreted, the universal law formula generates a complex and powerful (non-egoistic) normative theory. Thus, one cannot simply move from the first to the second. Henry Allison (1991) suggests that Kant's account of transcendental freedom (CPrR 27–41) fills this gap.

Roughly, Allison argues that transcendental freedom presupposes that a justifying reason must be a universally and unconditionally valid practical law. A justified action must not simply conform to such a law; it must be adopted because the agent accepts the law as a binding and motivating reason for action. So morally justified action must not simply conform to universal laws, the law must also be the agent's justifying reason for action.

So far so good; but now Allison must show that this last requirement generates the formula of universalizability. To show this progression Allison returns to the concept of transcendental freedom. In considering Kant's famous example of false promising, he writes,

> To adopt a maxim such as false promising in virtue of its assumed universality of application is not to adopt it because of its conformity to universal law, where the latter is understood as an unconditional practical law. On the contrary, such a policy is deemed reasonable in the first place only because of certain presupposed ends, which derive whatever justification they might have from the agent's desires. . . . But this conflicts with Kant's central claim that 'the legislative form, insofar as it is contained in the maxim, is the only thing which can constitute a determining ground of the [transcendentally free] will.' (1991: 12)

The basis of this central claim is that transcendental freedom presupposes "motivational independence"; that is, the maxim of a free action can never have a material principle as its determining ground (1991: 10–11). But now Allison's response falls prey to the apparent ambiguity in Kant's distinction between form and matter.

If transcendental freedom requires motivational independence, then the determining ground of the will cannot be a subjective desire-based principle; "it must be sought in a higher order maxim," as Allison puts it. It does not follow, however, that the supreme principle of morality is the formula of universalizability, as Kant (and Allison) insists. There are thus *two* gaps in Kant's argument. The first gap can be filled, with internalism and transcendental freedom. Once this gap is filled both rational egoism and all forms of desire-based individual relativism are seen to be unfit for the moral law. But this still leaves a further gap in the derivation of the moral law. We can conclude that moral principles will have an unconditional and universal legislative form, but we are not justified in concluding that the legislative form alone, without the derivation of the objective end of action, provides an adequate specification of the supreme principle of morality.

As we shall see in the next chapter, Kant's argument for the objective value of rational nature and the formula of humanity fills this second gap. So if the formula of humanity is best interpreted as a consequentialist principle, as I will argue, then Allison's argument would not conflict with a consequentialist interpretation of Kantian ethics. In short, the Kantian refutation of consequentialism must follow from the derivation and correct interpretation of the formula of humanity.

IV.   UNIVERSALIZABILITY AND CONSEQUENTIALISM

One might assume that the formula of universal law is indeed inconsistent with consequentialism because, quite simply, it is not a consequentialist principle. But this conclusion does not follow. The question, of course, is whether consequentialist principles fail the universalizability test. In fact, it is an open question whether deontological constraints are even universalizable.

Discussions of universalizability have focused on commonsense, intuitive, ordinary, day-to-day moral principles and egoistic exceptions to these principles. Since consequentialists typically defend these secondary principles and since consequentialist justifications of these principles are typically not even considered, these arguments simply are not relevant to the validity of consequentialism. There seems to be an assumption that an adequate response to the rational egoist and to Hegelian "empty formalism" objections is also a sufficient response to all forms of consequentialism. But this assumption is never articulated; it is not explained; and it seems quite unjustified.

Deontological or agent-centered constraints are structurally different from consequentialist principles.[9] Constraints prohibit breaking a promise in order to prevent more promise-breaking, or harming the innocent in order to prevent others from harming the innocent. The challenge and problem for the advocate of basic deontological constraints is to provide a rationale for principles with this structure. One thus wants to know: How does the formula of universal law provide a rationale for these deontological principles? Kantian deontologists have not addressed this question and the answer is not at all obvious.

For example, why assume that I cannot universalize the maxim of breaking a promise *in order* to prevent more promises from being broken? If I act on the maxim and, at the same time, will that my subjective maxim hold like a law of nature for all rational beings, then the practice of promise-keeping will not be undermined and dissolved. Indeed, if the agent is not confused about the consequences of the action, the practice of promise keeping will be strengthened. The same reasoning applies to the maxim of killing the innocent in order to prevent others from killing the innocent.

More generally, the excellent recent work on the formula of universal law does not demonstrate that universalizing a fundamental underlying maxim, or adopting a disposition to maximally promote the good, involves a contradiction either in conception or in will.[10] Furthermore, it is hard to see how universalizing a fundamental consequentialist principle could involve a practical contradiction. If I break a promise because doing so will do the most possible good, and I have a fundamental commitment to maximizing the good, why is this not universalizable? In a world where everyone acted on the basis of the same fundamental underlying consequentialist maxim, the practice of promise-keeping, say, would tend toward an optimific equilibrium of coordination and principled exceptions. So there is no contradiction in acting on the maxim, or internalizing the disposition, and willing such a world.

Of course, the Kantian deontologist would here appeal to the Kantian requirement to respect persons. But that is precisely the point: Universalizability alone does not rule out consequentialism. The dispute between consequentialist and deontologist turns on the derivation and correct interpretation of the formula of humanity. We shall thus return to these issues and the sacrifice of the innocent in particular, in chapters 6 through 8, after we have completed the main argument for the consequentialist interpretation of the formula of humanity (chapters 4 and 5).

So on the one hand, there is a clear case for the universalizability of consequentialist principles. On the other hand, the refutation of principles that involve exceptions for oneself simply does not show that one must adopt constraints on the maximization of the good. Indeed, it would seem that the universalization of agent-centered constraints would involve a contradiction in will. By hypothesis, a world with basic constraints would make promise-keeping or truth-telling less reliable means of achieving particular ends. Of course, the empirical hypothesis is somewhat implausible; but it is the deontologist who insists on the use of such empirically implausible cases to "test" consequentialist principles.

In addition, recent accounts of universalizability emphasize the important role of our "finitude" in the derivation of some duties. According to these accounts, as a finite being with needs, I will necessarily want the help of others when I am in need. This is the basis of duties of beneficence and mutual aid.

Why wouldn't basic deontological constraints, which lack a consequentialist rationale, conflict with principles that are based on the necessary needs of finite rational beings? (The derivation and interpretation of "imperfect" duties is discussed in chapter 6.)

Of course, there are complex and tangled issues about the correct specification of maxims, and the role of natural needs and ends, in the interpretation of the universal law formula. This short discussion of consequentialism and universalizability is thus far from complete. Since Kantian consequentialism is not based on these considerations, the goal of this brief discussion is simply to raise some questions and to block an all-too-premature dismissal of consequentialist principles.

The argument of chapters 2 and 3 is now complete. Once again, let me emphasize that I have not disputed the *deontological foundational or justificatory* aspect of Kant's moral theory; and I have acknowledged that Kant often emphasizes the non-consequentialist aspects of common sense morality. The basic question that I have been addressing is whether or not Kantian internalism provides good grounds for rejecting consequentialist normative theories and accepting basic agent-centered constraints. We have seen that, thus far, Kant's arguments do not provide any good reasons for rejecting consequentialist normative theories.

NOTES

1. See Andrews Reath (1994) and Christine Korsgaard (1992).

2. Allen Wood's explanation of Hegel's "empty formalism" objection to Kant's ethics seems to make a similar mistake; see Wood (1989): 454–83. According to Wood, Hegel argues that to pursue an end is necessarily to act from a motive other than duty and thus from empirical desires (pp. 462–64). Since Kant insists that all actions have an end and also that any action that has an end as its determining ground is a heteronomous principle of self-love, it seems to follow that moral action is conceptually impossible. Kant's presentation of his argument surely invites this type of interpretation and thus also this objection. There is nothing in Kant's argument, however, that excludes the more charitable and plausible interpretation, which distinguishes between empirical subjective ends and objective ends that are rationally required.

3. On this point, see Korsgaard (1989b).

4. Of course, Kant still recognizes that "virtue must be acquired (that it is not innate)" (MM 477). For a fuller discussion of the relationship between the commands of pure practical reason and the teaching of virtue, see "Teaching Ethics" (MM 477–84).

5. In an earlier article on this issue, I implied that Kant was a psychological egoist about non-moral motivation and thus took a form of hedonistic egoism as his primary

target. Christine Korsgaard (1989) convinced me that Kant's argument does not depend on his particular psychological views. In particular, Kant's hedonism involves the non-moral determining ground of the will, not the *purpose* of the action. His psychological views thus do not commit him to psychological hedonism or non-moral psychological egoism. For an excellent discussion of this issue, see Andrews Reath (1989a).

6. On this point, see chapter 2, section III.

7. As we shall see in the next chapter, Kant's derivation of the formula of humanity provides a transcendental argument for the objective value of rational nature as such and thus also the internalist justification of a consequentialist categorical imperative.

8. Paton translates "the universal conformity of its actions to law as such" as "conformity of actions to universal law as such." There is a difference between "universal conformity to law" and "conformity to universal law." Since Paton's version seems to best fit Kant's argument, I will use it in what follows. Kant makes the same move in the second section. He writes, "there remains nothing but the universality of a law as such with which the maxim of the action should conform. This conformity alone is properly what is represented as necessary by the imperative. Hence there is only one categorical imperative and it is this: Act only according to that maxim whereby you can at the same time will that it should become a universal law" (GMM 421). This is Ellington's translation, which is essentially the same as Paton's.

9. See chapter 1, section III.

10. I have in mind the work of Onora O'Neill, Christine Korsgaard, and Barbara Herman. See Nell (now O'Neill) (1975), esp. ch. 5, and O'Neill (1989a). For a development and defense of the "practical contradiction" interpretation, see Korsgaard (1985): 24–47. See also Herman (1989): 411–20, (1985): 414–36, and (1993b). Herman's position lends itself to a consequentialist interpretation, but she rejects this interpretation. Her reasons seem to involve her interpretation of the dignity principle and a general skepticism about maximizing rationality. These issues are discussed in chapters 5 and 7.

4

RATIONAL NATURE AS AN END-IN-ITSELF

Kant insists that all rational beings are necessarily committed to the value-conferring power of rational agency and thus also to the unconditional value of rational nature as such. Our own internal conception of ourselves as free, rational agents must somehow, according to Kant, result in a recognition that all rational beings are ends-in-themselves, and that we are thus rationally required to act so as to treat humanity (or rational nature) always as an end and never simply as a means:

> If then there is to be a supreme practical principle and, as far as the human will is concerned, a categorical imperative, then it must be such that from the conception of what is necessarily an end for everyone because this is an end in itself it constitutes an objective principle of the will and can hence serve as a practical law. *The ground of such a principle is this: rational nature exists as an end in itself.* In this way man necessarily thinks of his own existence; thus far it is a subjective principle of human actions. *But in this way also does every other rational being think of his existence on the same rational ground that holds also for me; hence it is at the same time an objective principle, from which, as a supreme practical ground, all laws of the will must be able to be derived.* The practical imperative will therefore be the following: Act in such a way that you treat humanity, whether in your own person or in the person of another, always at the same time as an end and never simply as a means. (GMM 429, emphasis added)

Kant's derivation of this conclusion provides the central argument of his moral theory. As Kant emphasizes, if there is no such end, then the categorical imperative is not possible (GMM 425–29). As we shall see, the argument for the end-in-itself justifies a two-tiered theory of value that gives priority to the capacity of rational agency over the value of happiness. In addition, in the next chapter, we shall see that this argument justifies a distinctly Kantian form of normative consequentialism.[1] The absolute and unconditional value of rational nature actually generates a consequentialist normative principle. Clearly this conclusion is controversial. To avoid it, however, Kantian deontologists must explain and justify an interpretation of unconditional value that justifies basic deontological constraints. Chapters 6, 7, and 8 will focus on the conceptual problems with the deontological alternative, but for now it may be useful to pause and reiterate and emphasize the common ground that is shared by the Kantian consequentialist and deontologists.

First, as should by now be clear, my approach to Kantianism focuses on the structure of Kant's arguments and views his internalism as basic. Kantian internalism, in a rough and very condensed nutshell, is the view that moral requirements necessarily provide all rational agents with overriding reasons for actions; and given that reasons must be capable of motivating a rational agent, if an agent recognizes the reason-giving force of a requirement, she will be motivated (to the extent that her action is determined by reason and justified) to follow the requirement. From this it follows that all rational requirements must have a source internal to the agent. The Kantian consequentialist two-tiered theory of the good is rooted in this thoroughly Kantian approach to ethics.[2]

Second, a Kantian two-tiered value theory is radically distinct from both hedonist and preference-satisfaction versions of utilitarianism. As a result of that difference, Kantian consequentialism is much more intuitively plausible than utilitarianism. Of course, consequentialism itself—even Kantian Consequentialism—has counter-intuitive implications. As we have seen, however, intuitive plausibility does not provide a Kantian justification of a normative principle. Nonetheless, although intuitive plausibility does not constitute a justification of a normative principle, as it turns out, the Kantian approach does provide a justification for the common intuition that rational nature is more important than mere pleasures and pains. Many standard intuitive objections to utilitarian consequentialism are thus avoided in a straightforward and *theoretically motivated* fashion. A two-tiered consequentialism follows from Kantian premises, and it is more plausible than either utilitarianism or Kant's own rigorism, including his account of the uncompromising nature of specific duties (for example, his prohibition against lying to a murderer to save a friend). In addition, we must not forget that consequentialism also provides indirect justifications of virtuous character traits and of common deontological secondary principles. So, in short, Kantian consequentialism is the most intuitively plausible position that is consistent with a Kantian internalist foundation.

In the last two chapters, we focused on the first part of Kant's argument—that is, his particular form of internalism and its implications—and we concluded that since one can adopt a consequentialist normative principle because of a conception of the rightness of the principle (even if one is not naturally inclined to promote the good), a consequentialist normative principle may have a "determining ground" that is in the requisite sense formal. Kant's argument thus far only shows that moral principles *presuppose* an objective determining ground of the will. The derivation of the end-in-itself and the formula of humanity, on the other hand, *reveals* that the objective determining ground of the will is rational nature as such. The formula of humanity thus provides the key to the normative content of Kantian internalism, and we must now show that it too is consistent with consequentialism. In fact, we shall see that the most straightforward interpretation of the argument entails consequentialism.

I.   THE KANTIAN CONCEPTION OF THE END-IN-ITSELF

Since we are looking at principles of action, and since actions always have a purpose (namely, the effect the action aims to bring about), we need to discover a purpose or end that a good person recognizes as binding. Now, the only sort of purpose that can internally bind an agent is an end that the agent is bound to hold—that is, an end that a rational agent must adopt. We will follow Kant and call such an end an objective end. The concept of a moral duty, or of a categorical imperative, plus the nature of rational agency, entails that there must be an objective end of rational action—that is, something that is an end-in-itself. More precisely, if there are rationally binding moral requirements, then there is something that is an end-in-itself.

Since we are looking for an end that binds rational agents, and since we have already seen that external laws are not necessarily rationally binding, it follows that only the internal perspective of a rational agent can generate something that is an end-in-itself. The objective end of rational action must be a necessary presupposition of rational agency itself: it must be an end to which any person adopting and pursuing any other end is thereby committed.[3]

Another way of looking at this point is to return to the notion of a purpose and the determining ground of the will in adopting a purpose. The determining ground is the "condition" of the value of the purpose or end of the action. If the condition is itself only conditionally good, then the justification of the action depends on the additional condition. The full justification for the action requires that at some point there is an unconditioned condition of value. Only something that is unconditionally valuable can provide an unconditional, sufficient, determining ground for action. So if there is ever a sufficient justification for action, then there must be something that is unconditionally valuable.

Much more needs to be said about the structure and soundness of this type of argument. In particular, the logical relationship between something having conditional value and the value of the condition needs to be spelled out. Why assume that the condition of the value of X is itself valuable? Why assume that the unconditioned condition of all value, if there is such, is a lexically higher value than the value it conditions? In section III of this chapter, I will have more to say about these issues.

Another issue—one that I will *not* discuss—is the basic assumption that there must be an unconditioned condition of value, if anything is to have value at all. Kant's approach is part of the tradition that assumes that infinite chains and circular chains of justification are unacceptable. There is a large and lively meta-philosophical debate about this issue, but I shall leave the whole matter aside. We cannot cover everything, and these background issues are not relevant to our primary goal, which is to provide the strongest and most charitable reconstruction of the argument for the end-in-itself and to show that it generates normative consequentialism.

It is crucial that we avoid a standard mistaken interpretation of the Kantian approach. We should not follow the many critical commentators and assume that Kant's notion of an end-in-itself is simply the notion of something that is valuable as an end.[4] Clearly, Kant's conception of rational nature is not the only possibility for such an end. Happiness is also a plausible example of something that is valuable as an end. Kant and Kantians, however, agree with this point. In particular, Kant believes that happiness is desirable as an end and that, when the conditions of its value are met, it is objectively good. The concept of an end-in-itself, of the unconditioned condition of value, is not simply the concept of a thing that is valuable as an end, rather than as a means. The objective end of practical action is something that provides the condition of the value of all other ends. An end-*in-itself* is an end whose value is not conditioned by anything else; it is a self-sufficient end that provides the unconditioned condition of the value of all other ends.[5]

The Kantian conception of value is complex. As Christine Korsgaard has argued, it involves "two distinctions in goodness."[6] On the one hand, Kantian value theory distinguishes instrumental goods (or means) and final goods (or ends), and on the other hand, it distinguishes extrinsic and intrinsic goods. According to Kant, pleasure, for example, is a final good or end; it is something desired for its own sake and not as a means to something else. But it is only extrinsically good, because its goodness is conditioned by a good will. Since pleasure is not unconditionally good, it is not intrinsically good. But it may nonetheless be a valuable end or final good. If something is an intrinsically good end, then it is, as Kant put it, an end-*in-itself*. Something can be a good end, not a mere means or instrumental good, and still not be an end-in-itself.

Typically, at least in this century, these two distinctions in goodness have been considered equivalent; that is, intrinsic goods are equated with final goods or ends, and extrinsic goods are equated with instrumental goods or means. It is thus a commonplace to contrast intrinsic and instrumental goods, as if intrinsic were the opposite of instrumental.

There are two theories of the good that appear to justify this conflation of the two distinctions. First, there is a subjectivist account of the good, which maintains that if we value/desire something for its own sake, then it is intrinsically good. On this account, to say that something is "intrinsically good," insofar as it means anything at all, simply means that it is valued/desired by someone as an end. In fact, a subjectivist value theory maintains that *nothing* has intrinsic value—X only has value if the extrinsic fact that it is valued/desired obtains, so nothing has intrinsic value. Incidentally, subjectivism seems to maintain that all values have a condition—namely, that they are desired—but the condition itself is not something that is taken to be valuable. (Of course, "subjectivism" seems more plausible if we assume that desire-satisfaction itself is intrinsically good. We might call this position "objectivist subjectivism.")

On the other hand, there is an objectivist view, which also equates the two distinctions in goodness. This view maintains that only things with intrinsic value are valuable as ends. As Korsgaard points out, "In this case we have a significant, and rather metaphysical, claim about ethics and moral psychology: namely, that choice is or ought to be a response to an attribute that we perceive in things—the attribute of intrinsic goodness."[7]

Neither of these alternatives fits the Kantian internalist account of the nature of moral judgments.[8] The subjectivist account cannot explain why we are bound to promote certain ends, and it provides no account of objective ends, the existence of which, we have seen, is presupposed by moral judgments—at least as the Kantian conceives of them. The objectivist account provides a thoroughly externalist account of the objectivity of morals. If objective values are properties of things, how can a rational agent be internally required to regulate his or her conduct in response to these objective values? According to Kantian internalism, if an agent is required to do something, then the agent has a sufficient reason for action, and the source of the reason must involve the agent's will. If all rational agents similarly have a reason, as they do in the case of moral requirements, then the source must be a necessary feature of rational agency itself. Since the objectivist position assumes that intrinsic value is a property of things, not a property of the will, it is diametrically opposed to the entire Kantian approach.

Of course, the mere incompatibility of these positions and Kantianism is not an argument against objectivism or subjectivism; the Kantian objection to these positions, however, is explained in the appendix. The point now at issue is simply that the conflation of these two distinctions is inconsistent with Kantian moral theory and that to ignore the "two distinctions in goodness" thus leads to serious misinterpretations of the derivation of the end-in-itself.

If we are to understand the Kantian position, we must distinguish final goods (or ends) and intrinsic goods (or ends-in-themselves). Although unfamiliar, the distinction is really quite simple: First, a final good is a thing that is valuable for its own sake, rather than as a means to something else. Final goods contrast with instrumental goods, which are means to other goods. Second, an intrinsic good depends on nothing else for its value. Intrinsic goods contrast with extrinsic goods, which presuppose some other factor, or condition, for their value. Thus, an extrinsic good can be a final end, but it cannot be an end-in-itself (because its value presupposes some other condition).

Since moral requirements are unconditional requirements, the concept of a moral requirement demands that there is something that is unconditionally valuable, or an end-in-itself, which provides the condition of the value of all other good ends. Since moral requirements are universal—that is, they apply to all rational beings—moral requirements presuppose that the end-in-itself is an objective, not merely a subjective, unconditioned condition of all value. Furthermore, as we shall see below, if an objective end is to provide universal reasons for action, its source must be an internal and necessary feature of agency itself, and this feature must be the value-conferring power of rational choice itself.

Although the Kantian distinction between good ends or final goods and intrinsic goods or ends-in-themselves is not that familiar, the Kantian idea it is meant to capture is very familiar. When Kant says that a good will is the condition of the value of happiness, he is not saying that happiness is a means to a good will! And he is clearly not saying that a good will is a means to happiness. The point is not that either happiness or the good will is only instrumentally good. The point is that the goodness of happiness presupposes a good will, and thus happiness is an extrinsically valuable final end.[9]

Kant is not the only theorist to recognize that a simple means-end contrast does not adequately capture the relationships between good things. G. E. Moore's concept of an organic unity (that is, a complex whole whose intrinsic value is greater than the sum of its parts) or the less metaphysical notion of a constitutive or contributory means (that is, a part that is not itself an end but is a necessary part of a complex whole that is an end) are attempts to capture the complexities of goodness. Kant's distinction between conditional or extrinsic, final goods and the unconditional or intrinsic good—the end-in-itself—functions in a fashion somewhat similar to these more common distinctions. Unlike Moore's concept of an organic unity, however, the distinction between conditional and unconditional goodness reflects the logic of dependence of the conditionally good on the unconditionally good: You do not add a good will to happiness and stir to get something that is good without qualification; the goodness of happiness depends on the unconditional goodness of the good will.

Similarly, the notion of a constitutive means does not accurately reflect the relationship of justification between the unconditioned and the conditioned. A good will is not best described as a constitutive *means* to the end of valuable happiness; it is indeed a precondition of the value of happiness, but it is simply misleading to assimilate this type of justificatory condition with the typical means-end relationship. Ends justify means, but the value of happiness, for example, is conferred upon it by its condition, which, as we shall see, is the justified choice of a rational agent. A condition of value and a constitutive means are thus disanalogous: Intrinsic value confers value on extrinsic goods, whereas ends confer value on means. So the end-in-itself, the unconditioned condition of all other value, is the source of all value; and this idea is not captured by the notion of a constitutive means.[10]

II.   THE DERIVATION OF THE END-IN-ITSELF

As we have seen, the Kantian conception of a moral requirement entails that an internal feature of the agent's perspective is the source of the requirement. We have also seen that moral requirements presuppose an objective determining ground of the will—that is, an end-in-itself. So the argument for the end-in-itself will have to be a transcendental argument, an argument concerning the necessary condition for the possibility of an intentional state—for example, experience, or consciousness, or, in this case, rational action. The derivation must show that the internal perspective of a rational agent requires the agent to recognize the end-in-itself—otherwise the agent's own actions will not be justified by the agent's own judgment. The end-in-itself must be a necessary condition of justified action itself.

Of course, as Kant emphasizes, this argument is a big hypothetical: The idea is that *if* there are moral requirements or fully justified actions, then there must be an end-in-itself. Even if Kant is right that rational nature itself turns out to be the only possible end-in-itself, and even if I am right that the argument leads to consequentialism, morality may still be an illusion. The third section of the *Groundwork* is supposed to complete the argument. The derivation of the end-in-itself is a transcendental argument, and it is thus part of Kant's metaphysical, a priori justification of morality. I will not, however, take on the task of fully defending the metaphysical basis of morality. My task is more modest— although I gather that it is substantial enough.

So, getting back to the derivation of the end-in-itself, the transcendental argument must begin with the internal perspective of a rational agent and all of the day-to-day value judgments that each agent assumes justify his or her actions. It then explores the necessary conditions that are presupposed by these value judgments until it discovers the final determining ground, the unconditioned condition of all rational action—the end-in-itself. The trek to the unconditioned condition of value, the end-in-itself, is thus fairly straightforward. Since the unconditioned justifies the conditioned, we need to pursue a *regress*, as Korsgaard has put it, from the conditioned toward the unconditioned.[11]

Let me explain. We need to start with something that we value and then consider the conditions under which that thing is valuable. For example, if I am thirsty for a cold beer, then beer has value as the object of my desire. My desire is a condition of the value of the beer. But the satisfaction of my desire for a beer is itself only conditionally good. If it is lunchtime and I am working on a book manuscript that I need to finish, then it is not a good idea for me to have a beer with lunch, because it will make me drowsy. In cases like this one, I reject the satisfaction of the desire as a sufficient reason for action.

In the beer example, the satisfaction of this particular desire conflicts with what I take to be a larger, more valuable project. The success of this larger project functions as a limiting condition on the value of my other desires. Although this requires some argument (which will soon be provided), Kantians maintain, first, that the condition of the value of all such projects is the rational choice or affirmation of the agent and that this condition has no other condition; that is, it is the unconditioned condition of all value, the end-in-itself. Second, Kantians maintain that the value-conferring power of rational choice, whether the rational nature is one's own or another's, is a condition of the value—that is, the reason-giving force—of all other ends. Rational nature as such, not simply my own rational nature, is a limiting condition or (objective) constraint on the pursuit of all other (subjective) ends.

So, the regress argument moves from the value of any end whatsoever, first, to the necessary conditions of the value of any end, which is the value-conferring power of an agent's reflective endorsement of the end, and then to the conclusion that rational nature as such is an end-in-itself, which is presupposed by any rational choice. Therefore, a person's reflective endorsement of ends must acknowledge that rational nature is the end-in-itself, for otherwise the person's choice is not rationally defensible.

The rest of this section presents the two main parts of Kant's transcendental argument. In the next chapter, I argue that Kant's argument requires a consequentialist interpretation of this conclusion. The regress argument itself is a reconstruction and defense of Kant's own derivation of the formula of humanity. The consequentialist interpretation of the conclusion is a deviation from the otherwise standard derivation.

The first part of the derivation concludes that my rational nature is the unconditioned condition of the value of my ends. We have already reviewed, in the beer example, the beginning of this argument. The immediate goal of most actions is an object or an effect that is desired by the agent. In all such cases, the value of the object is conditioned by the desire, thus it is not unconditionally valuable. In addition, the desire itself is valuable only if the satisfaction of the desire is valuable. After all, the reason that it is good to desire something is that desires move us to action. So the object is conditioned by desire, and a desire is good only if satisfying the desire is good. Since the satisfaction of the desire, or inclination, is the condition of the value of the object, we must ask whether desire-satisfaction is viewed by the agent as unconditionally valuable. The

Kantian answer, of course, is no. The mere existence of a desire does not show that it is good to satisfy the desire, and the mere fact that an act would satisfy a desire does not show that it would be good to satisfy the desire—that is, it does not show that satisfying the desire would be justified.

At the very least, the value of the satisfaction of the desire depends on whether or not the agent affirms, or identifies with, the desire. There are some desires that one wants to have and others that one does not want to have. In deciding what to do, we assume that it is up to us which desires will effectively guide our actions. Of course, a desire may overpower the will, but then the agent does not act on reason and does not successfully determine the bodily behavior at all.[12] Rational action, which is action that the agent takes to be justified, presupposes some type of practical freedom.

Kant says, famously, says that the "inclinations themselves, being sources of needs, are so far from having an absolute value such as to render them desirable for their own sake that the universal wish of every rational being must be, rather, to be wholly free from them" (GMM 428). Many readers do not share Kant's *apparent* repudiation of the value of inclinations. It seems to reflect an alienation from one's all-too-human self and a total rejection of the rewards of passions and pleasures that bring much joy and fulfillment to life.

Now, there is no need to read this passage of Kant's as claiming that a rational being strives to have no inclinations, to be free of them in the sense of being rid of them. First, Kant says that because the inclinations are "sources of needs," they are not desired for their own sake but are rather something that we wish to be free from. Now, a person may wish to be needed, but can one rationally wish to have needs? To have a need, perhaps, is simply to have something one wishes to eliminate. So a rational person would not desire, for their own sake, sources of needs.

Second, and more important, the idea in this passage is that we want to be free of the inclinations in a more political sense. As a free and rational being, one wants to be free from the inclinations in the sense that one does not want to be commanded or ruled by them. This is a familiar idea that goes back at least to Plato and is clearly expressed by Rousseau: "the impulse of appetite alone is slavery and obedience to the law one has prescribed oneself is freedom."[13] Similarly, Kant is simply stating that it is the universal wish of any rational being (which is any being that can set itself ends) to control her inclinations and thus determine which desires will provide reasons for actions and which will not. I believe that there is nothing remarkable about this claim. Indeed, it strikes me as a conclusion that follows directly from the very idea that a rational being is a being that sets herself ends. Since setting oneself an end involves deciding to be its cause, if my capacity to act is determined by causes that I cannot control, then I cannot deliberately set myself an end and thereby act as its cause. So it must be a universal wish of every rational being to control this potentially "powerful counterweight" to my own control of my actions.

Perhaps I should emphasize that this conclusion does not deny that inclinations may be desirable. It does not even deny that some desires may be valued for their own sake. It does, however, deny that the basis of the value of inclinations is simply that one has them and that they are sources of needs.

So Kant seems to be making a reasonable point in the previous passage: Inclinations *alone* do not provide a sufficient justification of action and thus cannot provide the unconditional determining ground of a free, rational will. Indeed, as the following quote shows, whatever the correct interpretation of the other passage may be, this is clearly Kant's considered view:

> Natural inclinations, *considered in themselves*, are *good*, that is, not a matter of reproach, and it is not only futile to extirpate them but to do so would also be harmful and blameworthy. Rather let them be tamed and instead of clashing with one another they can be brought into harmony in a wholeness which is called happiness. . . . But only what is opposed to the moral law is evil in itself, absolutely reprehensible, and must be completely eradicated.[14]

As finite rational beings, we should strive to shape our inclinations in a way that will bring us a happiness that is compatible with duty. We must thus strive to eliminate only those inclinations that are in opposition to doing what we believe is right. Contrary to first appearances, Kant's view is quite reasonable and humane. Humeans and Aristotelians should find nothing objectionable in this view of the value of the inclinations.

One might, however, object to even this perhaps modified Kantian subordination of the inclinations. In particular, one might argue that individual inclinations do not provide reasons for action but that the maximal satisfaction of all of one's desires—that is, happiness—is nonetheless the condition of the value of individual inclinations. When one rejects an inclination, one does so because acting on it would undermine the satisfaction of other inclinations. The objection concludes that happiness, understood simply as the aggregate sum of the inclinations, is the condition of the value of the inclinations.

Kant has various things to say about happiness. Indeed, as Paton has argued, Kant has two different conceptions of happiness.[15] The first view is of happiness as the sum total of one's inclinations or as the greatest possible amount of pleasure. From this perspective, the good act is the act that is the most efficient means to this non-rationally given end. The second is of happiness as an ordered and harmonious set of ends. On this view, reason must not simply determine the means to a given end; it must also integrate the inclinations and their ends into a conception of happiness. This involves an "ideal of the imagination," as Kant puts it. We must imagine what it would be like to realize different possible sets of ends. This process of imagination can result in significant revisions in the original set of inclinations and ends; it will alter the strength and even the very existence of particular inclinations. So although the entire process presupposes that we start with a given set of inclinations, the particular inclinations and their relative intensities are far from immutable.

According to this more plausible and considered view of Kant's, happiness is not simply an aggregate satisfaction of given inclinations. Individual inclinations are evaluated in light of larger projects, plans, aspirations, and self-conceptions. Typically, one does not discover one's conception of oneself or one's goals by calculating how to maximally satisfy the sum of one's inclinations. The sum of inclinations typically does not, and clearly need not, provide the condition of the value of individual inclinations. A simple aggregative model of happiness does not capture either the hierarchical structure of the human will or the complex nature of human happiness.

Of course, it is possible that an agent will decide to evaluate individual inclinations by judging the net effect on the total satisfaction of inclinations. But nonetheless, even in this case, the agent determines his or her conduct only by making it an end—by choosing—to maximally satisfy inclinations. In short, inclinations can provide the agent with a reason for action only if the agent adopts the end of satisfying the inclinations.[16]

It follows that in at least some minimal sense, human happiness, or the good for a person, is a rational concept. John Rawls's concept of a rational life plan is one familiar attempt to capture this idea.[17] The good life for me is the life I would choose if I knew what it was like to live all the various lives that are open to me. This notion needs to be refined and developed, but the main idea is that it is the agent's rational choice (or affirmation) of a set of ends that makes the ends valuable. Similarly, all of the "corrected" preference or "rational" desire views of practical reason concede, more or less, this basic Kantian point. In Kantian terms, the value of our inclinations and the objects of inclination are conditioned by the value-conferring power of rational choice itself.

So the regress from the conditioned to the unconditioned shows that happiness is the condition of the value of the inclinations. Happiness, however, presupposes the value-conferring power of rational choice. Indeed, the Kantian insists that as a rational agent deciding what to do, I must necessarily assume that my (idealized) rational choices justify my actions—if my actions are justified at all.

In deciding what to do, I evaluate alternatives to see which end I will pursue. In choosing to pursue an end, I am affirming that it is pursuit-worthy, that it is either instrumentally valuable or valuable as an end. But as we have already seen, the action cannot be called for or practically justified by an external law, because then it would not provide a reason for me to do the action. I thus cannot become obliged simply by recognizing a natural or non-natural property. The determining ground must be an internal source.

The regress from the conditioned to the unconditioned reveals that this source must be rational nature itself. Rational nature, the power of rational choice, is the unconditioned condition of all value. When an agent deliberates about ends, she takes herself to be a self-originating source of valid claims, to use Rawls's expression.[18]

The next step in the argument is familiar. A finite rational being necessarily conceives of his or her existence as an unconditioned condition of value. As such, it is a "subjective principle of human action." But "in this way also does every other rational being think of his existence on the same rational ground that holds also for me; hence it is at the same time an objective principle, from which, as a supreme practical ground, it must be possible to derive all the laws of the will" (GMM 429). I take it that Kant's idea here is that just as I must conceive of my rational nature as an end-in-itself, so too, and for the exact same reason, must every other rational being conceive of her rational nature as an end-in-itself. Rational nature as such thus provides an end that all rational beings must necessarily recognize as an end-in-itself.

Now, if rational nature has the power to confer value, it has this power whether it is my rational nature or anyone else's. Or to put the point differently, if I believe that my rationally chosen ends provide reasons for action, then so too must I recognize the rationally chosen ends of others as reasons for action. If I must think of my rational nature as an end-in-itself, then I must also think of rational nature as such as an end-in-itself. It is rational nature as such, or the value-conferring power of rational choice itself, not simply my rational nature, that I must take to be an end-in-itself if my rationally chosen ends are to have value and provide reasons for action.[19] Thus we get Kant's famous conclusion: All rational beings are required always to treat rational nature as such, and thus humanity in particular, never simply as a means but always at the same time as an end (GMM 429).

The basic idea in the move from the subjective perspective to the objective principle is familiar, and I assume the rational egoist response is also familiar. The egoist can maintain that each person's actions are justified if each person pursues her *own* rational good. At best, the egoist might concede to the Kantian that each rational agent must treat her *own* rational nature as an end-in-itself and must recognize that every other rational agent must also conceive of her *own* rational nature as an end-in-itself. However, this does not show that each rational agent must conceive of rational agency as such as an end-in-itself.

The Kantian does not accept this halfway step. If my actions are unconditionally justified, then my reasons for particular actions also constitute reasons for other agents. If I think that realizing an end is justified, then I think that others *at the least* have reason not to interfere with my pursuit of that end. The considerations that suggest that happiness presupposes the value-conferring power of rational choice do not suggest that it is only my own rational nature that has value.

This point is not about the "necessary" approval or disapproval of an impartial spectator—there is no necessity in this sense, and even if there were, it would not necessarily provide reasons for action. And it is not a logical point about the rational structure of the universe—the Kantian is not claiming that there is a logical relationship of contrariety between my valuing my own rational nature and my not valuing the rational nature of others. This point about what it is for an agent to recognize a reason for action and to think of her ends as valuable.

This point describes what it is like from the *inside*, so to speak, to think of one's ends and oneself as valuable. As Thomas Nagel might put it, I simply cannot think of myself as having the power to confer value on my ends and at the same time think of myself and my ends as having no significance in the practical deliberations of other agents. But if this is so, it is also true that I must recognize the significance of other agents and their rationally chosen ends. If my capacity to set myself ends, and my chosen ends themselves, provide reasons for others, so too must the others and their ends provide reasons for me.[20]

Now these Nagelean considerations leave open the nature and weight of the practical significance, for me, of others and of their ends. It is, of course, widely maintained that I have greater reason not to harm others than I have reason to help others. Similarly, in deliberating about what to do, most will admit that the ends of others count, but they also insist that other's ends do not count as much as one's own ends. These familiar and intuitively plausible points, however, must be justified. As I have continually emphasized, the consequentialist, and even the utilitarian, have typically provided a justification of these commonsense views about deliberative procedures and accountability. A Kantian consequentialist can also explain and justify many of these resilient intuitions.

The approach that all Kantians must take in determining the weight and significance of others and their ends, however, should be clear. As Kant puts it, if the value of my rational nature and my ends has "the same rational ground" as that of other persons and their ends, then I must recognize others and their ends as having the same value. Let us call this the equal-value principle: If the values of X and Y are based on the same rational ground, then they have the same value. An argument for consequentialism, based on this principle, will be developed in the next chapter.

In chapters 2 and 3, we discussed Kant's account of the motive of duty and his claim that it must be a "formal" principle rather than a "material" principle. We saw that a material principle is adopted because of a contingent desire for an end and that a "formal" principle is adopted because it is required. As Kant claims, the determining ground of a morally worthy action is the agent's conception that the action conforms to a law (or an unconditional requirement).

There is really nothing especially mysterious about such non-desire-based principles (see the appendix). The main idea is that my own evaluation of my desire-based reasons for action, say *D at t*, necessarily commits me to recognize "autonomous" or "pure" reasons for action, say *R at t*, *where R at t* need not be antecedently included in my set of desires, *D at t-1*, either as an end or as a means to an end. The relationship between *R* and *D* is a relationship of condition and conditioned, not means and end; that is, *D* provides reasons for action only on the condition that *R* is also taken to be an end (in a sense that we will have to spell out). If *D* has motivational force and if I am determined by reason, then *R* will also have motivational force. Just as there is a rational *transmission of motivation* from ends to means, there is also a rational transmission of motivation from an agent's ends to the necessary conditions of their reason-giving force. If the practical argument for the necessary ends is rationally compelling, then the rational mechanism is no more mysterious in the case of categorical imperatives than it is in the case of hypothetical imperatives. In the one case we are moved to take the necessary and available means to an end (or abandon the end), and in the other case, we are moved to perform all of the actions required by the principle we must accept, if we value anything at all.[21]

It is plausible to maintain that this form of argument is the basis of the irrepressible conviction that others must count my ends as significant and that thus I must also count their ends as significant. The more specific intuitions—that action counts differently than omission, for example, and that I may give disproportionate weight to my own ends, including those of my family and friends—are then to be derived as secondary principles and virtues of character.[22]

So understood, I have come (rather slowly) to find this point quite compelling (although still not conclusive). My concern, however, is not to settle conclusively the familiar questions about this step in the argument.[23] My primary concern is the normative implications of the argument, if it is indeed sound. More specifically, assuming that the Kantian argument withstands the egoist's challenge, what type of normative principle follows from the argument?

III.   THE PRIORITY OF RATIONALITY

Kant's theory of value has a complex structure: Rational nature confers value on ends, and it is thus the unconditioned condition of the value of happiness. It is thus assumed to follow, from this structural feature, that the value of rational nature is lexically prior to the value of happiness.[24] As I have argued and will continue to argue, this distinctly Kantian conclusion does not conflict with consequentialism. Even if rational nature is lexically prior to happiness, Kantian foundational theory would nonetheless justify a consequentialist normative theory. It is worth noting, however, that the argument for the conclusion that rational nature is unconditionally valuable is not as clear as one might wish. As a result, many hedonist or preference-satisfaction consequentialists may be reluctant to endorse the lexical priority of rationality. In this section, we shall more closely evaluate the structure of Kant's theory of value.

The issue here, however, is not whether Kantians should be consequentialists. One might say that the question is, instead, how Kantian about value theory should consequentialists be? Whether one accepts Kant's value theory or a modified Kantian value theory, consequentialism still follows from Kantian internalism.

Although for practical purposes the concept of lexical priority is apt, we are now in a position to see that the two tiers of value are *not* distinct and unconnected types of value. The relationship between the tiers is more appropriately conceived as an interdependent relationship that, as we shall see, includes an internal structural priority.

Kant's argument maintains that rational nature is unconditionally valuable *because* it is the condition of all value. What is the basis of this inference? The crucial part of Kant's argument relating to this inference is roughly as follows:[25] Without the capacity for rational choice there could be no judgment that anything has objective value. Furthermore, value is not something that exists in the world prior to and independent of the judgment of any rational agent. Thus, if there is no judgment that something has value, then there is no thing that has value. Thus, rational nature is unconditionally valuable, because it is the condition of all other value. Since having unconditional value and existing as an end-in-itself are equivalent, it follows that rational nature exists as an end-in-itself. The argument concludes that rational beings, and the conditions necessary for their existence, may never be sacrificed in order to promote happiness or any other conditional value. Unconditional value is lexically prior to conditional value. Since rational nature, R, is the condition of the value of happiness, H, it follows that R must be lexically more valuable than H.[26]

Now, an additional principle is necessary to arrive at the conclusion that rational nature cannot be traded off against other values. An obvious candidate is the following *(lexically) higher value principle:* If something is a necessary condition of all other value, and if its value is itself unconditioned, then it is a (lexically) higher kind of value than the value it conditions.

The argument assumes that the unconditioned necessary condition of all value must be a *higher kind* of value. Is this a plausible principle? In cases that do not involve a necessary condition of *all* value, the inference is not plausible. For example, assume that a necessary condition of tomatoes' being valuable is that there are beings that are hungry. It does not even follow that the existence of hungry beings is valuable at all. The tomatoes are conditionally valuable because they are a means to some other good. Logically speaking, the condition of value is not necessarily valuable. So there must be a special relationship between a conditional final good, like happiness, and the condition of its value, rational nature.

In addition, even if one grants that the condition of all value is rational nature, why should it follow that rational nature is *unconditionally valuable*? From the premise that ends are valuable only if they are rationally chosen, it may follow that rational nature brings value into the world, but it does not seem to follow that rational nature itself must have unconditional value. For that matter, why must it have any value at all? Let us assume that the condition of all value must have some value: Why not insist that rational nature has value only if it in fact brings value into the world? Finally, perhaps as the unconditioned condition of all value, rational nature must have *as much* value as it confers; but on what basis can we conclude that rational nature must have a (lexically) *higher* value than the value it confers?

In short, rational nature has some kind of priority over conditional value, since it is the condition of all value; but it is not at all clear why its priority presupposes that it is even independently valuable—much less lexically more valuable.

Korsgaard sometimes writes as if value is some stuff and as if rational beings are full of this value and are the "source" of this stuff. She writes, "goodness, as it were, flows into the world from the good will."[27] This is, I assume, simply a metaphor, but it is clearly ill-chosen. After all, "the primary advantage of the Kantian theory of goodness," she writes, is supposed to be that even "intrinsic value . . . is not ontological"[28]—that is, value is not stuff in the world at all. Since Kantian value is not ontological, rational beings do not need to be full of value to be a condition of value. Since prior to rational choice there is no value, it would be preferable to say that value is the result of the exercise of rational nature. If we are moved by practical reason, and thus on "grounds that are valid for every rational being," then the object of our action is good (GMM 413). In this sense, value is the object of a rational will, but it is still not some stuff that is produced by our rational choices.

Why then should one conclude that rational beings have value independent of, and over and above, the value they confer? Why does conferring value on ends presuppose that the conferrer is valuable? Must I confer value on myself in order to confer value on my ends? This seems to be the idea, but why must it be so? Even if it is so, it is not clear how this generates the lexically higher value principle. Even if I must think of myself as valuable if I am to confer value, why must I think of myself as having lexically more value than the value I confer?

In response to this objection, Korsgaard has suggested that the key to understanding Kant's position is to focus on the transcendental nature of the argument.[29] Kant's argument is a transcendental regress argument that starts with the internal perspective of a valuing agent. As we saw above, the argument concludes that only through the rational affirmation of desires do those desires become sources of value for a rational agent. Rational choice, from the perspective of the agent, is the unconditioned condition of value. The agent thus necessarily thinks of his or her own rational nature as a self-originating source of value. Now, here is the crucial claim: If an agent believes that the rational choice of ends justifies the ends chosen, then the agent must also place a *special kind of value* on rational nature itself.[30]

The argument next maintains that for the very same reason, each must recognize the equal status of all other rational beings as self-originating sources of value. It follows that a justified action presupposes as its condition that rational nature as such has an absolute value, and thus the action must be compatible with this condition. In this sense the agent cannot justifiably act against rational nature as such, because to do so would undermine the agent's own reason for action.

So rational nature has a special kind of value, and thus it presents an absolute limiting condition on justified action. Although rational nature is lexically prior to all other values, it is not an end that competes with our rationally chosen ends, because the value of rational nature is not independent from its exercise. The two tiers of value are not really separate and competing types of value. So an interdependent picture of the relationship between conditional value and the end-in-itself is called for.

Again thinking about the justification of an action from the inside, the recognition that value is conditioned by rational choice does not entail that rational nature has value independent of the exercise of the capacities it makes possible. Rational nature is not supposed to be something that has value in the sense that more of it in the world is always better than less.[31] Similarly, the mere existence of a rational being does not add positive value to the world, for value is not out in the world at all. Value exists only from the internal perspective of an agent. We should say instead that if I am to be justified in acting at all, I must recognize the significance of my rational nature and thus also the rational agency of other persons. The end-in-itself would then rightly function as a regulative constraint (or limiting condition) on actions and as a condition shaping the choice of ends, but not as an independent end of action. This conception thus dovetails nicely with the Kantian conception of duty and the distinction between the purpose of an action and the reason why an agent has that purpose ("the determining ground of the will"), which was developed in chapter 2. Rational nature and the exercise and pursuit of rationally chosen ends thus involves an integrated and mutually dependent relationship. Rational nature has a special kind of value, but it is not really an independently valuable end at all.

We must, after all, remember what rational nature is: According to Kant, a rational being sets itself apart from the rest of nature by its capacity to set itself ends and thus to act according to its conception of a law or principle. Rational beings are end-setters in the sense that they have the capacity to be autonomous or self-legislating—which, for our purposes, is just the capacity to deliberate about one's ends and to act according to principles that one sets oneself (rather than simply being determined by instinctive or naturally given ends). A rational being is a being that is moved by its conception of justificatory reasons for action. To value rational nature above all else involves valuing this capacity in oneself and in others. This includes at least a commitment to act on the best available reasons. Much more needs to be said about the practical import of the idea that rational nature is an end-in-itself. It would seem, however, that it need not imply that we must always put our future capacity to choose above the ends that we have chosen. Indeed, we should put our rationally chosen ends above our future capacity to choose whenever there is *good reason to do so*. If there is a good reason for me to sacrifice my personal ends, I should do so. If the sacrifice of my life is truly called for, I should sacrifice myself and my future rational capacities. In subsequent chapters, we shall see whether there are indeed good reasons for these types of sacrifice. More trivially, if there is good reason to get light-headed drinking champagne in celebration of a momentous event, then one should do so—even if doing so temporarily diminishes one's rational capacities. Although such a permissive view may not be Kant's own view, it is surely a sensible view, and it is all that the best interpretation of the priority of rationality requires.

Although I will not pursue these points any further, it would seem that if one accepts Korsgaard's basic interpretation of Kant's theory of the good, one should endorse an interdependent interpretation of the lexical priority thesis. Rational nature has a conceptual and structural priority over particular ends, but it does not have independent practical value. It is manifest in rational choice and is a structurally prior part of a justified action, but it is the activity of rational choice that presupposes its value. In this sense, rational nature is the unconditioned condition of all value.

Let me confess, however, that I find these issues perplexing and even a bit mysterious. Quite clearly, the nature and basis of the unconditional value of rational choice demands a more thorough analysis.[32] Nonetheless, despite remaining questions about the details of Kant's theory of value, Kantian value theory does involve a significant priority of the unconditionally valuable—rational nature—over the conditionally valuable—happiness. In what follows, we will refer to this complex relationship between the two tiers of value as one of lexical priority.

One final comment about this more controversial aspect of Kantian moral theory: Surely some non-Kantians will still have serious reservations about the lexical priority thesis. Nonetheless, it is sensible to set these reservations aside. If lexical priority fails, a more familiar form of consequentialism, more like preference-satisfaction utilitarianism, can all the more easily be generated. If it succeeds, consequentialism still follows. Lexical priority clearly fits Kant's own view, however, and the point is to show that it does not tell against consequentialism. It thus makes sense, in this context, to accept the thesis in order to see what follows.

NOTES

1. Normative consequentialism, as I explain in chapter 1, involves the *structure* of the basic normative principle, not the arguments used to *justify* the principle. For our purposes, a normative theory has a consequentialist structure if the basic normative principle, whatever its justification, is a requirement to promote the good, and if it does not include basic agent-centered constraints on the maximization of the good. So understood, egoism and act utilitarianism are consequentialist normative theories.

Of course, such theories can include a recognition of the significance of secondary principles, decision procedures, character traits, and personal projects that do not directly aim at the good. Since I am not concerned with generating a complete topology, I leave aside the question of how one should classify various rule or indirect versions of consequentialism. Although I will defend maximization, a theory without constraints that does not require the maximization of the good is still consequentialist. The point of interpreting normative consequentialism in this particular way is to emphasize the main difference between Kantian deontologists and typical consequentialists.

2. Kantian internalism and its role in Kant's argument are developed and explained in chapter 2 and the appendix.

3. Even a person deciding to do nothing is thereby adopting an end. One cannot avoid this argument by intentionally not pursuing ends. Of course, if one is incapable of intentionally pursuing ends, or even if one does not recognize that it is up to him what he chooses to do, then this argument cannot get started. The argument is addressed to rational beings and, we might add, beings with a conception of themselves as capable of controlling their conduct.

4. See, for example, Fred Feldman (1978): 121–23, and John Hospers (1982): ch. 5.

5. From the structure of the argument, it could turn out that there were plural unconditioned conditions of value—different kinds of unconditioned value that condition different kinds of ends. This would raise interesting complications, but since there is only one kind of unconditioned value, I leave aside the qualifications in the formulation of the argument required by the possibility of multiple ends-in-themselves.

6. For a more thorough discussion of this issue, see Korsgaard (1983): 169–95 and (1986c): 486–505. See also Paton (1951b, 1951c). My understanding of these distinctions is based on Korsgaard's account of the nature and significance of these two distinctions.

7. Korsgaard (1983): 171.

8. See chapter 2 and the appendix for a fuller discussion of this issue.

9. As Robert Johnson has pointed out, it may be rather hopeless to limit the use of 'intrinsic' in this way; perhaps it would be best to stick with the more awkward and unfamiliar concept of unconditioned value and say that there are two kinds of intrinsic value: conditional final ends and the unconditional end-in-itself.

10. Korsgaard (1983) develops the contrast between Kant's view and Moore's organic unities and the concept of a constitutive means. See also Paton (1951c). For a comparison of "Aristotle and Kant on the Source of Value," see Korsgaard (1986c).

11. The structure of Kant's argument is set out in Korsgaard (1986a):183–202, esp. pp. 194–97. The following discussion of the value of happiness, however, departs from her reconstruction.

12. This way of putting the point follows Frankfurt's hierarchical account of freedom (1971). I am not, however, committed to the specifics of his account. In particular, my discussion aims for neutrality on the sufficiency of a compatibilist account of free will. For an excellent discussion of a rather minimalist account of Kantian autonomy, see Tom Hill (1989).

13. Rousseau, *Social Contract* (1762): bk. 1, ch. 8.

14. REL 51.

15. Paton (1951b), esp. 163–67. The discussion that follows is also influenced by Andrews Reath (1989): 42–72, esp. 55–59. Onora O'Neill's discussion of "principles of rational intending" is also relevant to this issue; see O'Neill (1989b), esp. 91–93.

16. On this point see Henry Allison (1990): 115, 126–27.

17. In addition to Rawls's original discussion of this issue, see Richard Brandt (1979); Stephen Darwall (1983): Chs. 8, 9; Peter Railton (1986); and Allan Gibbard (1991).

18. Mark Okrent has suggested that there is an interesting parallel between the Kantian position and naturalistic accounts of the good. The good of an organism is whatever is conducive to or part of the natural life of the organism. Persons, however, are rational beings whose lives are not naturally determined. Nonetheless, the good for us is still determined by the kind of beings that we are—that is, by our finite rational nature. The good for a person is constituted by whatever is conducive to or part of the person's rationally chosen life plan.

19. For a similar interpretation of this argument, see Hill (1992a): 144–45.

20. Thomas Nagel (1970, 1992).

21. In addition, unconditioned, pure practical reason does not involve a separate intelligible world, and it does not require a commitment to some form of contra-causal freedom. Even if we are compatibilist about freedom, we can nonetheless agree that pure practical reason provide us with a "higher vocation" than the rest of nature, because we can be moved by our conception of an unconditioned reason for action. This form of "autonomy of the will" does provide a reasonable basis for our clear sense of responsibility and accountability for our actions.

22. I would like to thank Jay Rosenberg for demonstrating how one might misread an earlier version of the last argument. He thus encouraged me to clarify the structure of the argument. I say a good deal more about these issue in the next two chapters.

23. On this issue see, for example, Foot (1978); Nagel (1970); Gewirth (1978); Williams (1981b); Darwall (1983); Gauthier (1985); Korsgaard (1986b, 1989b); Falk (1965); and Allison (1990).

24. This assumption was stated explicitly in Stephen Engstrom's comments on a paper of mine at the Pacific Division meeting of the American Philosophical Association in San Francisco, March 1987. Korsgaard also assumes that the argument shows that rational nature has a special kind of value; Barbara Herman (1989) maintains that the categorical imperative procedure shows that rational nature is lexically more valuable than happiness; and Thomas Hill assumes that there is some basis for the dignity-price distinction in Kant's ethics (and this distinction is clearly an elaboration of the concept of the end-in-itself). In each case, the distinction amounts to more than just lexical priority, because each of these people also thinks that rational nature has a special kind of value, but I am here concerned with the priority claim. The relationship between Kant's dignity principle and deontological constraints is discussed in chapter 7.

25. This reconstruction is based on Korsgaard (1986a), esp. 195–97.

26. This last way of the putting the point is taken from Stephen Engstrom's comments on a paper of mine at the Pacific Division meeting of the American Philosophical Association in San Francisco, March 1987.

27. Korsgaard (1983): 181.

28. Ibid., 195.

29. Professional correspondence, 1988. This objection to the higher value principle is made in Cummiskey (1989).

30. This seems to be why Kant says that rational nature has a dignity that is beyond all price. Although Kant does not adequately explain his concept of dignity, it does seem to signify, at least, the lexical priority of rational nature. Again, the distinction between dignity and price is discussed more fully in chapter 7.

31. This point is developed more fully in chapter 5, section II.

32. There are other important questions about Kantian value theory that we have not discussed, the most significant of which is the status of pleasures and pains of non-rational beings. This question is part of the broader issue of the nature of the conditional value of happiness. In the future I hope to have more to say about this issue.

In particular, it seems possible to defend the value of non-rational pleasure by focusing on the derivation of the formula of humanity. In reconstructing the regress argument, we discussed Kant's assertion that a rational being necessarily wishes to be free of inclinations. I maintained that this need not be interpreted as a wish to be disembodied but that, rather, it can be interpreted as echoing Rousseau's view that as rational beings, we want to be in control and not controlled by our inclinations. As we have reconstructed Kant's argument, it does *not* seem to require the problematic and controversial thesis that some inclinations do not provide a basis for prima facie reasons for action. Inclinations may be fine sources of justified actions as long as, first, they do not conflict with one's deeper commitments and, second, they are compatible with the reciprocal rights of others.

Although I am not prepared to defend the point, it seems to me that when I recognize the value, the prima facie reason-giving force, of my pleasure and the absence of my pain, my rational nature has nothing to do with the pain's disvalue; it is pain as such that I see as bad, not simply the pains of a rational being. So pain is bad, and provides a conditional reason for action, because rational beings do not like pain; but it is *pain* that is thus disvaluable—not simply the pains of rational beings. This is just the beginning of a sketch of a view; but if some such view could be worked out, it would provide a better, more direct account of our responsibilities to non-rational sentient beings.

5

A DERIVATION OF
CONSEQUENTIALISM

We have seen that normative consequentialism is fully compatible with Kant's theory of justification, his account of the motive of duty, his account of the formality of the moral law, and even the formula of universal law. We will now see that there is also a natural consequentialist interpretation of his theory of the good. But as I have said, a stronger conclusion seems surprisingly to follow: The philosophically favored interpretation of the formula of the end-in-itself certainly seems to be consequentialist. Although one might impose a deontological interpretation to the formula, there is no reason to do so, and there is good reason not to do so. So although the Kantian argument for consequentialism is not a mathematical deduction, it should provide considerations capable of determining the intellect.

First, in this chapter, the basic Kantian rationale for a consequentialist principle of right is presented. Second, in chapter 6, we consider the nature and basis of the Kantian duty of beneficence and Kant's distinction between perfect and imperfect duties. Then, in chapter 7, alternative deontological interpretations of Kantian normative theory, which emphasize *respect* for the *dignity* of persons and the Kantian ideal of the kingdom of ends, are considered and rejected. In chapter 8, we focus on the familiar and central problem of the sacrifice of the innocent.

I.   REVIEW OF THE PREVIOUS ARGUMENT

We have covered a lot of ground, so let's briefly review the argument of the last three chapters: Since moral laws or requirements apply equally to all rational beings, they cannot be based on mere subjective inclinations (chapters 2 and 3). The "determining ground" of the good will—that is, the reason why the agent adopts and acts on the principle of action—thus cannot be a mere subjective end (chapter 3). If the determining ground of the principle (the maxim) is not the end (the matter) of the action, then, Kant suggests, only the *form* of the principle remains as a possible determining ground. A universal and unconditional requirement (or moral principle) has the form of a *law* of action (or freedom). As a result, Kant suggests that a principled (or dutiful) person acts on the basis of the mere *idea of law as such*, which includes the idea of avoiding practical self-contradiction. Since an intentional action always presupposes a principle of action, which Kant calls a maxim of action, one can avoid practical self-contradiction if one acts only on maxims that are compatible with the nature of law as such (chapter 3). I have argued that the idea of acting on universalizable maxims, or of avoiding practical self-contradiction, is a necessary condition of moral action but that moral obligations also presuppose that there is an objective end, or determining ground, of rational action, because only such an end can provide the requisite unconditional and universal determining ground of the will (chapter 4).

Now, Kant was an internalist: Moral reasons necessarily motivate rational agents, and only a necessary characteristic of rational agency itself can necessarily motivate all rational agents. The Kantian conception of a moral requirement entails that the agent's perspective and motivational capacities must be the source of moral requirement (chapter 2 and the appendix). Yet, unlike Humeans, Kant argues that moral requirements (the idea of a categorical imperative) presuppose an objective determining ground of the will—an end-in-itself (chapters 2 through 4).

This brings us to the transcendental regress argument. In thinking of my ends as valuable, I necessarily assume that there is an unconditioned condition of their value. But only something that is good absolutely and without any qualifications can provide the unconditioned condition of all value. If we pursue a regress from the conditioned to the unconditioned, we discover that setting oneself ends necessarily presupposes that one takes oneself to be the unconditioned condition of the value of the ends one sets. Thus, Kant concludes that as a rational being, I necessarily conceive of myself as an end-in-itself, and for the exact same reason, I must also conceive of all other rational beings as ends-in-themselves (chapter 4).

II.   THE EQUIVALENCE ARGUMENT FOR CONSEQUENTIALISM

We now need to fill out the practical significance of the idea that rational nature is an end-in-itself and establish that it provides an objective end or moral goal for a consequentialist principle of right. The distinctive characteristic of rational nature, as opposed to mere animality, is "the capacity to set oneself an end" (MM 392; GMM 412). Human beings are end-setters, and this end-setting capacity is itself to be treated "as an end and never simply as a means" (GMM 429). Thomas Hill has pointed out that to treat rational nature "merely as a means" is "to fail to treat it in some other appropriate way while one is treating it as a means." This other appropriate way is nothing more nor less than treating rational nature also as an end. So treating rational nature as an end is both necessary and sufficient for treating it not simply as a means.[1]

So, what is it to treat rational nature as an end? We have seen that rational nature is not an ordinary end or purpose of an agent but is, rather, the source of the value of other ends. The justified pursuit of any end whatsoever presupposes the value-conferring power of autonomous rational choice. If the value of all other ends depends on this capacity, then it has a special kind of value—an absolute and unconditional value, according to Kant. As Hill and others have argued, if a capacity has such a special kind of value, "one must seek to preserve, develop, and exercise [it]," and one must do so in a way that also recognizes the same special value of other rational beings.[2] Since rational nature is the source of the value of all other particular ends, its value should take priority over that of other ends. The conditions necessary for the flourishing of both my own and others' rational nature is thus a limiting condition on the value of all other ends.

Although the special value of rational nature is aptly described as a limiting condition or constraint on all other ends, the flourishing of rational nature is nonetheless an end that we must promote. As Onora O'Neill has explained,

> a necessary and hence universal constraint or limit on the pursuit of goals is constituted by the need to maintain the conditions of the pursuit of other goals, that is, the need to maintain agency throughout the universe of moral agents under considerations. A major part of what is required to maintain agency consists in not undercutting or destroying it. . . . However, the agency of finite beings is too vulnerable for us to be able to secure it merely by guaranteeing that it is not undercut or destroyed. . . . Finite rational beings also need positive support from others if they are to remain agents.[3]

If rational nature has absolute value and is an end-in-itself, then we must see to it that we do not act in ways that undermine rational agency, and we must also see to it that it is preserved and protected, so that its development and exercise are possible.

It may appear that what we have here is a negative duty not to undermine agency and a positive duty to promote agency. Although there is something to this idea, the supposed negative duty is really a duty to see to it that rational nature is not undercut or destroyed. If there is something we can do that will prevent the rational agency of others from being undermined or destroyed, and if rational nature has absolute and unconditional value, then we should do what is necessary to preserve it. Typically this will involve my not destroying or undercutting the agency of others, but it will also require that I prevent others from destroying or undercutting agency. Both the negative and the positive duty are really aspects of a requirement to promote the generally necessary conditions for the flourishing of rational agency. The idea that rational nature is an end-in-itself that has absolute value thus amounts to a supreme moral goal that we are required to promote: We should strive to promote the conditions that are needed for the general development and exercise of rational agency, or, more briefly, we are required to promote the flourishing of rational nature. Of course, we must also recognize the value of others' ends and thus promote the realization of the permissible ends of rational agents.

This is the first point in the derivation of consequentialism, but from this (dual) moral goal and relatively uncontroversial consequentialist principle, we do not get a full-blown consequentialist normative theory. The Kantian deontologist will insist that this moral goal only grounds an imperfect duty, which is rigidly constrained by perfect duties, so this moral goal does not lead to consequentialism. We thus need to show that we are required to maximally promote this moral goal. In chapter 6, we will also examine the concept of imperfect duties, and the idea that the pursuit of moral goals is limited and constrained by perfect duties. Furthermore, it will be objected, the special value of rational nature is such that it is incompatible with any consequentialist maximizing principle, because rational nature has a dignity that cannot be captured by any consequentialist aggregative principle.[4] We thus need to show, first, that rational nature is indeed the kind of ("agent-neutral") value that can ground a consequentialist principle of right. And second, in chapter 7, we need to look more closely at alternative interpretations of the dignity of rational nature and the requirement to respect it in others. Clearly these objections to consequentialism reflect Kant's own conception of beneficence as an imperfect duty and also his conception of the absolute value and dignity of humanity. So in the next two chapters, Kant's normative views need to be considered and evaluated. I hope to show now, however, that there is a straightforward and sensible consequentialist interpretation of the Kantian conception of rational nature as an end-in-itself.

The formula of the end-in-itself is constituted, at least in part, by the complex moral goal of promoting the flourishing of rational nature and the realization of permissible ends. In order to more fully specify this normative principle, we need to return to the derivation of the end-in-itself in order to see what normative conclusions follow from the derivation. If one accepts the Kantian argument for the end-in-itself, one is committed to the *equal* significance of all rational beings and their happiness (interpreted as the satisfaction of an ordered set of rational desires). The central Kantian move from the subjective perspective to the objective requirement is based on this principle. The Kantian idea, roughly, is that the actions of any person, in the final analysis, have the exact same rational basis and justification as any of my justified actions. Rational nature is thus the source of all value, and it thus has the absolute value

that is presupposed by the idea of morality as a system of categorical imperatives. Basically, if I am to think of myself as a source of value, I must also think of
all other agents as sources of value. Whatever value I thereby attribute to myself
and my ends, I thus must also attribute to each other agent and her ends. In
short, all agents have equal practical significance or equivalent value. We will
call this argument the "equivalence argument."

In chapter 1, a consequentialist normative theory was defined as one that
requires the promotion of the good, without including any agent-centered
constraints on the maximization of the good. The equivalence argument and the
two supporting arguments that follow it (the indirect proof in section III of this
chapter, and the derivation of the principle of beneficence in chapter 6) are
supposed to establish the first component of consequentialism. Chapters 7 and 8
then try to establish the second component. The two parts are connected,
however, because the basic strategy is to show that a Kantian should accept the
first component, but the rationale for the first component generally undermines
arguments for basic agent-centered (or deontological) constraints.

The equivalence argument concludes that in choosing, ordering, and pursuing my own ends, I am rationally committed to the equal significance of other
persons. A concern for the equal status of other rational agents functions as a
higher-order regulative condition on the rational affirmation and ordering of
ends and a limiting condition on particular actions (chapter 2, section V). As an
initial approximation, this means, first, that the pursuit and realization of ends
that I endorse should be consistent with the necessary conditions of rational
agency in myself and others; and second, that the rationally chosen (or legitimate) ends of others must count equally with my own ends.[5] It would seem to
follow that in promoting the flourishing of rational agency and happiness, we
should be strictly impartial and count all equally.

This brings us to the second point. The key move in the argument is from the
equivalence of the ultimate determining ground of all subjective principles to
the objective principle, which asserts the equal objective value for each rational
agent of rational nature as such. The capacity for rational choice, which makes
me an unconditioned condition of value, is a capacity of rational nature as such,
and thus all rational beings are similarly unconditioned conditions of value. The
idea here is that rational nature is an "agent-neutral" rather than an "agent-
relative" value, to use Nagel's terms; that is, roughly, rational nature is a value
for any rational agent.[6] The egoist halfway stop, or subjectivist alternative,
insists that each person's happiness or rational nature is a good for that person.
On this view, the good is relative to the agent. The Kantian view is that anyone's
rational nature is an end for any agent in the sense that each agent has a reason to
treat the rational agency of any other agent as an end. On this view, the good is
not relative to a particular agent, and in this sense it is an agent-neutral value.
(This point will soon be discussed more fully.) As a result, a two-tiered conse-

quentialist principle provides a perfectly reasonable conception of treating rational nature as an end-in-itself.

This brings us to the third point and the initial consequentialist conclusion. The equal value of all rational beings implies that all rational beings are equally significant in deciding what to do. Thus, I must choose courses of action that reflect this equal value. Clearly, the most straightforward way to do this is to treat the value of all such beings equally. And the obvious way to do that involves striving as far as I can to promote the necessary conditions for, first, reflective rational choice, and, second, the effective realization of rationally chosen ends. The first part of this principle does not require us to maximize rational being or our rational capacities. Rational nature is not something that we are to maximize in that sense. It does, however, require the maximal promotion of the conditions that are necessary for the flourishing of rational agency. The second part of this principle may require something like the maximization of rational-desire-satisfaction or corrected-preference-satisfaction.

More accurately, however, desires and preferences come ordered and ranked in various complex ways. One should avoid an overly atomistic conception of a person's ends. Conceptions of the good include higher-order synthesizing principles that order and adjust individuals' ends. We should think of an "agent's ends" (which we are to make our own) as referring to an ordered cluster of ends that the individual aims to realize in the course of a life. And we must be aware that individuals regularly revise and adjust their ends in response to circumstances, changing tastes, and evolving ideals. This is why the duty to make others' ends one's own should be filled out as a requirement to promote the conditions that are generally necessary for the effective realization of ends. The idea is that each person's ordered set of ends must be given equal consideration.

Once again, for various reasons, the best means of promoting the good typically involves paying particular attention to our own ends, commitments, and attachments. Nonetheless, the legitimacy of doing so follows indirectly, not directly, from the Kantian conviction that rational nature as such is an end-in-itself (see chapter 2, section V).

It will be objected that the end-in-itself is supposed to provide a constraint on the pursuit of goals, rather than a requirement to promote the good. This objection is based on a confusion. In the consequentialist interpretation, rational nature as such and the legitimate ends of others are indeed constraints on the pursuit of my subjective ends. This brings us to the fourth point. A constraint in this sense is fully compatible with a consequentialist normative principle. As I argued throughout chapters 2 and 3, consequentialism can be "duty-based" in this sense. More specifically, as we shall see, we are *required* to maximally promote the conditions necessary for rational agency and happiness. Consequentialism, so understood, is a constraint on all subjective and "arbitrary" ends. Clearly, one can argue that morality constrains one's inclinations, or merely subjective projects, without being committed to agent-centered constraints on the maximization of value. Hence, there is nothing in the argument thus far that rules out a consequentialist interpretation of the requirement to treat rational beings as ends-in-themselves and not merely as means only. So normative consequentialism is consistent with the derivation of rational nature as the end-in-itself.

The fourth point, however, is that for the Kantian consequentialist, the requirement to promote the flourishing of rational nature is an agent-centered requirement; it is even an agent-centered constraint on the maximization of one's *own good*. Indeed, *the maximization of happiness is also constrained and limited by this requirement*. What distinguishes Kantian consequentialism from standard deontology is simply that it does not recognize any additional agent-centered constraints on the maximization of *the good*. It is worth noting that there is no practical difference between agent-centered and agent-neutral requirements, if all the requirements have a consequentialist structure. (For more on this point, see the appendix.)

Since we have provided a clear rationale for a requirement to promote the two tiers of value, the deontologists must provide a rationale for the *additional* agent-centered constraints that they wish to defend. In subsequent chapters, the problems with justifying these additional constraints on the consequentialist requirement will become clear.

Since the requirement to promote the flourishing of rational nature and the permissible ends of others is based on the absolute and unconditional value of rational nature, this end must take priority over all other ends. If we value rational nature above all else, then we should strive to *maximally* promote the flourishing of rational nature. In order to further see that this is so, let us look more closely at the concept of setting oneself an end.

Consider Kant's discussion of the hypothetical imperative: According to Kant, it is a requirement of rationality that one must either take the necessary and available means to one's ends or abandon the ends. Indeed, if one has set oneself an end, one must be willing to take some sufficient means to that end. Kant takes this to be analytic, because it simply spells out what it is for a rational agent to make something an end.[7] Now, as Hill explains, the hypothetical imperative is not itself a maximizing principle, because it always leaves one the option of simply abandoning an end rather than continuing to promote it.[8] Nonetheless, the difference between hypothetical and categorical imperatives, as we have seen, is that for the former the ends are subjective and contingent, and thus can be abandoned, whereas for the latter the ends are objective and necessary, and thus cannot be abandoned. It remains a principle of rationality, however, that one must take the necessary and available means to any ends one sets oneself.

Again, this is simply what it is to set oneself an end, rather than to wish or hope for something. If I set myself the end of skiing, then I am committed to taking the necessary means to achieve this end. Now, of course, this does not mean that I must *maximize* how much I ski in my life, as if I had no other ends. Often I will choose to pursue some other end instead. Skiing is one of my ends, but it has a proper place in my overall conception of the good. In addition, my end is not simply to ski; rather, it is to do *some skiing* this winter (or more skiing this winter than last winter). Typically, one thinks, "I only went skiing twice last winter; I plan to go more (or about ten times) this winter." If I have really set myself this end, then I must do something to *make it so*. If I do nothing, then I have not really set myself the end; it is simply an idle wish. When I set myself an end, and thus will the end, I am thereby committed to achieving the end. In contrast, compare the quite different thought, "I *wish* I could ski more this winter"—here there is no commitment to doing anything to actually make it so.

This brings us to our fifth point. As a rational agent, I must either take the necessary and available means, and some sufficient means, to my ends or abandon (or alter and adjust) those ends. Since the ends required by the categorical imperatives are necessary, and thus cannot simply be abandoned, one must take the necessary and available means to these ends. (If the ends conflict, then one must alter and adjust the ends as required by the end-in-itself.) But this is simply to say that insofar as one is determined by reason, one must do all that one can to promote the ends of morality. But "to do all that one can do" is to do the maximum that one can do; so I am rationally required to *maximally promote* the objectively valid ends of morality. We have already seen that the special value of rational nature suggests, even to Kantian deontologists, that one must strive to promote the flourishing of rational nature. It now follows that I am required to strive to maximally promote this end.[9]

Nonetheless, although I am required to maximally promote this end, I do not have to set myself the end of maximizing my rational capacities, or maximizing the use of my rational capacities, or maximizing the number of rational beings. As Kant recognized, the absolute value of rational nature does not entail that rational nature is something to be produced so that the world will have more value (GMM 437), and it also does not imply that human life must always be preserved (MM 333, 349, 423–24).[10] The value of rationality should not be thought of as something independent and detachable from the particular ends and concerns of the individual (chapter 4, section III). The idea is that each agent, if she is to think of her ends as providing reasons for action, must recognize rational nature as the source of all value and hence as having a special value itself. (We will return to this point in a moment.)

These five points constitute the core of the positive argument for the consequentialist interpretation, but there are many points of clarification that are still necessary, and many objections and alternatives that must be addressed. The rest of the book will build on the equivalence argument and respond to the most important and common objections to the consequentialist interpretation. Let us begin this task with two points of clarification.

First, I have insisted that the consequentialist interpretation does not presuppose that Kantian value is some stuff and that we are to produce as much of this stuff as possible. The stuff view is a familiar view, but it does not capture the Kantian conception of value. The Kantian conception of value, as I understand it, is a "person-affecting" conception of value, to use Derek Parfit's phrase. The idea is that each existing person in virtue of his rational nature (or humanity) has a claim to equal consideration. The idea is not that rational nature is an intrinsic value from the point of view of the universe, so the more of it the better. The idea is that all persons, in virtue of the value they place on their own nature, are committed to the equal value of other persons.

The difference between these two conceptions of value undermines the "population objection" to Kantian consequentialism—that is, the objection that the Kantian consequentialist view requires us to maximize the total number of rational beings. Rational nature is not some stuff such that, if there is more of this stuff, then the universe has more intrinsic value. Kant seems to be making this point when he states that rational nature or humanity is not an end to be produced by our actions but is instead a "self-existent" end (GMM 437). As Hill explains, "The point, apparently, is that whenever humanity exists it is an end by virtue of what it is and to say that humanity is an end is not to say that something which does not yet exist should be produced or that the quantity of something desirable should be increased."[11] The idea is that rational nature is an end in the sense that persons who exist (and persons who will exist) provide constraints on the subjective ends of any autonomous rational agent.

Second, it might be objected, by Korsgaard for example, that I have conflated two distinct notions of agent-neutral value. We must distinguish, she has argued, between an objective realist and an intersubjectivist interpretation of agent-neutrality.[12] The above "straightforward" interpretation presupposes that values can be added "across the boundaries between persons," but this presupposition is only plausible if one believes that neutral values are "out there" in the world independent from any subject, she argues. For the objective realist, legitimate subjective values or reasons will be derived from the prior and independent objective ones. On the other hand, Korsgaard claims,

> on an Intersubjectivist interpretation, neutral reasons are shared, but they are always initially subjective or agent-relative reasons. So, on this view, everything that is good or bad is good or bad *for* someone. This makes it natural for an Intersubjectivist to deny that values can be added across the boundaries between people. My happiness is good for me and yours is good for you, but the sum of these is not good *for* anyone, and so the Intersubjectivist will deny that the sum as such is a value.

This is an important objection, and the response to it should help clarify the Kantian consequentialist position. What exactly is the problem with the consequentialist position supposed to be? Given Korsgaard's own transcendental regress argument (see chapter 4), we start from the subjective ends of particular agents, but we discover that each agent is committed to the "neutral" value of all other agents. Even though initial values are always "subjective," the shared neutral values are required by the reasons that support the "initial" subjective values. Agent-neutral reasons are inescapable, necessary requirements of agent-centered practical reason. In short, although *all reasons are agent-centered*, and objective reasons are thus derived from subjective concerns, objective practical reasons *are not agent-relative in any significant sense*.

This point does not presuppose that neutral value is "out there"; indeed, it is incompatible with such an interpretation. The Kantian idea must be that *I* am committed to the value of all other agents and their ends, if I think my ends are justified at all, and the same is true for all other agents. So my rationally chosen ends are good—that is, they provide *me* with reasons for action—only if I also take the rationally chosen ends of any other agent as also good, in the sense that they also provide *me* with reasons for action. So, contra-Korsgaard, the combination of these two goods is good for someone (that is, it provides someone with a reason for action). Indeed, the good of every agent is, in an important sense, a good for each agent (that is, it provides a possible reason for action for each person).

Now, of course, the combinatorial principles are more complex than a simple summing operation.[13] Indeed, I do not even simply sum up my own ends. I combine them into a coherent whole by weighing the significance, the costs, and the possibilities and then ordering them according to my best judgment. Morality adds the additional complexity of giving equal consideration to other persons and their ends. Thus, the ordered set of ends of each agent ought to be shaped by a fundamental moral sensibility: If I am committed, first, to the equal status of all and to the equal significance of the permissible ends of others, then I may have to revise and shape my ends, commitments, and projects in light of this fundamental commitment. So the idea is not to hold all subjective ends fixed and then maximize. The consequentialist idea includes and incorporates the regulative role of the end-in-itself in shaping and reinforcing the attachments of a morally good agent (see chapter 2, section V).

The idea is not to simply sum; rather, it is for each agent to revise in light of the value of all, and then, after suitable revisions, to count all equally. Again, this concept does not imply that in one's day-to-day life, one should treat all ends equally, in the sense that one should not distinguish between sets of ends and directly promote the particular ends of oneself and others. There are good "neutral" and impartial reasons to adopt partial secondary principles and virtues. Mill was quite clear on this point:

> The great majority of good actions are intended not for the benefit of the world, but for that of individuals, of which the good of the world is made up; and the thoughts of the most virtuous man need not on these occasions travel beyond the particular persons concerned, except so far as is necessary to assure himself that in benefiting them he is not violating the rights, that is, the legitimate and authorized expectations of any one else.[14]

As we shall see in chapter 6, Kant also emphasizes this point.

To conclude, the essence of the move from the subjective to the objective, in the derivation of the end-in-itself, involves a denial of the significance of the "boundaries between persons" *in the particular sense that is necessary to avoid consequentialism.* The basic idea is that the value of others and their ends has the same basis as the value that I place on myself and my ends; that this is a neutral value in the sense that each person must recognize the equal value of others and their ends; and that thus each person is required to promote the conditions necessary for the flourishing of rational agency and the realization of ends. Since rational nature is an absolute value that thus takes priority over all other ends, we are required to do all that we can do to promote this end.

Nonetheless, the Kantian consequentialist recognizes that the good for each person is determined by the person's own conception of his or her happiness and that each person matters because each person takes himself or herself to be a source of value. Korsgaard claims that this idea implies that values cannot be added across the boundaries of persons, but it simply does not imply this. On the contrary, it naturally suggests, as Kant claims, that each person must treat all persons as self-originating sources of value and therefore recognize that others' legitimate ends count just as much as one's own. The integration and combination of my own initial ends and the ends of others thus provide my "agent-centered," yet nonetheless "neutral," practical reasons.

For the Kantian consequentialist, like the deontologist, rational nature has a special kind of value. Nonetheless, Kant does not embrace an *unconstrained* consequentialist interpretation of his conclusion, and in subsequent chapters we will examine Kant's own view and the more familiar deontological interpretation of it. In particular, we will examine Kant's concept of the dignity of humanity and the significance of the Kantian concept of respect for persons (chapter 7). We will also consider Kant's own principle of beneficence and his distinction between perfect and imperfect duties (chapter 6), between maxims of action and maxims of ends (chapter 8), and between duties of justice and duties of virtue (chapter 8).

It is important to realize, however, that Kant's normative distinctions cannot simply be assumed. They must be justified, and the intuitive plausibility of these distinctions does not provide a sufficient justification. In time we will address these distinctions and the important issues they raise. My goal at this point is to present the *positive rationale* for Kantian consequentialism. In subsequent chapters, I will respond to the many objections to this interpretation, and I will also argue against the more popular non-consequentialist alternatives—including Kant's own rather extreme interpretation, which we must not forget is rejected even by most Kantian deontologists.

In this section, we have seen that the crucial move in Kant's argument from the subjective to the objective point of view must be based on the agent-neutral value, or reason-giving force, of rational agency as such. I have claimed that the move from the unconditional value of my rational nature to the objective value of rational nature as such depends on the justificatory equivalence of all instances of rational nature. I have suggested that the appropriate conclusion is that both rational nature and rationally chosen ends are agent-neutral values. The formula of the end-in-itself—that is, always treat rational nature as an end and not a means only—thus demands that we maximally promote these Kantian values. It remains to be seen whether Kant's argument provides a rationale for any additional deontological constraints on this basic consequentialist principle.

III.   AN INDIRECT PROOF OF CONSEQUENTIALISM

In addition to the above equivalence argument, I offer the following indirect proof that rational nature must be an agent-neutral, not agent-relative, reason for action. Consider the agent-relative alternative: Let us assume that the duty to think of oneself as an end-in-itself is interpreted as an agent-relative reason for action. Now, the transcendental regress argument moves from an agent's assumption that his or her rational nature is an unconditioned condition of value to the claim that rational nature as such is the end-in-itself. So if the objective end of action is agent-relative, then this must be a consequence of the subjective conception of the significance of one's own rational nature.

It has been argued, for example, that my conception of myself as an end-in-itself generates a requirement to avoid all maxims that would undermine my rational existence.[15] After all, the argument continues, according to the Kantian position, if one is to act at all, then one cannot without practical self-contradiction treat oneself as subordinate to the ends of one's action, because one's self is the source of the value of the ends and must thus be an objective end of all of one's actions. Since an objective end is an end that is demanded by the idea of conforming to law (or practical reason) as such, and since the only way to avoid practical self-contradiction is to always treat oneself as an end-in-itself, it seems to follow that preserving *my existence* as a rational being is an objective and unconditional constraint on all my actions. Since any consequentialist principle may require that I sacrifice myself for the sake of the good, this conclusion conflicts with all consequentialist interpretations of the Kantian conclusion.

Although this move may avoid the Kantian consequentialist conclusion, it surely does not generate the desired deontological alternative. If one interprets the argument in this way, the move from subjective to objective generates a supreme requirement that each rational being preserve his or her rational existence. We still get a consequentialist normative principle, but the supreme good is now my self-preservation! And this leads directly to an extremely minimalist, radically Hobbesian normative conclusion: Since I cannot sacrifice myself, *because* I must in every maxim of action will my own rational existence, it would seem that for the same reason, I cannot rationally will a maxim that permits my death (either as a means or as an end). It follows that each rational being is required to do whatever is necessary to preserve itself.

There are two points here. First, the argument makes self-sacrifice forbidden; it is impermissible for me to sacrifice myself to save others. Second, it also requires me to sacrifice others to save myself, because I am required to avoid all actions that undermine my existence. Consequently, if necessary, I may lie, cheat, steal, and kill without a qualm. Indeed, it would be my duty to do so. So this "Kantian" argument entails an implausible Hobbesian conclusion.

Of course, the objection may simply be assuming that one also gets some form of the doing allowing or intending foreseeing distinction; but this assumption is simply pulled out of thin air. After all, the argument maintains that my supreme end must be my self-preservation. If an action is a necessary and available means to this end, then why would I not be required to do the action? It is all too common to simply assume some such distinction, because we all find the distinction intuitively obvious, but the point at issue is whether there is any Kantian non-consequentialist justification of some such distinction.[16]

Clearly, this particular Kantian attempt to avoid consequentialism was not intended to transform Kant into a Hobbesian. The important point is that there is a general lesson to be learned by this utter failure. Clearly, the Kantian must recognize that sacrificing oneself for the sake of others is not categorically forbidden.[17] Most Kantians believe, and Kant believed, that I may be required to die if preserving my life requires killing others, and that it is sometimes permissible to sacrifice oneself for the sake of others. We were led down the Hobbesian path because at first it seemed that such sacrifices involved subordinating oneself to another object—that is, using oneself as a means only. The Kantian must insist that there is a confusion in conceiving of self-sacrifice in this way. The important Kantian point is that I cannot sacrifice myself for a mere arbitrary, subjective, non-moral end. Sacrifices that are sanctioned by duty are entirely another matter.

Surely there are situations in which the only way to act consistently with one's fundamental commitments will involve sacrificing one's own finite existence. In particular, any available action that does not result in my death may require that I do something seriously wrong (or fail to do something that I am really required to do). (In more Kantian jargon, the mere idea of avoiding practical self-contradiction simply does not exclude the possibility of dying as a possible means of avoidance. If all my other alternatives result in practical self-contradiction, then perhaps in dying I can avoid practical self-contradiction.) Since the point is to never act contrary to reason, we need an independent argument showing that all maxims that require my death are never rationally justified maxims.[18] And, of course, what goes for me, by the equivalence thesis, goes equally for all others; others may also be required to risk death or face certain death.[19]

How then does the Kantian avoid the extreme Hobbesian conclusion? In the move from the subjective to the objective in his derivation, Kant writes, "every other rational being conceives its existence on the same rational ground which is valid for me." The idea here must be that the reasoning that leads me to the conclusion that I am an objective end also entails that every other rational agent is also an objective end. Indeed, the above derivation of the Hobbesian conclusion is an indirect proof that the Kantian must conceive of rational nature as an agent-neutral rather than agent-relative value.

Kant's conclusion is that as a rational agent, I must necessarily will rational agency as such as an end-in-itself. The regress argument claims to show that rational choice—the capacity to self-consciously set oneself ends—is necessarily the source of all practical value or reasons for action (if there is any value at all), and that rational nature is an end-in-itself, and thus a rational constraint on action, whether the rational agency is my own or any other being's. This does not imply that I must always will the continued finite existence of anyone, including myself.

I have argued that Kant's derivation of rational agency as the objective determining ground of a rational action requires an agent-neutral interpretation. The equivalence argument and the indirect proof establish that the consequentialist interpretation follows naturally and easily, no bells or whistles, from the structure of Kant's argument. Again, it remains to be seen whether there is an alternative interpretation that justifies deontological constraints on the duty to maximally promote the good.[20]

IV. THE KANTIAN CONSEQUENTIALIST NORMATIVE PRINCIPLE

There is a significant degree of common ground between Kantian deontologists and Kantian consequentialists. Both agree that treating rational nature as an end-in-itself suggests "that one must seek to preserve, develop, exercise, and 'honor' rational agency in oneself and to respect it in other human beings."[21]

From this, after considerable argument, the consequentialist concludes that the basic normative principle is a requirement to maximally promote the conditions necessary for the flourishing of rational nature and happiness. Despite the absence of deontological constraints, one should not underestimate the differences between Kantian consequentialism and classical utilitarianism.[22]

It should now be clear that the foundation, the internalist justification of the consequentialist normative principle, is thoroughly Kantian. In addition to this foundational difference between classical utilitarianism and Kantian consequentialism, there is also a significant *normative* difference. In order to see that this is so, we need to more fully articulate the Kantian consequentialist normative principle.

In practice, the special value of rational nature implies that I must respect it in myself and others. First, if rational choice confers value, then my actions should reflect this. So respect for my own rational agency includes choosing actions, practices, and policies that I believe to be the most justified. Second, I must also seek out justifications and develop my capacities to evaluate my options and ends. If I value my rational nature, then I must develop and exercise my rational capacities, then follow my best judgment. (This may, of course, include deciding not to deliberate too much, or deferring to others that seem to be better judges of the issue at hand). Third, if I am to satisfy the first two principles, I must develop the character traits necessary for successfully judging and doing the right thing. In these ways, I respect and promote my own rational nature, and I also manifest the unqualified value of a good will (chapter 2, section III).

In addition, since we value rational agency as the source of all other values and conceptions of the good, our principles of action should reflect this value. So, first, each agent should promote the conditions necessary for forming, revising, and effectively pursuing a conception of the good. Second, since all agents are equal, each agent should adjust his or her personal ends in light of the equal status of all other agents and their ends. Third, since others' ends are just as important as my own, each agent should recognize the equal value of the ends of others, and thus promote the happiness of others—provided that the ends of others are not inconsistent with the previous two conditions and are thus permissible.

As a practical matter, the first two requirements generate moral claims to liberty, to security, and to subsistence, and the third requirement generates a moral claim to the all-purpose means that are necessary for well-being or happiness. These requirements generate rights, in Mill's sense: Society (or, more generally, others) ought to protect individuals in the possession of these goods. Individuals should be protected in the possession of these primary social goods because doing so will most likely promote the flourishing of rational nature and happiness.[23] Of course, in deciding difficult cases of conflict between individuals, or between rights to subsistence, liberty, security, and well-being, we must adjudicate in light of the equal status of each person and his or her interest in realizing a self-chosen conception of the good.

Should we count all of a competent agent's ends equally, or should we count only an agent's rationally chosen ends? The conditions for the autonomous, reflective endorsement of ends should be promoted, and self-reflection should be encouraged. Nonetheless, each agent is the final judge of his or her own conception of the good. There is no standard of the good life that is independent from the informed, reflective choice of the person who will live the life (chapter 4). The good is simply the object of informed, autonomous, rational choice.[24] So within the constraints of morality, the person is the final authoritative judge of his or her own good. Of course, human beings are not fully informed and perfectly rational, so an individual's desires do not perfectly coincide with what she would judge to be good, for her imperfect self, if she were fully informed and perfectly rational.[25] We should, however, generally presume that others' ends are rationally chosen, provided, again, that they are permissible. The response to a perception of imperfect rationality should involve a reasonable attempt to provide the missing information or to point out the perceived error in reasoning. Yet, given that each individual is the source and final judge of her own conception of the good, we should recognize this fact by honoring the individual's own judgment of what is indeed good for her. In short, if we are to respect each person's capacity to set ends, then we must also respect the (permissible) individuality that results from the exercise of this capacity.

This is the full statement of the Kantian consequentialist normative principle. More simply and less accurately, the basic normative principle is a requirement to maximally promote two tiers of value: rational nature and happiness, where rational nature is lexically prior to happiness.[26] In what follows, the short version will stand in for the more detailed statement of principle.

As a result of the priority of rationality, the Kantian consequentialist can agree with the Kantian deontologist's insistence that respect for the rational nature of persons is more important than simply maximizing happiness. Many of the familiar objections to utilitarianism are thus avoided in a straightforward and theoretically motivated fashion. For example, the pleasures of the Coliseum cannot outweigh the fundamental interests of the victims. The luxuries generated by slavery cannot justify the sacrifice of the liberty of the slaves. More generally, in the distribution of resources (or primary social goods), each should be assured a satisfactory minimum of the basic goods necessary for life, liberty, and self-development before happiness is maximized. (These claims are developed in chapter 9.)

On the other hand, Kantian consequentialism may require us to sacrifice life or liberty in order to protect the lives or liberty of others (chapter 8). This basic intuitive objection to consequentialism remains. The important point, however, is that this intuitive objection has no defensible Kantian basis. Thus, if one rejects deontological intuitionism, then an indirect consequentialist account of our deontological intuitions and commitments is the only reasonable justification that remains.

Although the arguments of this chapter and the arguments that follow do not have the rigor of "moral geometry," they do provide a strong case for normative consequentialism. Indeed, I am convinced that if a form of normative consequentialism does not follow from Kantian internalist foundational considerations, *nothing* does. One should note, however, that even if the argument for consequentialism is not conclusive, we still have seen that the familiar assumption of a fundamental opposition between Kantian approaches to moral theory and consequentialist approaches is mistaken. Any Kantian rejection of consequentialism must be based on rather subtle and quite controversial details in the interpretation of the formula of the end-in-itself. This is *not a minor point.* If the defender of deontological constraints simply insists that neither consequentialist nor deontological principles clearly follow from Kant's argument, then the defender must also grant that Kantian ethics and consequentialism are not fundamentally incompatible. Indeed, we would then be faced with two different interpretations of the formula of the end-in-itself, and we would be left with no Kantian reason to choose one rather than the other. Nonetheless, although a tie of this sort would itself be significant, I do believe that the weight of consideration, in the final analysis, establishes consequentialism as the philosophically favored interpretation of Kantian ethics.

V.   CONCLUSION

Most Kantians believe that there is a duty—at least an imperfect one—to promote the happiness of others and that the greater the sacrifice, the greater the virtue. As I have emphasized, Kant explicitly and repeatedly states that this is his view—indeed, he almost never misses an opportunity (GMM 398, 423, 430, 441; MM 326, 385–86, 388, 389, 393–94, 398, 402, 452–53). Since, in general, Kantians recognize that the objective justification of the value of an end gives rise to a requirement to promote the end, the Kantian cannot simply deny that considerations of objective value generate agent-neutral requirements. The nonconsequentialist Kantian is thus faced with quite a challenge. We need an explanation of the asymmetrical treatment of the conditional but objective value of happiness and the unconditional and objective value of rational nature. We also need an explanation of the equal practical significance of each person that does not generate the consequentialist interpretation. But this explanation must avoid the implausible Hobbesian duty to preserve oneself at all costs. All Kantians must recognize that some sacrifices are called for—there is some duty to aid those in need—and Kantians should grant that significant sacrifices are not only permissible but are also a sign of virtue. Although Kantian deontology is intuitively plausible, it is not at all clear how it is supposed to follow directly from the derivation of the end-in-itself.

The widespread assumption that Kant's argument generates agent-centered constraints on the pursuit of the good appears to be indefensible. Even most of their defenders agree that deontological constraints on the maximization of value presuppose a non-value-based rationale (see chapter 1, section III). But as we have seen, the preceding argument is thoroughly value-based. For structural reasons alone, consequentialism should follow from this type of Kantian argument.[27] *Consistent Kantian internalism entails normative consequentialism* (if it entails anything at all). We must now consider some important objections to this conclusion. In the end, however, we shall see that there is no Kantian rationale for rejecting this result.

NOTES

1. Thomas Hill ([1980] 1992a): 41–42.

2. Hill writes, "One must seek to preserve, develop, exercise, and 'honor' rational agency in oneself and to respect it in other human beings" ([1991] 1992a: 204). The concept of respect and Hill's interpretation of Kant's distinction between price and dignity are discussed in chapter 7.

3. Onora O'Neill (1989c): 139.

4. See, for example, Herman (1993b) and Hill (1980, 1991a). According to Herman, "As the final end of rational willing, rational nature as value is both absolute and nonscalar. It is absolute in the sense that there is no other kind of value or goodness for whose sake rational nature can count as a means. It is nonscalar in the sense that (1) it is not the highest value on a single scale of value, and (2) it is not additive: more instantiations of rational nature do not enhance the value content of the world" (p. 238). As we shall see, the Kantian consequentialist can agree that the value of rational nature is absolute and even non-scalar in this sense. According to the Kantian consequentialist, the special value of rational nature implies that we should maximally promote the flourishing of rational nature. Although "more instantiations of rational nature do not enhance the value content of the world," as we shall now see, a concern for the absolute value of rational beings does suggest that one should count each person equally and, if one is in a position to do so, save as many as people as possible. (This last claim is developed and defended more fully in chapter 8.) Hill's account of the dignity principle is explained and discussed in chapter 7. His account of imperfect duties is discussed in chapter 6.

5. Nonetheless, individual virtues, commitments, decision-making procedures, or other secondary principles need not be strictly impartial, provided that it is possible to impartially justify these secondary principles, etc.

6. See Nagel (1986): ch. 9. Nagel recognizes that deontological constraints are formally puzzling because they involve agent-relative reasons that are not based on agent-relative interests or the character of the interest that they respect. His own account thus relies on the "apprehension of a normative truth" and an appeal to the doctrine of double effect. Nagel's realism conflicts with the Kantian internalist approach to justification. For a discussion of this issue, see Korsgaard (1992, 1993). On the doctrine of double effect, see Kagan (1989). Since the idea that rational nature is an end-in-itself provides a moral goal, the Kantian approach justifies the *pro tanto* or prima facie requirement to promote the good, a requirement that is central to Kagan's defense of consequentialism.

7. For a thorough discussion of Kant's views on this topic, see Thomas Hill (1973). See also Onora O'Neill (1989b), esp. 89–94.

8. Hill ([1989b] 1992a): 130.

9. For criticisms of maximizing rationality, see Michael Slote (1985, 1989); see also Michael Stocker (1990), esp. part 4.

Some may be inclined to reject maximizing rationality and thus disinclined to saddle Kant with such a position. I will not here respond to these objections, but I do not find them convincing. In addition, Kant does not argue against maximization; indeed, he often seems to assume that ends can be summed and that happiness is simply a "maximum of well-being" (GMM 418) or the satisfaction of the sum total of one's inclinations (GMM 405). Indeed, as we saw in chapter 3, he argues that all subjective activities and ends can be measured on the same scale of value, because all are based on our susceptibility to pleasure (CPrR 21–23). In short, maximizing rationality is plausible enough; Kant seems to embrace it and certainly does not argue against it; the recent arguments against it are not convincing; and the preceding interpretation of the categorical imperative involves a reasonable conception of maximization. (Again, we still need to see if Kant's arguments generate constraints on maximization.)

Finally, although the debate over maximization may be important and interesting to some, its relevance to the justification of deontological constraints is not obvious. It would seem that even non-maximizing views (sometimes called "satisficing" views) of rationality still need to justify basic constraints in order to avoid consequentialism and still vindicate commonsense morality (see chapter 1, section III). Of course, one may reject maximizing consequentialism because one generally rejects maximization, but this simply is not the classic Kantian problem with consequentialism, which is our concern. On this last point see Rawls (1971), esp. pp. 22–27, and Nozick (1974): 28–35, 48–51.

10. See also Hill ([1980] 1992a): 43–44, 51.

11. Ibid., 43–44.

12. Christine Korsgaard (1993), esp. sections I, II. Andrews Reath has also raised this objection to the consequentialist position. On intersubjectivism, also see Stephen Darwall (1983).

13. I have benefited here from discussions with Andrews Reath.

14. J. S. Mill ([1861] 1961): ch. 2.

15. This objection comes from Richard McCarty's paper (1992), which responds to Cummiskey (1990).

16. For a thorough discussion of these distinctions, see Shelly Kagan (1989).

17. Kant addresses this issue, and he clearly implies that self-preservation is not always a duty (GMM 423, MEJ 235, DOV 423–24).

18. Of course, this argument only sanctions my voluntary death when it is morally permissible or required. It remains impermissible to sacrifice my rational nature for the sake of *mere* subjective ends. If, however, I am enduring significant suffering and there is no reasonable hope of relief, then I do not see how I am sacrificing my rational nature in choosing to die. In such a situation, my suffering is already stealing my rational nature. The freely chosen decision to die may be the last great act of rational choice; it may reflect one's last affirmation of the life one values. Death with dignity is not an empty phrase, for acceptance of death itself can signify a reverence for one's rational nature. Similar considerations may apply to the permanent loss of one's rational capacity. A Kantian should distinguish morally unacceptable suicide and morally permissible euthanasia— even active euthanasia.

This conclusion does not conflict with Kant's own discussion of suicide. In discussing suicide, Kant carefully formulates his examples. He objects to the idea of one taking his life when he is in despair as a result of a series of misfortunes. Kant's conclusion is quite reasonable: I should not kill myself simply because the continuation of my life "threatens more evil than it promises pleasure." His reasoning for this conclusion in the *Groundwork* is suspect, but the conclusion that follows is sensible, and it follows from our reconstruction of Kant's argument. Suicide is usually wrong, but there is nonetheless a Kantian right to die.

19. In chapter 8, we see that this conclusion also entails that each agent may be required, by an equal concern for the value of all, to sacrifice some to save others.

20. John Taurek (1977) has presented a clever and surprisingly influential argument that the numbers do not count. Let us thus briefly consider whether his argument undermines Kantian consequentialism. Taurek presents two basic considerations in support of his thesis that the numbers do not always count. His first argument *assumes* that one may give disproportionate weight to one's own interests, compared to the interests of others, in deciding what to do. He then uses this assumption to derive the conclusion that others also need not be counted equally in deciding what to do. Since he presents no argument for the initial assumption and we have seen that there are good Kantian grounds for rejecting it, this first argument in no way challenges the consequentialist interpretation. We will revisit the question of the legitimacy of the assumption, however, in the next chapter, when we discuss the nature and comparative status of Kant's imperfect duties.

Taurek's second argument is based on the counter-intuitive implications of simple aggregative utilitarianism. This time, however, the rhetorical question is how many headaches equal a life, or how many mild headaches equal a severe migraine headache. It is clearly counter-intuitive to think that if killing someone or giving someone a migraine headache will (somehow) eliminate enough mild headaches, then the action is justified. Taurek suggests that the following principle accounts for this clear intuitive judgment: A person cannot be required to suffer a greater loss for the sake of any number of individual lesser losses. Very roughly, we cannot eliminate any number of mild headaches if doing so requires subjecting even one person to a greater headache.

Now, the intuition about the relative status of life versus mild headaches is indeed gripping. The conclusion, however, which essentially posits a lexical ordering of pains, is not even plausible. So what should we conclude? I believe that the correct account of these matters is captured by the two tiers of value (and other secondary principles). Life and liberty should not be lightly traded against mere discomfort. Of course, extreme pain, like a migraine, undermines rationality and is thus also a more serious matter than simple discomfort or discontent. There is no need, however, to rashly conclude that all pains are to be lexically ordered. If we wish to justify the above intuitions, the significance of the priority of rational capacities is the obvious place to which to turn.

So the numbers do count. If I have the end of helping others in need, then I should save others if I can (by permissible means and without unreasonable sacrifice). For the purpose of this discussion, I assume this qualification throughout (in chapters 6 and 8 we will consider the force of this proviso). If I save one person and then I can save one more, then I should save the second person too. I have a reason to save each, and no countervailing reason not to, so I should save each. Now, given that I should save each, if I can save both at once, then I should save both. This is all quite obvious, I hope. Since I should save all I can save, it is wrong not to save someone if I can. It thus seems to follow that I should save as many as I can save—the numbers do count. Of course, the hard cases, where some must be sacrificed to save more, remain (and will be discussed at length in chapters 6, 7, and 8).

21. Hill ([1991a] 1992a): 204.

22. Hill has claimed that all consequentialist interpretations of Kant's theory are just "another version of an all too familiar type: namely a theory that first assigns a quantity of intrinsic value to various possible outcomes and then treats the right decision as a function of these value assignments" ([1991a] 1992a: 205). It should now be clear that this claim is simplistic, if not simply false.

23. J. S. Mill ([1861] 1962): ch. 5, and ([1859, 1869, 1879] 1989).

24. Compare Mill ([1859] 1989): ch. 3.

25. This way of putting the point is derived from Peter Railton (1986): 163–207.

26. On the priority relationship, see chapter 4, section III.

27. There is an analogy here with Scheffler's account of the paradox of deontology (1988). The paradox is generated by the combination of a neutral or impartial perspective, maximizing rationality, and agent-centered constraints. Kantian deontologists are also committed to this apparently inconsistent triad: namely, the objective end of rational nature as such, the hypothetical imperative (which replaces maximizing rationality), and deontological constraints.

6

THE (NOT SO) IMPERFECT DUTY
OF BENEFICENCE

Kant's derivation of the formula of humanity provides a clear rationale for an unconstrained Kantian duty to maximally promote the good. In the next two chapters, I will further develop the Kantian argument for consequentialism. In this chapter, we will consider some textual questions and arguments that focus on the principle of beneficence and Kant's use of the then-common distinction between perfect and imperfect duties. As far as I can tell, Kant's rather uncritical and undeveloped views about the nature and priority of perfect duties and his more plausible views about the limits of justifiable coercion prevented him from even considering an unconstrained consequentialist principle of right. This is not, however, a criticism of Kant; we should not expect our central concerns to be his.

Of course, Kant's application of his normative theory reflects his strong deontological intuitions. The point is simply that Kant does not consider and thus does not respond to the current controversy about the justification of agent-centered constraints. Furthermore, his uncompromising application of the categorical imperative rests on comparatively minor points, like the distinction between perfect and imperfect duties, and not his theory of justification, or his insistence on an a priori method in ethics, or even his account of the motive of duty. So Kant was a deontologist, not a consequentialist; but the basis of his deontology is not to be found in the distinctively Kantian aspects of his moral theory.

Although the nature of imperfect duties and the distinction between perfect and imperfect duties is not philosophically very interesting, it is historically and textually important. So far, I have argued that Kant's foundational theory does not even purport to refute normative consequentialism. I have also argued that there is a natural consequentialist interpretation of the formula of the end-in-itself. In contrast to these arguments, Kant's position on the relationship between perfect and imperfect duties clearly conflicts with consequentialism. Now we must see if Kant has good grounds for his non-consequentialist position.

My argument—that he does not—has three parts. The first part defends a robust but possibly constrained interpretation of the imperfect duty of beneficence. Many Kantians assume that the imperfect duty of beneficence is a rather undemanding duty that only requires that one help others "sometimes to some extent."[1] According to this view, there is no general duty to promote the happiness of others, thus there is no general consequentialist requirement that would conflict with other deontological constraints. In contrast, I am convinced that Kant believed that imperfect duties, as a set, do *not* include an option or a prerogative, to use Samuel Scheffler's term, to give more weight to one's own personal projects than can be justified by an impersonal regard for the good of all.[2] Of course, the robust view of imperfect duties, which will be explained and defended in the following section, does not itself generate consequentialism, because even robust imperfect duties, according to Kant, are strictly constrained by perfect duties.

Thus, the second part of my argument considers three interpretations of the distinction between perfect and imperfect duties and finds that each interpretation quite clearly fails to provide a basis for constraining the duty of beneficence. Although this chapter is rather textual and somewhat scholastic, in the next two chapters we shall consider the more general and philosophical Kantian justification of such an unlimited and unconstrained duty of beneficence. In the end, we shall see that there are no good Kantian grounds for constraining the duty of beneficence. The Kantian (but not Kant's) justification of an *un*constrained principle of beneficence constitutes the third part of the argument.

So the first part of the argument, which takes up the first three sections of this chapter, develops and defends the robust interpretation of the principle of beneficence. The second part of the argument—the fourth section of this chapter—rejects the relevance of the perfect/imperfect duty distinction. Finally, in the next two chapters, I argue for the unconstrained interpretation by further developing the Kantian (not Kant's) rationale for it. Philosophically, the third part is the most important.

I.   THE PRINCIPLE OF BENEFICENCE

The formula of humanity, with its corresponding two tiers of value, is the basic normative principle of Kantian ethics, it thus provides the basis for all moral judgments. Following Barbara Herman, we can say that it justifies *deliberative presumptions* against certain kind of acts (negative duties) and supports the adoption of certain types of ends (positive duties).[3] Kant calls these deliberative presumptions "grounds of obligation" (MM 224).

Kant took care to point out that the formula of humanity could be approached from two different directions:

Now humanity could no doubt subsist if everybody contributed nothing to the happiness of others but at the same time refrained from deliberately impairing their happiness. This is, however, merely to agree negatively not positively with *humanity as an end in itself* unless everyone endeavors also, so far as in him lies, to further the ends of others. For the ends of a subject who is an end in himself must, if this conception is to have *full* effect in me, be also, as far as possible, *my* ends. (GMM 430)

Clearly, one of the best ways to further the ends of others is not to interfere with their choice and pursuit of ends; that is, each agent should adopt a presumption in favor of mutual non-paternalism, non-interference, and non-aggression. Non-interference with the legitimate ends of others is clearly important; but equally important is a social context that encourages the development of one's capacities and provides a reasonable expectation of happiness. Of course, each person must form and revise his or her conception of the good within the constraints generated by the circumstances and the equal claims of all others; but within these obvious constraints, there is a social duty to provide the necessary conditions for the effective pursuit of rationally chosen ends.

Typically, the satisfaction of this duty requires the construction of institutional structures and coordinated social practices, not simply individual actions. Still, individual actions are also called for. If an individual is in a position to help others, and the individual has a reasonable expectation of success without comparable losses, then the individual has a positive duty to provide assistance. The duty of mutual aid follows from the general duty to make others' ends my own; and this general duty, Kant explains, is an essential part of the idea of treating humanity as an end-in-itself. This last duty follows directly from the duty to promote the necessary conditions of others and their ends. Nonetheless, since there is so much controversy over duties to aid, let us look more closely at its basis.

Human beings are vulnerable creatures; we are finite rational beings, as Kant would say. Our vulnerability or finitude is a condition of our existence as rational choosers and pursuers of ends. In choosing and pursuing any end, we must also will the necessary conditions of our rational agency; for one who wills the ends must also will the necessary and indispensable means to that end. This is Kant's hypothetical imperative of rationality or consistent willing: Will the necessary means or abandon the end![4] So, since (1) rational agency is the unconditioned condition of the value of all ends and is thus a limiting condition on all actions; and (2) life and liberty are typically necessary conditions of the agency of finite rational beings; and (3) the preservation of life and liberty may require the assistance of others; it follows that (4) each rational agent must recognize a reason for helping other rational beings secure the necessary conditions for the development and exercise of their rational agency.

Similarly (but a bit more roughly), since (1) the value of our ends is based on the value-conferring power of rational agency as such, the mutual maximal satisfaction of ends is a limiting condition on one's realization of her ends; and (2) the realization of ends typically requires means over and above the agent's own body and mind; and (3) the maximal satisfaction of ends may require the assistance of others, it follows that (4) each rational agent must recognize a reason to make others' ends her own, thus it is a duty to help others whenever one is in a position to help without a comparable loss to oneself.

Thus, we have an initial Kantian justification of a two-tiered positive duty of beneficence. Kantians must recognize a clear deliberative presumption to aid the needy and promote the happiness of all.

It is important to distinguish this type of justification from a similar and influential explanation of the Kantian duty to aid. According to some recent interpreters, my own vulnerability provides a *condition* of my duty to aid. I am obliged to aid others because I must recognize my own vulnerability as a reason for willing that I receive aid. The idea behind this type of interpretation is to focus on the demands of rational willing and then show that "there are certain things a *human* rational will cannot rationally will, given the conditions of human willing."[5] According to this interpretation, I have a duty to aid because I am vulnerable.

The problem with this alternative interpretation is that it implies that non-vulnerable beings would have no responsibilities to vulnerable beings. This interpretation thus does not adequately account for the equal practical significance of all agents. It is also not Kant's considered view—even if it is entailed by some of his discussions of mutual aid. Of course, Kant does say that since an infinite being does not have inclinations, it also does not have "duties," but nonetheless, Kant clearly would acknowledge that even such a being must adjust its actions in light of the objective value of rational nature as such.

In my interpretation, on the other hand, human beings have a claim to aid because humans are vulnerable, but I am not required to aid others because I am vulnerable. I am required to aid others in need because other agents and their ends are limiting conditions on rational action. As a rational agent, I am committed to the unconditional value and value-conferring power of rational nature as such—and this is the source of my duty to aid, not the contingent fact that I happen to be vulnerable too.

The important point is that all rational beings have the capacity to set themselves ends. It is this capacity that represents the basis of the reason-giving force of an agent and her ends, and thus only this capacity to set and pursue an end is necessary to generate the duty of all other rational beings to respect such agents and their ends. Our vulnerability clearly determines much about how we ought to be treated; but even the invulnerable must treat us accordingly. It follows that even if an infinite rational being does not have "duties," such a being still acts according to its conception of an unconditional principle and necessarily respects the unconditional value of rational nature as such. Infinite beings have responsibilities rather than duties. All rational and autonomous agents must endeavor, insofar as they can, to make the ends of others their own.

II. THE ROBUST INTERPRETATION OF IMPERFECT DUTIES

It is all too common for philosophers to ignore Kant's explicit account and interpret the principle of beneficence as a fairly lightweight, undemanding imperfect duty. Yet as we have reconstructed Kant's argument, it generates a robust duty of beneficence, a duty that is limited only by our other duties. This also seems to be Kant's own conclusion. He states that I am required to make others' ends *my own;* that to help others *when one can* is a duty; and that one should endeavor *insofar as one can* to promote the happiness of others (GMM 398, 423, 430, 441). Nonetheless, despite Kant's rather explicit language, it is common to maintain that Kant's position on the duty of beneficence is really rather weak and undemanding.

It is, of course, common to think of beneficence as more or less optional. It is thus not surprising that champions of commonsense morality would look to Kant's concept of imperfect duty to capture this widely held view. Furthermore, the apparent dissolution of the supererogatory under the extreme demands of consequentialism has provided the basis for ongoing and lively controversy. As a result, some Kantians have endeavored to demonstrate that Kantian beneficence is not very demanding and that it thus leaves a moral space for the supererogatory—that is, actions that are above and beyond the call of duty, in the sense that the action is good to do yet not required by duty. The textual basis for this interpretation of Kantian beneficence is Kant's classification of beneficence as an imperfect duty. However, this meager and inadequate textual support fails to provide any rational basis for such an interpretation.

Kant states that an imperfect duty includes *a certain latitude for the inclination* to determine the required action. Since these imperfect duties include a greater latitude than perfect duties, Kant contrasts these "wide" duties with the "narrow" duties of justice (and respect) (GMM 421n; MM 390). The different possible distinctions between perfect and imperfect duties will be discussed more fully in section IV below. The central idea behind these claims, however, is that an imperfect duty is a *duty to adopt an end* rather than to do or omit a (type of) action. The duty to adopt an end, however, does not "specify precisely in what way one is to act and how much one is to do by the action for an end that is also a duty" (MM 390). Imperfect duties do not specify exactly what or how much one must do. Thus, many Kantian deontologists rashly conclude that one need not do much of anything at all to satisfy an imperfect duty.

Apparently, it is quite natural to read Kant's comments about imperfect duties, latitude, and inclinations as implying this kind of conclusion. Indeed, perhaps under the influence of an article by Thomas Hill, it has become somewhat of a dogma that Kantian beneficence, since it is an imperfect duty, only requires that one help others "sometimes to some extent."[6] We shall see, however, that the textual support, not to mention the philosophical basis, for this *anemic interpretation*, is inversely proportional to the conviction of those who defend it. Indeed, the textual case for the more *robust interpretation*, which I have suggested follows from Kant's argument, is quite clearly the stronger.

As I have continually emphasized, the robust interpretation is compatible with a derivative, more moderate and nuanced set of secondary principles that guide one's actions and decisions in the concrete context of day-to-day life. These more specific day-to-day virtues and secondary principles, however, must be derived from the more basic general principles, which will include the robust principle of beneficence.

In contrast to the anemic interpretation, the robust interpretation maintains that "one ought to do a beneficent act whenever one can, unless one chooses to follow instead some other principle of imperfect duty" (Hill [1971] 1992a: 151). The robust interpretation permits the agent latitude to determine a particular course of action in light of the various principles of imperfect duty that apply to the particular circumstance.

In defense of the robust interpretation, consider, first, that this is quite clearly how Kant describes the latitude of imperfect duties. He writes, "But a wide duty is not to be taken as a permission to make exceptions to the maxim of actions, but *only as permission to limit one maxim of duty by another* (e.g., love of one's neighbor in general by love of one's parents), by which in fact the field for the practice of virtue is widened" (MM 390, emphasis added). The defender of the anemic interpretation must attempt to creatively explain away what this passage seems to say—despite the fact that what it clearly seems to say is quite reasonable and consistent with Kant's main argument.

To this end, Mary Gregor and Hill claim that the context implies only the anemic interpretation. We are told that in the above "controversial passage . . . what Kant seems to be saying is that, whereas we may (and indeed must) restrict the number of times we are prepared to act on one maxim (e.g. to develop our talents) by adopting another maxim (e.g. to promote the happiness of others), we may not let our concern for one maxim keep us from adopting another" (Hill [1971] 1992a: 152). Now this conclusion seems true, indeed obvious, and it is also entailed by the passage—but it simply is not what the passage in question says. The passage says that the wideness of imperfect duties is "only a permission to limit one maxim of duty by another"; that is, we may not take the wideness of imperfect duties as a permission to make non-duty-based exceptions to the demands of imperfect duty; in more Kantian jargon, we cannot make inclination-based exceptions to the maxim of actions that would promote the obligatory end. We can, however, let inclination determine which imperfect duty we will act on and to what extent.

Kant's imperfect duty of beneficence is thus quite clear: One must endeavor insofar as one can to promote the (permissible) ends or happiness of all, provided, of course, that this is consistent with one's other duties. This proviso includes, first, a permission to limit one imperfect duty with another imperfect duty and, second, a requirement that perfect duties constrain imperfect duties.

In addition, the context of the "controversial" passage does not imply the anemic interpretation. Kant goes on to say: If one "brings closer to narrow duty (duties of right) the maxim of complying with wide duty (in his disposition) so much the more perfect is his virtuous action" (MM 390). Since we are to strive for our moral perfection, we are supposed to make perfectly virtuous action one of our ends. The idea is that one should make it a principle to develop the strength of character that would result in all of one's actions being self-governed by the ends that are also duties.[7] Indeed, in explaining the imperfect duty of moral perfection, Kant says it is a duty "only of *wide* obligation" because it prescribes only the maxim "to strive *with all one's might* that the thought of duty for its own sake is the sufficient incentive of every action conforming to duty" (MM 393, emphasis added). According to the anemic interpretation of imperfect duties, we should find Kant saying that one must "sometimes to some extent" strive to be more virtuous, but if on a particular occasion one is inclined to satisfy one's inclinations instead, that is fine. Whatever else Kant may seem to be saying, he is quite clearly and emphatically endorsing the robust interpretation of imperfect duties.

Hill offers two objections to the robust interpretation. First, he argues that Kant's rejection of the "fantastically virtuous" man "who allows *nothing to be morally indifferent* and strews all of his steps with duties, as with man traps" (MM 409) is incompatible with the robust interpretation because then a person would "never be free from obligation" (Hill [1971] 1992a: 152). Of course, here Hill seems to forget that a virtuous person has succeeded in adopting the obligatory ends and thus does not wish to be free from obligation. Similarly, a rational person wishes to be free from the inclinations which are an obstacle to duty, not from the demands of duty itself. But even leaving aside these details (which involve the conception of autonomy that is at the heart of Kant's moral system), if we examine the rest of the passage in question we see that it provides no support for the anemic interpretation. Kant continues, "it is not indifferent to him [the fantastically virtuous person] whether I eat meat or fish, drink beer or wine, supposing that both agree with me. *Fantastic virtue is a concern with petty details* which, were it admitted into the doctrine of virtue, would turn the government of virtue into tyranny" (MM 409, emphasis added). Quite clearly, all this passage suggests is that the "doctrine of virtue" is not concerned with "petty details." So this passage does not support the anemic interpretation over the robust interpretation—unless, of course, one wishes to suggest that the pains and projects of others are "petty details."

More important, one is not likely to promote the ends of others by tyrannically interfering with or judging all of the details of their lives. Indeed, in Mill and others, we find convincing arguments for a principle of respect for individuality and diversity even if one's only goal is to maximally promote happiness. The robust interpretation is not only textually compatible with this passage; it also justifies the passage.

Second, Hill rightly points out that Kant limits the duty of beneficence to others with a principle of beneficence to oneself; that is, I may sometimes refrain from making others happy in order to make myself happy. What could be more reasonable? But, Hill asks, does this not conflict with the robust interpretation of beneficence? I think the answer is that it does not conflict with a charitable interpretation, but it nonetheless shows the need to formulate the principle more fully. The amazing thing, however, is that this passage, which is supposed to undermine the robust interpretation, quite clearly refutes the anemic interpretation.

Kant gets himself into a bit of linguistic jam by claiming that there can be no "duty" to promote one's own happiness—because, for Kant, duty implies the opposition of inclination, and happiness (which is the sum total of inclinations) cannot be opposed by inclination. The central question this passage raises, however, is whether one ever has good reason to promote one's own happiness. Given that Kant focuses so exclusively on "duty" rather than on what we "ought" to do, or what we have "good reason" to do, this question easily becomes unnecessarily confusing. At any rate, given Kant's account of duty and inclination, one's own happiness is not included in the imperfect duty to promote happiness. But if the principle of beneficence did not include oneself, it would lack universality; as Kant says,

> since all *others* with the exception of myself would not be *all*, so that the maxim would not have within it the universality of law, which is necessary for imposing obligation, the law making benevolence a duty will include myself, as an object of benevolence, in the command of practical reason. . . . lawgiving reason, which includes the whole species (and so myself as well) in its idea of humanity as such, includes me as giving universal law along with all others in the duty of *mutual benevolence, in accordance with the principle of equality,* and *permits* you to be benevolent to yourself on the condition of your being benevolent to every other as well. (MM 451, some emphasis added)

So the imperfect duty of beneficence is a duty to promote the happiness of all, not just others, in accordance with the principle of equality. I am required to give equal regard to all, including myself. Although this is a refinement or clarification of the robust interpretation, which brings it more in line with the principle of utility, it does not lend any support to the anemic interpretation. After all, the conclusion now is that I may promote my own happiness, rather than the happiness of others, provided that doing so is compatible with a mutual and equal regard for the happiness of all others. This is a far cry from the idea that "sometimes to some extent" I ought to promote the happiness of others.

III.   SUPEREROGATION AND IMPERFECT DUTIES

It might be objected that a Kantian account of supererogation depends on the anemic interpretation of imperfect duties.[8] This interpretation leaves plenty of room for actions that are recommended by moral considerations (and thus good to do) but are not required by duty. Specifically, as Hill suggests, if someone has regularly and to a reasonable extent done the type of actions required by imperfect duty and yet continues to perform the actions for moral reasons, then the actions go beyond the demands of duty and are thus supererogatory.

One must not be misled, however, by the apparent simplicity of this conclusion. First, we need a much fuller account of the difference between requirements and recommendations.[9] Specifically, are recommendations categorical imperatives? Do they involve objective ends? As these questions suggest, we need not only an explanation but also a Kantian justification of this distinction. Finally, if this position is supposed to conflict with indirect consequentialist accounts of supererogation, then familiar consequentialist considerations cannot provide the rationale.

Second, as a result of its radically indeterminate nature, the anemic interpretation seems to make supererogation too easy. All that has been said suggests that whenever one has already helped others "at some time to some extent" yet continues to help others, as the years go on, the action is supererogatory. As Hill describes supererogation, it involves "an agent who has adopted the relevant principle of wider imperfect duty and has often and continually acted on that principle" (Hill 1992a: 169). But the plausibility of this characterization involves a sleight-of-hand. Although such an agent may be the *best candidate* for supererogation, the account of imperfect duty on which the concept is based implies that *anyone* who has "at some time and to some extent" acted on the principle of imperfect duty is also performing an act of supererogation. After all, they have done all that the principle of imperfect duty *demands of them*, and yet, for moral reasons, they choose to do more.

Third, Hill's view raises some peculiar questions about the maxim of the action in question. Since a supererogatory action is not demanded by duty, what should we say about the agent who erroneously, given Hill's account, is motivated by his or her sense of duty? As Hill acknowledges, if supererogatory acts are "beyond duty" yet motivated by a "sense of duty," then the agent would be confused rather than heroic or admirable.

Hill responds by distinguishing "a motive to do one's duty" and "a motive to do what is demanded or encouraged by moral considerations." The supererogatory involves actions encouraged but not demanded by moral principle. Of course, this simply raises many of the questions mentioned above. One wants an explanation and justification of why our own moral principles, which we give to ourselves, only encourage but do not require us to do actions that they recommend.

Hill's response is simply not satisfactory. After all, it never explains the status of the "supererogatory" action that is motivated by duty. Are we supposed to conclude that the individual who dove into the icy Potomac River to save the lives of the victims of an airplane crash did not perform a supererogatory action, simply because he thought this response to the situation was demanded of him by moral reasons? I think not.

So the anemic interpretation is philosophically unsound because it does not follow from any apparent Kantian argument; it is textually unsound because it conflicts with Kant's explicit account, and the robust interpretation is an equal or superior match for the surrounding text; and it does not provide a plausible account of supererogation because it is both too anemic and too underdeveloped. There is thus no basis for rejecting the robust account of imperfect duties.

We must now turn to the priority of perfect duties over imperfect duties. It has seemed to many that even if beneficence is a robust imperfect duty, perfect duties nonetheless provide significant deontological constraints that conflict with all versions of consequentialism. In recent terminology, according to this approach, Kantian ethics includes constraints but not options or prerogatives. Although this does seem to be a correct textual interpretation of Kant's position, we shall now see that the distinction between perfect and imperfect duties cannot provide a rational basis for such an interpretation; even if it was Kant's view, it is not the most defensible Kantian view.

IV. PERFECT AND IMPERFECT DUTIES

Even Kantians who, like Alan Donagan and Jeffrie Murphy, insist on a deontological interpretation of Kant's normative theory have pointed out that the formula of humanity is a teleological principle.[10] As a teleological principle it naturally lends itself to a consequentialist interpretation. Of course, both Donagan and Murphy nonetheless insist that Kant's normative theory is not consequentialist. According to these Kantians and many others, Kant avoids consequentialism because he correctly distinguishes between perfect and imperfect duties. Indeed, it is clearly tempting to appeal to Kant's distinction between perfect and imperfect duties to resolve apparent conflicts of duty and thus avoid the Kantian consequentialist conclusion. As we shall see, however, this approach, like many other temptations, brings no true satisfaction.[11]

There are many possible interpretations of the moral relevance of this distinction. I shall focus on three interpretations—two accounts that are suggested by Kant's comments and one familiar account from Mill.

As Paton, Donagan, and Bruce Aune have argued, the perfect imperfect distinction involves the freedom or discretion we may exercise in complying with our imperfect duties but not with our perfect duties.[12] Kant explains that a perfect duty "permits no exception in the interest of inclination" (GMM 421n), whereas an imperfect duty allows a certain play-room, "a latitude for free choice in following (complying with) the law, that is, that the law cannot specify precisely in what way one is to act and how much one is to do" (MM 390). The individual has a certain amount of discretion in deciding how imperfect duties are to be satisfied. Following Kant, I will refer to duties with this property as "wide" duties and duties without this property as "narrow" duties (MM 390). The perfect imperfect distinction thus essentially involves the narrow wide distinction.

Kant's explanation that perfect duties involve maxims of actions and imperfect duties involve maxims of ends helps clarify the distinction (MM 389). Some maxims of duty have to do with specific actions we must perform or omit, and other maxims of duty have to do with ends we must adopt. When we adopt an end, there are many possible means, possible actions, that may further the end. For example, there are many equally deserving charities that I could now aid with a donation. The imperfect duty of beneficence requires me to have the general end of assisting deserving charities, but it does not tell me exactly which charity to assist and exactly how much I must give. In this sense, an imperfect duty permits a degree of freedom or discretion in how it is satisfied. Perfect duties, on the other hand, require one to omit or perform specific actions. We are, for example, simply prohibited from stealing or killing or failing to pay our debts. Some perfect duties, rather than simply prohibiting actions, require actions to be taken. As a result, some perfect duties may be carried out in various ways—I may pay a ten-dollar debt with ten ones, or two fives, or one ten, and so on—but a definite action to a specific person is still required. In contrast, imperfect duties, which involve maxims of ends, permit a significant degree of freedom for the agent to choose which definite actions are required. The wideness of imperfect duties and the narrowness of perfect duties is to be interpreted in one of the following three ways.

1. As a result of this difference, one might argue that in cases where one must choose between a perfect and an imperfect duty, the wideness of the imperfect

duty means that it is less weighty or binding than the narrow perfect duty. Although Kant never presents this type of argument, his comment that in cases of conflicting "*grounds* of obligation . . . the stronger *ground of obligation* prevails" (MM 224) may suggest this sort of argument.

This argument is not convincing, however. What does the wideness or latitude of imperfect duties have to do with their obligatory strength? Consider, for example, the obligatory end of aiding those in need: Why would our obligations to all of the people whom we can aid be lessened simply because we cannot help all those in need? Granted, if ten people need assistance and I can help only three, I cannot help all of those in need; but I am still obligated to help three of the ten. For example, if I am on a boat and I see ten people fall overboard and the only thing I can do to help is throw the three available life preservers to three of the ten, then I can aid only three of the ten. I may use discretion in deciding which three to aid; in this sense, there is a certain latitude or freedom in how the obligation is fulfilled. But this freedom is not logically convertible into a weaker ground of duty. We must sometimes choose whom to help, but we are nonetheless obliged to help all we reasonably can. The wideness of imperfect duties does not provide a justification for believing that perfect duties are more weighty than the imperfect.

According to Kant, imperfect duties are also wide in the sense that they do not tell us "how much one is to do by the action for an end that is also a duty" (MM 389). One might take this to imply that it is up to each individual to determine how much self-sacrifice imperfect duties require. However, Kant explains that the freedom for inclination to decide how much must be done in furthering the obligatory end "is not to be taken as a permission to make exceptions to the maxim of actions, but only as a permission to limit one maxim of duty by another (e.g., love of one's neighbor in general by love of one's parents), by which in fact the field for the practice of virtue is widened" (MM 390). Thus, in the above example, if my parents are two of the ten who have fallen overboard, I may (and perhaps must) throw two of the three life preservers to my parents.

Although intuitively we think that perfect duties are more binding than imperfect duties, the mere wideness of imperfect duties provides no support for this intuition.

2. Alan Donagan has suggested that although the wideness of imperfect duties does not make them less binding, it does explain the priority of perfect duties in regulating actions. According to Donagan,

> A perfect duty is simply a duty not to do, or not to omit, an action of a certain kind: not to murder, or to lie, not to omit to pay a debt. By contrast, an imperfect duty is always a duty to promote a certain general end; and since carrying out such a duty does not exclude any specific acts of commission or omission, it cannot be simply a duty not to do, or not to omit, an action of a certain kind.

Since perfect duties prohibit specific acts of commission or omission, and since imperfect duties do not prohibit specific acts, promoting the general ends of the imperfect duties cannot require violating a perfect duty that prohibits specific acts. Donagan thus concludes that if we recognize that the perfect imperfect distinction involves the difference between prohibiting specific acts and promoting general ends, then we see that perfect and imperfect duties simply cannot conflict.[13]

Donagan's argument, unlike the first argument, does not presuppose that the imperfect duties are less weighty simply because they are wide. Indeed, since there are no perfect imperfect conflicts, one type of duty need not outweigh the other.

The possibility of conflicts of perfect and imperfect duties is eliminated, according to Donagan, because the duty to promote a general end does not "exclude any specific acts of commission or omission." Is this argument convincing? Specifically, does promoting a general end really not require any specific acts (i.e., really not exclude any specific acts of omission)?

According to Kant, if one wills an end, then one also wills the necessary means (GMM 417). Thus, if one wills the happiness of others as an end, one must also will those actions that are necessary means to their happiness. It follows that to do or omit specific acts can be inconsistent with the promoting of a general end. The duty to promote the happiness of others requires me to do (not to omit) those actions that are necessary to promote the happiness of others. If, for example, I can save someone from serious harm at no comparable cost to myself, the duty to promote the happiness of others requires me to act.

It might be objected, however, that the wideness of imperfect duties implies that no specific act is a necessary means to the objective end. Donagan might argue that if one does not further an objective end because the only means of doing so involves violating a perfect duty, then one does not violate an imperfect duty at all: One can always fulfill the imperfect duty in some other way, thus one never needs to violate a perfect duty to fulfill an imperfect duty. For example, I never need to violate a perfect duty to help someone in need, because I can always help that person at some other time or help some other person at some other time and thereby fulfill my imperfect duty. Since perfect duties leave no play-room or latitude, and since imperfect duties can be satisfied by any action that furthers the objective end, the duty to promote objective ends simply does not require violation of a perfect duty. Thus, imperfect duties do not conflict with perfect duties.

Perhaps it was this sort of argument, rather than the first argument, that Kant had in mind when he claimed that one ground of obligation may be stronger than another and that there are thus no unresolvable conflicts of duty; but leaving aside the question of textual exegesis, this argument has significant problems of its own.

First, the argument maintains that one never needs to violate a perfect duty for the sake of an imperfect duty because the imperfect duty can always be filled in some other way. Shelly Kagan has pointed out, however, that it might be the case that the wide duty is such that for all of the alternatives that would promote the objective end, each given alternative would violate some perfect duty. Thus the wideness of imperfect duties cannot entail that they can be filled without violating a narrow perfect duty. So there still could be significant conflicts between the demands of an imperfect duty and one or more perfect duties.[14] In such cases of conflict, there is no reason for concluding that perfect duties provide a stronger ground of obligation.

The second problem with this argument is that the perfect imperfect distinction does not correspond to the positive-negative distinction. Simply put, we may have "narrow" positive duties that would then be perfect duties; for example, as we shall see, beneficence can be a perfect duty in this sense. If the perfect imperfect distinction is supposed to provide a Kantian rationale for a priority of negative over positive duties, it is necessary for the two distinctions to correspond. In Donagan's terms, if the duty of beneficence excludes specific acts of omission, then beneficence is a perfect duty. If beneficence is a perfect duty, then one cannot appeal to its imperfect status to explain why it cannot conflict with other perfect duties.

The conclusion that there are narrow positive duties follows even on Donagan's own interpretation of the duty of beneficence. Donagan argues that the Kantian duty to treat others as ends-in-themselves generates a positive duty of beneficence: "It is impermissible not to promote the well-being of others by actions in themselves permissible, inasmuch as one can do so without proportionate inconvenience." In addition, he recognizes (in a context in which he is not discussing the perfect imperfect distinction) that the principle of beneficence requires of a person that "should he encounter another who then and there needs help which only he can give without disproportionate inconvenience, the principle of beneficence calls on him to give it."[15] It follows that it is sometimes impermissible to omit certain specific beneficent acts; thus, on Donagan's own terms, such acts are perfect duties.

It is easy to imagine cases where there is only one person whom I can aid and thus where the positive duty of beneficence is a narrow and thus perfect duty. Consider the following case: A ship has sunk off Bermuda, and a raft of survivors is hailed by another survivor in the water. In such a situation there is only one person needing aid and only one raft in a position to provide aid. Given the circumstances, there is only one person whom the persons on the life raft can aid. It is simply irrelevant that many people in the world also need aid. The wideness of the positive duty to aid permits a particular act of aid to be forgone for another act that promotes the same objective end, but there is no such latitude in this case. I cannot, for example, excuse my inaction in this case by intending to aid some other person on some other occasion. Since I can save both this person and another person on another occasion, if I fail to save one then I fail to fulfill my positive duty to aid. Thus, in this case, the only way to fulfill the positive duty to aid is to pull this drowning person onto the raft. In short, it is sometimes possible for us to aid all those whom we can aid, so the duty to aid will sometimes require a specific action and thus be a perfect duty.

Hence, Donagan cannot use the perfect imperfect distinction to explain why one can never kill, steal, or lie in order to aid specific persons in need. Even if there are no perfect imperfect conflicts, there would still be narrow positive duties of beneficence that could conflict with other negative duties not to harm, or steal, or lie.

Consider another case, adapted from Thomas Nagel, which involves a conflict of narrow positive and negative duties.[16] I have an accident, by no culpable fault of my own, on a deserted country road at night. Since the driver's side of the car was equipped with an air bag, I am unharmed. My two passengers, however, were not as lucky and are both seriously injured. I recall that there is a farm about a mile back up the road, and I run to it for help. To my dismay, however, the owner of the house will not provide assistance or loan me a car in the driveway. Assuming that I am capable and that there is no other apparent means of aiding the two injured passengers, should I forcefully steal the car from this one person in order to aid the two others? This case involves a conflict between negative duties of non-aggression and positive duties to aid. Whatever one's intuitions about this type of case, the perfect imperfect distinction is not applicable. Both sets of duties are narrow and thus perfect.

In many situations, the person or persons whom one has a duty to aid is clearly demonstrated by the circumstance. Although the duty of beneficence is often wide, it is also often narrow. Indeed, in any of the standard (realistic?) cases where I can save a given two only by killing one (i.e., there are no other two that I can save without killing the one, and there is no other way to save the two besides killing the one), both duties are narrow, thus the relative moral status of perfect and imperfect duties is irrelevant. Furthermore, in cases where these conditions, which narrow the duty of beneficence, do not obtain, a consequentialist would be required to save the two in a way that did not kill the one or would save some other two in a situation that did not require the killing of one. These are not isolated and uninteresting counter-examples, for a consequentialist will probably be required to kill one to save others only if the act of aid corresponds to a narrow duty.

Although Donagan appeals to our commonsense intuitions that killing, stealing, and lying are impermissible means of aiding the needy, the perfect imperfect distinction understood as the narrow wide distinction provides no Kantian rationale for limiting the duty of beneficence. Donagan's interpretation of the perfect imperfect distinction thus does not provide a Kantian justification for our commonsense intuitions.

The conclusion that positive duties can be perfect duties presents an additional problem for the first interpretation of the moral relevance of the perfect imperfect distinction. Even if we grant for the sake of argument that, because they are narrow rather than wide, perfect duties are more weighty than imperfect duties, one still cannot reach the conclusion that negative duties are more weighty than positive duties. Positive duties may be narrow and perfect and thus just as weighty and binding as narrow, perfect, negative duties.

3. There is one last interpretation of the perfect imperfect distinction that merits brief discussion. Jeffrie Murphy has argued, as did J. S. Mill, that the Kantian perfect imperfect distinction really involves the issue of correlative rights: Perfect duties correlate with assignable rights, which are violated if the duties are not honored; imperfect duties involve actions that one ought to do, but no assignable rights are violated if one fails to act. As Murphy puts it, in the case of beneficence "no one can demand by right that I make him happy, can regard himself as wronged if I fail to make him happy . . . [but] the person to whom I am bound in contract can demand by right that I honor it, can legitimately regard himself as wronged if I fail to honor it."[17] Of course the duty of beneficence is a duty to aid persons in need or in distress, not simply a duty to make others happy. Nonetheless, from the commonsense, intuitive perspective, the creditors have a correlative right to be paid, but the needy do not have a similar correlative right to be aided. Let us thus consider whether this last interpretation of the perfect imperfect distinction will supply the desired non-consequentialist conclusion.

Now, there are two possible entailments between correlative rights and the narrowness of perfect duties. One might maintain that it is the narrowness of the perfect duty that makes it correlate with an assignable right. On the other hand, one might maintain that it is the correlative right that makes a duty narrow and thus perfect: The fact that the duty correlates with a right entails that it is narrow and perfect. Either way, though, the desired deontological conclusion does not follow. The first proposal faces the same type of problems as Donagan's interpretation, and the second proposal presupposes an antecedent and problematic account of correlative rights.

First, we have just seen that our positive duties of beneficence can be narrow and thus perfect. It would follow that in such cases, we have a correlative right to beneficence. In fact, just as our positive duties can be narrow and perfect, our negative duties can also be wide and imperfect. Since negative duties include, in addition to not killing or stealing, such things as keeping promises, repaying debts, and telling the truth, which call for action and not simply inaction, situations may arise in which negative duties are wide and thus imperfect. What if, for example, I owe $1,000 to each of ten people but, through no culpable fault of my own, I only have $2,000? Since I cannot repay all whom I owe, I must decide whom to repay. Since 'ought' implies 'can,' my duty to repay my debts only obliges me to do all I reasonably and legitimately can do. It follows that I am only obliged to repay two of the ten, and I must use discretion to decide which two. There is no difference in latitude between this case and the case where ten people are each in need of $1,000 and I only have $2,000 to give away. Negative duties thus can be wide and imperfect.

Of course, I still owe the other eight $1,000 each, in the sense that if I came upon the money I would be obliged to repay them. But the same is true of my duty to aid. If I were to come upon another $8,000 that I could reasonably spare, then the obligatory end of aiding those in need would oblige me to aid the other eight. We think of the claims of the creditors as different from the claims of the needy. We say, for example, that the debt to the others is not discharged unless they are paid. But we may similarly say that the claims of the needy are not satisfied. One must thus independently show that the former duty is more weighty than the latter, because there is no difference in the wideness of the duties.

Intuitively, we believe that we must do more for the creditors than for the needy and that the creditors can demand more from us. The sacrifices that the duty of beneficence can demand of us are not as severe as the sacrifices required to pay our debts. We saw, in response to Donagan, that the distinction between duties not to do or omit specific acts and duties to promote general ends does not itself generate this intuitive conclusion. In the case of the present proposal, the narrow-wide distinction cannot account for commonsense intuitions about correlative rights. The duty of beneficence can be narrow and thus perfect, and the duty of contracts can be wide and thus imperfect. It would follow from the first proposal that beneficence might often generate correlative rights and contracts might not.

One might thus object that the second proposal is the correct one. The first proposal seems to have things backward: Narrowness does not entail rights. Instead, contracts are perfect duties, because contracts generate correlative rights, and it is the correlative right that makes the duty narrow. Beneficence, on the other hand, is an imperfect duty, because it is not generated by a correlative right, and it is for this reason that one has a certain latitude in fulfilling the duty of beneficence. This second proposal is much more plausible than the first, and it is probably the idea underlying Murphy's interpretation of the perfect imperfect distinction. Nonetheless, either this proposal presupposes an independent argument showing that contracts, but not beneficence, generate correlative rights or it clearly begs the question.

Mill, of course, provides an independent utilitarian account of the principles of justice, which he maintains exactly coincide with perfect duties, and of the nature and basis of the correlative rights. The principles of justice are social rules, enforced by sanctions, that protect individual rights. Mill maintains that to have a right is to have something that society ought to defend my possession of; and he argues that society ought to do so because doing so tends to promote the general happiness.[18] But leaving aside consequentialist explanations of why society especially ought to protect my possession of security and liberty and ought to enforce contracts, we need a Kantian rationale for limiting the scope of correlative rights. Since treating persons as ends-in-themselves involves both positive and negative duties, we need some non-consequentialist reason for assigning rights that correlate with negative duties but not positive duties. Thus, for a Kantian, drawing the perfect imperfect distinction in terms of correlative rights provides no normative guidance, for it leaves open the question of the nature and scope of assignable rights. If the arguments of chapters 3 and 5 are sound, then there is no reason, in principle, for a Kantian to limit the scope of assignable rights so that they correlate only with negative duties.

We have seen that, first, the wideness of imperfect duties provides no rationale for claiming that they are less weighty than perfect duties. Second, the perfect imperfect distinction does not coincide, in any intrinsic way, with the negative positive distinction; indeed, positive duties may be perfect duties. Thus even if perfect and imperfect duties do not conflict, perfect positive and perfect negative duties can conflict. In such conflicts, the perfect imperfect distinction does not provide a rationale for giving priority to negative duties. Finally, unless one has an independent argument showing that only negative duties correlate with rights, it will not do to argue that perfect duties involve assignable rights. As a result, we still have no reason for believing that the Kantian duty of beneficence does not correlate with the rights of the needy to all the assistance that we can provide without comparable loss.

The distinction between perfect and imperfect duties is not helpful in adjudicating conflicts of duty and justifying basic agent-centered constraints. So we have yet to find any Kantian basis for rejecting consequentialism.

NOTES

1. Thomas Hill ([1971] 1992a): 149.

2. Kant's imperfect duty to develop one's talents captures at least some of the alleged natural independence of the personal point of view (GMM 423, 430). Could recent theorists actually be rehabilitating duties to oneself?

3. Herman (1985): 428–29 and (1989): 415, 425.

4. For a defense of the hypothetical imperative, see Thomas Hill (1973) and Onora O'Neill, (1989b).

5. Barbara Herman (1989): 419; see also O'Neill (1989a): 100–101, 229–30. These discussions do not directly address the responsibilities of the non-finite (the invulnerable) to the finite (the vulnerable).

6. Hill ([1971] 1992a): 149. For Hill's more recent rational reconstruction of Kantian normative ethics, see chapter 7.

7. In addition, moral perfection, for Kant, involves developing the disposition to comply with juridical duties from the motive of duty (MM 220).

8. For a more complete discussion of Kant, Hill, and supererogation, see Marcia Baron (1987): 237–62.

9. On this issue, see Marcia Baron (1984).

10. Donagan (1977): 63; Murphy (1970): 70–76.

11. This section has been vastly improved by an extensive critique by Shelly Kagan. His comments, which were significantly longer than my original text, motivated a complete reworking of the arguments. As a result, many confusions and errors have been removed. For additional discussion (and a devastating critique) of Donagan's position, see Kagan (1987): 643–53. For a Kantian critique of Donagan's view, see Thomas Hill (1993).

12. See Paton's translation of the *Groundwork*, p. 137, note 53, n. 1. Paton (1947) emphasizes the overridingness of perfect duties, but as he comes to recognize, there must be some difference between the two types of duties that explains why the perfect duties override imperfect duties; Donagan (1977): 154–55; Aune (1979): 188–94. Aune's discussion is similar in several respects to the following discussion of perfect and imperfect duties. Since I read his book several years before I developed my position, I may well have been influenced by his account.

13. Donagan (1977): 154–55.

14. Shelly Kagan, professional correspondence.

15. Donagan (1977): 85–86. Donagan qualifies the principle of beneficence with the standard two limitations—permissible means and proportionate inconvenience. As I will explain in chapter 8, these limitations do not affect the point in question.

16. Thomas Nagel, (1980): 126–27 and (1986): ch. 9.

17. Murphy (1970): 51, but see also p. 146, where he argues that helping others in distress can be a perfect duty and thus subject to state coercion; J. S. Mill ([1861] 1962): ch. 5.

18. J. S. Mill ([1861] 1962): ch. 5, and ([1859] 1989).

7

RESPECT, DIGNITY, AND THE KINGDOM OF ENDS

There are many versions of Kantian ethics and even more supposedly Kantian objections to consequentialism. By considering three of the more sweeping and influential objections, we shall see that there are general conceptual difficulties with Kantian responses to the consequentialist interpretation. We will consider, first, the significance of the Kantian deontologist's emphasis on respect for persons; second, the relevance of Kant's distinction between price and dignity; and third, the formula of the kingdom of ends.

The typical arguments based on the first two distinctions simply beg the question against the consequentialist. It is certainly possible to interpret the notions of respect and dignity in such a way that they conflict with consequentialism, but the Kantian has provided absolutely no reason for doing so. The interpretation of the kingdom of ends formula is more complicated, and our discussion of it will lead to thorny questions about the limits of beneficence and the sacrifice of the innocent. In each case, however, the derivation of the formula of the end-in-itself does not justify deontological constraints. Therefore, the Kantian deontologist must assume the task of providing an independent justification for a fundamental deontological and agent-centered interpretation. Without such a justification, the deontological positions in question are simply question-begging and thus amount to nothing but groundless deontology.

I.   RESPECT FOR PERSONS

We begin with the Kantian emphasis on *respect* for persons. The bald assertion that consequentialists do not respect persons has become an all-too-common refrain from deontologists. Consequentialists obviously think that they show appropriate respect for persons by maximizing hedonistic happiness, or preference-satisfaction, or intrinsically valuable lives, or, as we have been suggesting, the two tiers of value. The deontologists, however, are not satisfied. They insist that maximizing value is not the same as showing respect, and they appeal to Kant's authority as support for this conviction. Since the inconsistency or incompatibility between respect for persons and concern for value is never explained, we must divine the nature of the consequentialist error.

Perhaps the idea is as follows: The formula of humanity essentially involves the concept of respect for persons, not the consequentialist concept of promoting the good. Respect for persons involves respecting the rights of persons; that is, respect essentially involves honoring agent-centered constraints on actions.[1] In order to respond to this objection, we must look more closely at the concept of respect. What is it to respect something or someone?

Stephen Darwall has argued that there are two kinds of respect: "recognition respect" and "appraisal respect." Recognition respect "consists in giving appropriate consideration or recognition to some feature of its object in deliberating about what to do." Appraisal respect consists in a positive appraisal of its object as a consequence of some intrinsic features of the object. Appraisal respect does not essentially involve any conception of how one's behavior toward that object is appropriately restricted. Since respect for persons is supposed to play a role in determining our conduct, the notion of respect involved is recognition respect.[2]

There are both a narrow notion of recognition respect, which is limited to moral recognition respect, and a more general notion of recognition respect. Moral recognition respect involves giving appropriate moral weight to the features of the object of respect in one's deliberations about what to do. To morally respect some object is to regulate one's behavior—that is, to constrain or conform one's actions in accordance with the moral requirements generated by the object. According to the most general notion of recognition respect, any fact that we consider in deliberation is a fact for which we are showing respect. This notion is so broad that it covers all uses of respect. (Indeed, it may be too broad.)

The demand that we respect persons is a moral demand that we regulate our conduct according to the moral requirements generated by the existence of persons. Now, as Darwall points out, recognition respect for persons is "identical with recognition respect for the moral requirements that are placed on one by the existence of persons." But, of course, this is precisely what is at issue between the consequentialist and the deontologist: What are the moral requirements placed on us by the existence of persons? The concept of moral recognition respect thus simply cannot help us discover the nature of the moral requirements generated by the existence of persons.

Kantian normative theories, and commonsense morality, often assume that respect for persons fundamentally involves agent-centered constraints rather than consequentialist considerations. The mere concept of respect, however, does not support this assumption. A consequentialist approach is prima facie as appropriate as an agent-centered approach. To assume otherwise is simply question-begging.

Indeed, if one insists that as a conceptual matter, respecting persons logically involves honoring agent-centered constraints, then one must provide a rationale for interpreting the formula of the end-in-itself as essentially involving the notion of respect rather than some consequentialist notion. The derivation and formula of the end-in-itself does not say anything about "respect" for persons. It says, "Act in such a way that you treat humanity, whether in your own person or the person of another, always at the same time as an end and never simply as a means" (GMM 429). The Kantian deontologist first rephrases this formula of the categorical imperative in terms of respect for persons and then insists that respect essentially involves honoring some particular set of agent-centered constraints. It should be quite clear that this terminological point is not even close to a Kantian refutation of consequentialism; it hardly counts as an objection at all. Indeed, so interpreted, deontology is simply imposed on the Kantian approach with no explicit logical connection or relationship with the derivation or even the language of the formula. Since the Kantian consequential-ist has produced an argument for the consequentialist interpretation, at least some competing argument is called for.

Finally, Kant does not use the concept of respect in the manner presupposed by the deontological objection. For Kant, respect for persons involves respect for the moral law within oneself or others. Kant writes, "Duty is the necessity of an action done out of respect for the law" (GMM 400). He goes on to explain that

> respect is properly the representation of a worth that thwarts my self-love. Hence respect is something that is regarded as an object of neither inclination nor fear, although it has at the same time something analogous to both. The object of respect is therefore nothing but the law—indeed that very law which we impose on ourselves and yet recognize as necessary in itself. . . . *All respect for a person is properly only respect for the law* (of honesty, etc.) of which the person provides an example. (GMM 402n, emphasis added)[3]

So Kant uses the notion of respect to distinguish moral motivation from the in-centives of self-love (broadly construed), but we have seen that Kant's account of the motive of duty is clearly compatible with consequentialism (chapters 2 and 3). Hence, Kant's concept of respect for persons also does not conflict with consequentialism.

In addition to this more "formal" use of the concept of respect, Kant also uses the concept in a more substantive and normative sense. In the *Metaphysics of Morals*, Kant contrasts the principle of practical love and the principle of respect. Kant writes,

> The principle of *mutual love* admonishes men constantly to *come closer* to one another; that of the respect they owe one another, to keep themselves *at a distance* from one another. . . . *Love* is not to be understood as *feeling*. . . . It must rather be thought of as *benevolence* (practical love), which results in benefi-cence. . . . The same holds true of the *respect* to be shown to others. It is not to be understood as the mere *feeling* that comes from comparing our own *worth*

with another's (such as a child feels merely from habit toward his parents, a pupil toward his teacher, or any subordinate toward his superior). It is rather to be understood as the *maxim* of limiting our self-esteem by the dignity of humanity in another person, and so as respect in a practical sense. (MM 449)

The concept of respect here is somewhat obscure. The contrast with practical benevolence suggests that Kant has more in mind here than the formal concept of respect for the moral law. Yet he does not adequately explain the practical significance of "the maxim of limiting our self-esteem by the dignity of humanity in another person." If this maxim expresses a recognition of the equal significance of other people as a source of value, just like oneself, then the Kantian consequentialist accepts the maxim. In addition, the practical significance of the two tiers of value—especially the recognition that each person determines the content of his or her own conception of the good (chapter 6)—captures much of the "practical sense" of respect for humanity (which is the capacity to set oneself an end). So, the Kantian consequentialist can clearly assent to the spirit of this distinction between benevolence and respect.

On the other hand, it does seem clear that Kant has more in mind than this. He does seem to be thinking of respect as the ground of negative duties that constrain positive duties (MM 450). The question remains, however: What is the basis of this more deontological claim? We have seen that the perfect-imperfect distinction does not support deontological constraints on the principle of beneficence (chapter 7), and we have just seen that the concept of respect itself provides no support: Respect for persons involves giving appropriate practical consideration to the fact that there are persons. The meaning of 'respect' cannot settle the issue of what counts as appropriate practical consideration.

In response, it might be objected that I have cast the deontologist's objection too narrowly. The point is that respect for the *dignity* of persons conflicts with the consequentialist interpretation, not simply respect *simpliciter.* For persons to exist as ends-in-themselves with a dignity above all price is for them to exist as objects of respect, and not simply as another value to be promoted. This is why Kant talks of "limiting our self-esteem by the *dignity of humanity* in another person" (MM 449, emphasis added). We thus need to consider Kant's conception of the dignity of persons and see if it provides the sought-after but elusive ground of deontological constraints.

II. THE DIGNITY PRINCIPLE

Kant famously claims that rational beings have a "dignity," not merely a "price." He writes,

> In the kingdom of ends everything has either a price or a dignity. Whatever has a
> price can be replaced by something else as its equivalent; on the other hand,
> whatever is above all price and therefore admits of no equivalent, has a
> dignity . . . but that which constitutes the condition under which alone some-
> thing can be an end in itself, has not merely a relative worth, i.e., a price, but
> has an intrinsic worth, i.e., dignity. (GMM 434–35)

As we have seen, according to the consequentialist interpretation of Kantian
moral theory, the distinction between dignity and price marks off the two tiers
of value and the lexical priority of rationality.

Thomas Hill, however, has argued that Kant's concept of dignity is meant to
mark off a more radical distinction between price and dignity. According to this
more radical distinction, dignity is not a value to be maximized, because things
with dignity cannot even be compared with each other; there is no scale of
equivalences for things with dignity, thus there is no appropriate maximizing
strategy. Indeed, the concept of dignity is meant to mark off the non-substitutability
of the intrinsic value of persons. Let us call this the *extreme interpretation* of the
dignity principle. According to this interpretation, unlike the *consequentialist
interpretation,* it is *not* permissible to sacrifice one person with dignity in order to
save *more* people.[4] The question is thus whether objects with dignity are not
equivalent to each other or are simply not equivalent to any other kind of object.

Hill does an interesting job developing his interpretation of the normative
implications of this Kantian thesis. He argues quite convincingly that one can
accept the extreme interpretation of the dignity principle and nonetheless avoid
Kant's own inflexible and unattractive conclusions about particular duties. One
might say that he develops a moderate version of the extreme interpretation. He
does not, however, discuss the Kantian basis or justification of the distinction
between price and dignity. His goal is to explain Kant's conclusion and to see
what follows from it; he does not focus on the nature and soundness of the
argument for his interpretation of the dignity principle. In order for us to
determine the correct Kantian interpretation of the dignity principle—which
may or may not be Kant's—we must evaluate the argument for the distinction
between dignity and price.[5]

As Kant uses the concept of "intrinsic value," it marks off the things that
depend on nothing else—that have no extrinsic conditions—in order to have
value. All the objects of our inclinations, whether desired as ends or as means,
are conditioned by desire; that is, they are only valuable because they are desired
by us. In this sense, both ends and means are equally extrinsically (not instrumentally) valuable.[6] Similarly, the value of desires and inclinations—insofar as
they provide reasons for action—is conditioned by the agent's rational choice or
affirmation of the desire. Only the value-conferring power of rational choice
itself has no further condition determining its value, thus only rational nature
has unconditional or intrinsic value.

Kantian value theory does support Kant's conclusion that the dignity of persons cannot be exchanged for anything that has a mere market price. The possessor of dignity is "infinitely beyond all price, with which it cannot in the least be brought into competition or comparison without as it were, violating its sanctity" (GMM 435). So rational nature is not simply one more commodity in the marketplace of competing inclinations.

Kant writes,

> Persons are, therefore, not merely subjective ends whose existence as an effect of our actions has a value for us: they are objective ends, i.e., exist as ends in themselves. Such an end is one for which there can be substituted no other end to which such beings should serve merely as means, for otherwise nothing at all of absolute value would be found anywhere. But if all value were conditioned and hence contingent, then no supreme principle could be found for reason at all. (GMM 428)

Kant's idea seems to be that if all values can be cashed in on a scale of value that is determined by the inclinations, then all values are substitutable for inclinations; but then, since inclinations can only support hypothetical imperatives—that is, conditional requirements—there would be no unconditional, objective end of action and thus no categorical imperatives—that is, no universal and unconditional requirements. Thus, if there are any moral requirements, then there must be a kind of value that is not commensurable with values determined by the inclinations. In short, the incommensurability of values is presupposed by the nature of moral judgment.

This is a very complicated line of thought, and it raises many of the issues that were discussed when we evaluated the thesis of the lexical priority of rationality (chapter 4). For our immediate purpose, however, we do not need to unpack all of the assumptions that lend support to this argument. The important point is that this line of argument establishes at best only the thesis that there must be an objective scale of value that is incommensurable with the values established by mere inclinations. It does not show that each person has a value that is incommensurable with the value of other persons. The conclusion that follows from Kant's argument is that there are two *types* of value that are incommensurable with each other, not that there is a type of value where each *token* of that type is incommensurable with every other token. Since type incommensurability is consistent with the consequentialist interpretation, Kant's argument for the two tiers of value provides no support whatsoever for the extreme interpretation.

It does, however, support the consequentialist interpretation. Since the moral demand to respect other persons is based on the equal moral status of all persons, Kant's argument presupposes the equal value, or dignity, of all persons. Such beings are comparable, and the comparison demonstrates the equal objective value of all. The equal value of all rational being provides a clear basis for a requirement to maximally promote the flourishing of rational agency (chapter 5).

Nonetheless, while the extreme interpretation must be rejected, the dignity-price distinction still accurately signifies the priority of rationality. If we refuse to sacrifice a person for the sake of the maximization of happiness or any other market value, then we have shown a "reverence" for such beings. But as we shall see more fully in chapter 9, this reverence is compatible with the sacrifice of some for the sake of other persons with dignity. It is mere dogmatic intuitionism or groundless deontology to insist that all such sacrifices are inconsistent with the equal dignity of all.

At times the dignity principle seems to function like an inkblot where each sees whatever conclusions he or she is predisposed to accept. If one believes that a particular way of treating people is morally unacceptable, then such treatment is inconsistent with respect for the dignity of persons. Too often, when a deontologist uses the dignity principle as a normative principle, the cart is put before the horse: This reasoning presupposes that we have a standard of unacceptable conduct that is prior to the dignity principle. The dignity principle cannot then provide the reason why the conduct is unacceptable.

The goal of the Kantian deontologist is to (directly) vindicate ordinary commonsense morality; but it is not at all clear how the dignity principle can even support the intuitive view that the negative duty not to kill is more stringent than the positive duty to save lives. How is the common view that we have only slight, if any, duties to aid those in desperate need consistent with the lexical priority of the dignity of persons over the price of the inclinations? Of course, on the one hand, it is commonly maintained that killing some persons to save many others fails to give due regard to the incomparable and absolute dignity of persons. On the other hand, it is maintained that respect for the dignity of persons does not require that one spend one's discretionary income on saving lives rather than on one's own personal projects. As long as one has done some minimum and indeterminate amount to help others, then one need not do any more.

So the Kantian deontologist wants to use the dignity-price distinction to resolve conflicting grounds of obligation in an intuitively acceptable way, but it is far from obvious why allowing a loss of dignity for the sake of something with price is consistent with the dignity principle.[7] In short, ordinary morality permits one to place the satisfaction of one's inclinations above a concern for the dignity of all. Consequentialists have produced indirect justifications for many of these common intuitive judgments; it would seem that those appealing to the dignity principle must rely on similar arguments.

Finally, even if one grants that saving two persons with dignity cannot outweigh and compensate for killing one—because dignity cannot be added and summed in this way—this point still does not justify deontological constraints. On the extreme interpretation, why would not killing one person be a stronger obligation than saving two persons? If I am concerned with the priceless dignity of each, it would seem that I *may* still save two; it is just that my reason cannot be that the two compensate for the loss of the one. Consider Hill's example of a priceless object: If I can save two of three priceless statutes only by destroying one, then I cannot claim that saving two makes up for the loss of the one. But similarly, the loss of the two is not outweighed by the one that was not destroyed. Indeed, even if dignity cannot be simply summed up, how is the extreme interpretation inconsistent with the idea that I should save as many priceless objects as possible? Even if two do not simply outweigh and thus compensate for the loss of the one, each is priceless; thus, I have good reason to save as many as I can. In short, it is not clear how the extreme interpretation justifies the ordinary killing/letting-die distinction or even how it conflicts with the conclusion that the more persons with dignity who are saved, the better.[8]

The reason for rejecting the consequentialist interpretation is the intuitively unacceptable sacrifices that it may require. But the Kantian has not demonstrated that the *more complex and mysterious* extreme interpretation follows from Kant's arguments, and it is far from obvious how token incommensurability is supposed to (directly) justify anything like ordinary intuitive morality. On the other hand, we have seen that the consequentialist interpretation, which requires only type incommensurability, follows naturally from the Kantian argument that justifies the dignity principle. Kantian consequentialism is the more simple and logical conclusion of Kant's own argument. Thus, it follows that *the burden of proof has been shifted from the Kantian consequentialist to the Kantian deontologist.*

III.   THE KINGDOM OF ENDS

Thomas Hill has also been developing a Kantian conception of moral reasoning that incorporates the dignity principle into the formula of the kingdom of ends. The result of this approach is a more Kantian version of John Rawls's hypothetical social contract theory.[9] Of course, Rawls's theory is limited to the derivation of principles of justice, but Hill maintains that Kant's kingdom of ends principle provides a more general model for deriving moral principles.

The formula of the kingdom of ends combines the main ideas of the other formulations of the categorical imperative. According to Hill, "it asks us to consider what we can (rationally) will as universal laws and requires us to act accordingly. It incorporates the injunction to regard humanity as an end in itself into the conditions of moral legislation; and the idea of autonomy is included in the same way."[10] More specifically, "the formula of the kingdom of ends enjoins us to follow those rules that we would make as legislating members of such a kingdom." The rules and principles adopted (1) must be "universal in form"; (2) the legislative perspective from which the rules are chosen must be one that "abstracts from the personal differences of rational being and also from all content of their private ends"; (3) the legislators must adopt rules under the assumption that they are "fully rational," in the sense that all the rules must be supported by reasons and that, as members of the resulting society, the legislators will follow the rules adopted; and, as Hill puts the point, (4) "the lawmakers must be autonomous. . . . They will be unmoved by appeals to authority and tradition. . . . They cannot even appeal to their antecedent moral convictions to guide them in making laws. They are the moral lawmakers: there are no moral truths to be discovered independently of their wills"[11]

These four negative conditions are clearly analogous to the "veil of ignorance" that is part of Rawls's "original position." The original position is a merely hypothetical, initial fair-choice situation (which replaces the classical state of nature).[12] Like Rawls, Hill and Kant now need to account for the motivations of these ideal lawmakers. The rules must be rationally defensible, but the lawmakers have not yet been given any ends, which are necessary to rationally justify any rules that are adopted. At this point Rawls introduces his "thin" theory of primary social goods, which are supposed to be all-purpose means (that is, things that anyone would want as a means to whatever else one happens to want). Rather than specifying a shared set of ends, the lawmakers (under the veil of ignorance) deliberate about the distribution of all-purpose means, like rights and liberties, powers and opportunities, and income and wealth.

Although Rawls's overall approach is extremely influential, there is, as he recognized, an extremely plausible argument that the legislators in the original position would choose the principle of average utility maximization (or a set of rules that maximize average utility). In order to avoid this result, Rawls argues that since they are under the veil of ignorance and since one's entire life prospect is at stake, the legislators would adopt a "maximin" decision-making strategy (that is, maximize the minimum). The goal of this strategy is to choose in such a way that the worst possible outcome will be as good as possible and thereby guarantee oneself a satisfactory minimum outcome. Rawls's argument for this thesis has not proved convincing.[13] In addition, there is much controversy about the basis and ranking of the primary social goods. This is all well-worn ground, and we are not concerned with the details of Rawls's theory. However, the striking thing to note is that these disputes have little to do with Kant's formula of the end-in-itself. For the Rawlsian approach, the rejection of utilitarianism does *not* turn on respect for persons or the unconditional value and dignity of rational nature. Despite the Kantian promise of Rawls's theory, the adequacy of utilitarianism turns on extremely complicated and controversial theoretic considerations. In the final analysis, there is nothing distinctively Kantian about Rawls's rejection of utilitarian normative principles.[14]

This brings us back to Hill's interpretation. Hill follows Kant much more closely and introduces a "fifth condition, namely, that in legislating each member regards himself [or herself] and every other member as an end in itself." From this Hill concludes that the "legislators regard the rationality of each member as unconditionally and incomparably worth preserving, developing, and honoring." Since all rational beings necessarily share this value, "they have reason for making general rules concerning the preservation, development, and *respect* for the rational personality of each member" (emphasis added). In addition, "persons necessarily have ends, and one way of showing our special respect for persons is to favor rules which enhance the opportunity to satisfy their ends."[15]

So far so good, but how does any of this conflict with a two-tiered consequentialist normative principle? How does any of this generate basic agent-centered constraints on policies that aim to maximally promote these values? Of course, the difference between Hill's view and consequentialism turns on the significance of his use of the notion of "respect" and on his interpretation of the unconditional value or dignity of rational nature. Since we have already discussed these conceptions, we have come full circle without result.

Rawls and Hill provide two distinct conceptions of the relationship between the dignity principle and the kingdom of ends formula. Both conceptions, however, are compatible with the consequentialist interpretation. First, there is Hill's conception, which asks what principles would be chosen by legislators who value rational nature as an end-in-itself. The answer to this question turns on an antecedent interpretation of the formula of the end-in-itself and on the correct interpretation of the dignity principle in particular. The kingdom of ends formula itself would not then provide an independent rationale for the thesis that deontological constraints are necessary, if the legislators are moved by a respect for the dignity of the individual. Second, as Rawls suggests, one might wish to use the kingdom of ends formula to "fill out" the content of the dignity principle. According to this alternative interpretation, we ask what principles the legislators for the kingdom of ends would agree to, and the result, whatever it is, respects the dignity of each individual. If the fundamental normative principle that the legislators choose is consequentialist, then consequentialism respects the dignity of persons.

Now, many people do find Rawls's theory convincing, but that is not really the point at issue. The point is that Rawls's approach does not demonstrate any fundamental problem with Kantian consequentialism. The question of whether one should maximize or maximin in the original position is remote from Kant's moral theory and his conception of rational nature as the unconditional end of moral action. More importantly, Rawls does not consider the two-tiered consequentialist alternative to his two principles of justice. The main advantage of the maximin strategy is supposed to be that it generates a more egalitarian, distribution-sensitive conception of justice. In the final chapter, however, we shall see that Kantian consequentialism can also account for the intuitive appeal of the egalitarian concerns that motivate Rawls's principles of justice.

Leaving Rawls's particular theory aside, the legislative ideal of the kingdom of ends, and the model of moral deliberation it instantiates, are generally acceptable to the Kantian consequentialist. Indeed, for the most part, the system is simply an overly compressed account of the model of justification that we have used to defend consequentialism.

Nonetheless, Hill would insist that the fundamental attitude of respect for the incomparable and irreplaceable dignity of each person is incompatible with the maximizing strategy adopted by consequentialists. He writes, "It is hard to imagine that a human being could maintain this attitude while deliberately killing another. . . . It is even more unlikely that human beings in general could authorize, approve, and carry out public policies of deliberate sacrifice of the innocent persons while continuing honestly to affirm an untarnished respect for human dignity."[16] As Hill explains, this is a psychological thesis, not a logical or conceptual claim. Since this is a contingent thesis with only intuitive support, it is a very difficult thesis to evaluate. Although the thesis does have a good deal of immediate appeal, on due reflection it should be rejected.

If one has internalized the commonsense prohibition on killing, then one will identify killing with a disregard for the equal status and rights of others. Of course, all agree that such attitudes and intuitions are generally a good thing that should be nurtured and encouraged. It is equally clear, however, that all sorts of horrific practices have intuitively struck people as consistent with respect for human dignity and, conversely, that perfectly acceptable practices have struck basically good people as an affront to human dignity. This is why utilitarians have long emphasized that intuitions and current moral attitudes must be scrutinized by a more critical form of moral thinking.

At the more critical level, consequentialists must acknowledge that the sacrifice of the innocent may sometimes be necessary and thus consistent with respect for the dignity of all. At the same time, it is acknowledged that in the real world even the best type of moral person may find it difficult to perform certain types of action because of the secondary principles and dispositions that a good person has internalized. If the call for such actions is exceedingly rare, then this is probably for the best. In other cases, however, changing or novel circumstances may require new secondary principles and virtues.[17]

A clear recent example of the latter would be the changing attitude toward euthanasia and the physician's role at the end of life. The concept of "death with dignity" is apparently out of moral reach, at least initially, for many who have internalized the earlier principles. Yet as the old scheme of principles shows itself to be obsolete—because, on critical reflection, it is seen that it has consequences that are inconsistent with respect for the dignity of humanity—attitudes change, new principles are shaped, and the intentional killing of the innocent coexists with "an untarnished respect for human dignity."[18]

In addition, Hill's thesis about the maintenance of a moral attitude of respect for persons focuses on violations of negative duties and does not adequately consider the consequences of violations of positive duties. His thesis is plausible only if one has internalized and uncritically accepts the commonsense priority thesis. The consequentialist, on the other hand, considers the absolute value of all those who can be saved, rather than simply focusing on those who will be harmed by positive action. In the next chapter, we will look more closely at how a Kantian should resolve conflicting negative and positive (grounds of) duty, and how a Kantian, who is committed to the dignity of all persons, should think about the sacrifice of the innocent.

Of course, if one only recognizes an anemic principle of beneficence or if one endorses the priority of negative duties, then the sacrifice of the innocent will not easily coexist with respect for dignity. In contrast, if one recognizes that the sacrifice in question is required by moral principles which show an equal concern for the dignity of all persons, then acting should not tarnish one's concern for human dignity. It is only when one antecedently believes that the sacrificed person is not morally required to accept or endorse the action that it seems to conflict with a regard for the dignity of the person. If my sacrifice is required by universal and unconditional moral principles (to which I am necessarily committed), then my sacrifice is not an affront to the dignity of humanity, thus it should not undermine or tarnish the agent's respect for human dignity.

IV. IMMORAL CONDUCT AND THE KINGDOM OF ENDS

Our discussion of the kingdom of ends, however, is not yet complete. Kant insists that even though a kingdom of ends has not been realized, one should still act as if one were a member of a possible kingdom of ends. Here is the controversial passage on this matter from the *Groundwork:*

> Such a kingdom of ends would actually be realized through maxims whose rule is prescribed to all rational beings by the categorical imperative, if these maxims were universally obeyed. But even if a rational being himself strictly obeys such a maxim, he cannot for that reason count on everyone else's being true to it, nor can he expect . . . the kingdom of nature to favor his expectation of happiness. Nevertheless, the law: Act in accordance with the maxims of a member legislating universal laws for a merely possible kingdom of ends, remains in full force, since it commands categorically. (GMM 439)

How is this somewhat utopian thesis compatible with the practical realism of consequentialism?

In this passage, Kant seems to be assuming that when I am deciding what to do, I should assume others' full compliance with the moral law. Full compliance theory assumes that everyone will in fact do their duty and then asks what principles should be adopted for a kingdom inhabited entirely by virtuous agents. So interpreted, the kingdom of ends formula also requires us to act in our world of imperfect beings as we would act if everyone always did exactly what they are supposed to do. According to this rather implausible interpretation of the categorical imperative, the idea seems to be that for a Kantian, the moral inadequacies of others have no impact on the content or details of moral requirements.

For a consequentialist, how much I am required to do will depend in part on how much others are likely to do. So, apparently, the formula of the kingdom of ends conflicts with consequentialism. This interpretation of the point of the relevant *Groundwork* passage, however, is quite implausible. Although this passage seems to neglect the problem of adopting *rules for dealing with conduct that violates the rules*, Kant elsewhere provides an account of coercion and punishment that reveals the inadequacy of this interpretation. (We will discuss Kant's account of justified coercion in the next chapter.) In general, however, like Hill, we reject this utopian interpretation as inessential to the main point of Kant's idea of the kingdom of ends.[19]

Fortunately, there is an alternative interpretation that is quite plausible. Although Kant's discussion of revolution and lying to murderers shows that he may not fully agree, Kantian moral and political theory requires that we respond and react to the moral failings of others: When I am determining the act that I am morally required to perform, I am duty-bound to consider the consequences of the immorality of others.[20]

The idea of the kingdom of ends simply requires that we do not use the unjustified actions of others as an excuse for our own moral failures. For example, if others are acting wrongly—stealing my property, for example—my own virtuous failure to steal as well will make me much poorer than I would be if all were honest or even perhaps if I stole too. Of course, if everyone were to act morally, then we would expect virtue to more fully correlate with happiness— we would expect a harmony and "a whole of all ends in systematic connection (a whole both of rational beings as ends in themselves and also of the particular ends each may set for himself)" (GMM 433). Nonetheless, Kant's point, in the controversial quote, is that even though the immorality of others may undermine our legitimate expectations of happiness, duty may require us to endure this unfortunate consequence. The immorality of others affects the particular content or details of our duty and the personal consequences of doing one's duty, but it does not weaken or lighten the demands of morality that may, as a result of the failures of others, fall heavily upon us.

In conclusion, neither Kant's concept of the dignity of persons nor the recent emphasis on respect for persons provides a non-consequentialist Kantian basis for resolving conflicting duties. In addition, Kant's conception of the kingdom of ends does not conflict with the consequentialist interpretation. Nonetheless, more needs to be said about the limits of justified coercion and of the sacrifices of the innocent.

NOTES

1. Although neither Alan Donagan nor Jeffrie Murphy explicitly argues that the concept of respect entails an agent-centered approach, both Donagan's assumption that the formula of the end-in-itself generates "prohibitory concepts" (1977) and Murphy's assumption that respecting persons essentially involves non-interference with the freedom of rational beings (1970) seem to presuppose such an entailment. The move from "respect" to deontological constraints is typically taken to be self-evident, thus the deontologist is apparently assuming an analytic or conceptual connection.

2. Stephen Darwall, (1977): 36–49 and (1983): 148–49; quotations are from Darwall (1977), esp. pp. 38, 45. One should note that I rely on a Kantian account of the concept of respect.

3. See also MM 403 and CPrR 38, 75–82, esp. p. 81 n. 3, where Kant also emphasizes this point.

4. This is essentially the interpretation developed by Thomas Hill (1980, 1991a). There are two alternative readings of this extreme view. The first claims that you can never kill one to save many. The second permits you to kill one to save many, but it denies that the reason it is permissible involves the comparatively greater value of the many over the one. We must appeal to some other reason that must be explained. Hill suggests that some other formula of the categorical imperative, specifically the formula of the kingdom of ends, might provide the reason. Hill's use of the kingdom of ends is discussed in section III. Hill does not explicitly defend the soundness of the Kantian position he develops. He maintains only that it is Kantian in spirit and not totally implausible; that is, he does not claim that it is Kant's view, and he also does not argue that it is a sound view. Clearly, however, it is supposed to be an improvement on Kant's own view. Since I am interested in rational reconstructions of Kant's moral theory, I will treat Hill's interesting suggestions as if they were a full-fledged defense of his conclusion.

5. This is not a trivial point. Hill, for example, approaches this issue by developing an interpretation that both avoids consequentialism and captures those aspects of Kant's conclusions that he finds intuitively plausible ([1980] 1992a: esp. pp. 49, 52). This sort of approach all too easily collapses into groundless deontology, as I have dubbed it. It is not sufficient to simply reconstruct Kant's conclusion or an intuitively more plausible simulacrum of it. One must show that the conclusion follows from Kant's argument, from a rational reconstruction of his argument, or from some other Kantian argument.

Clearly, one must take note of Kant's own conclusion in reconstructing the argument, but one cannot rule out reconstructions simply because they entail consequentialism.

Indeed, Hill's comment suggests that he thinks that normative consequentialism entails foundational consequentialism and externalism, so if one attributes normative consequentialism to Kant one must also deny Kantian internalism; thus, there is no Kantianism left ([1991a] 1992a): 205–6. At this point in our discussion, it should be clear that this inference is totally unjustified.

It will not do to simply object that *Kant* was not a consequentialist, because Kant also *clearly rejected* Hill's own more moderate view. For example, Hill takes it to be obvious that one should lie to a murderer to save a friend, and he takes it to be an open question whether Kant's theory, on his reconstruction, would permit the intentional killing of the innocent (despite the acknowledged fact that Kant would be horrified at the thought) ([1991a] 1992a: 218). It seems to me that only a conflation of normative and foundational consequentialism can explain this otherwise clearly question-begging approach to the consequentialist alternative.

6. See chapter 4, section I, for the intrinsic/extrinsic distinction.

7. I have not bothered to distinguish the doing allowing distinction from the intending foreseeing distinction. Similar points can be made about each. For a thorough discussion of these distinctions and the problem with justifying an intuitively plausible version of either distinction, see Shelly Kagan (1989): chs. 3, 4.

8. This point was suggested by Shelly Kagan.

9. John Rawls (1971). The discussion of Rawls that follows is addressed to those familiar with the main outline of his view.

10. Hill ([1972] 1992a): 62.

11. For elaboration of these points, see ibid., 59–61 and Kant, GMM: 433–34.

12. The veil of ignorance excludes all knowledge of natural talents, social assets, and particular conceptions of the good.The idea is to ask what principles of social cooperation and adjudication one would choose if one did not know these particular facts about oneself. The imaginary veil of ignorance is supposed to be a device for generating impartiality and fairness.

13. See Harsanyi (1975); Lyons (1976b); Barry (1973); Hart (1976); Narveson (1982); and Goldman (1980).

14. Andrews Reath has suggested that people have misunderstood Rawls on this point. Maximin does have a Kantian basis: Someone who values the ability to exercise her rational powers in a more or less absolute way would find it rational to adopt maximin in the original position. If something were of great value to you, you would not gamble with it or take chances. See Rawls (1971), esp. section 33.

Although this is a promising suggestion, it does not conflict with Kantian consequentialism. First, as we have seen, Kant's view is that each of us should value rational nature as such and not simply our own rational capacities. Second, the two tiers of Kantian consequentialism would also protect our rational powers from unreasonable trade-offs. Third, if I am indeed trying to preserve my own rational powers in the original position, and I am faced with the possibility of a situation where the powers of all cannot be preserved, then I am most likely to preserve my own rational powers by adopting the consequentialist approach of preserving as many as possible. Of course, this is also true if we have the more Kantian goal of equal concern for each person's rational powers. So we are still left with the standard questions about the maximin principle. (Again, I discuss the troubling problem of the sacrifice of the innocent in chapter 8.)

15. Hill ([1972] 1992a): 61.

16. Hill ([1991a] 1992a): 220. This is similar to Anscombe's earlier, more extreme position that if one is even willing to debate the intentional judicial killing of the innocent, then one "shows a corrupt mind" and thus may be dismissed and ignored; see Anscombe (1958): 16–17. For a response to Anscombe see Kai Nielsen (1972): 219–31; see also R. G. Frey (1978): 134–41. These and many other excellent articles are reprinted in J. G. Haber (1994).

17. R. M. Hare has most fully developed the practical significance of the intuitive and critical levels of moral thinking; see Hare (1981). I have also been influenced here by Peter Railton (1984) and Sarah Conly (1985).

18. I have served on medical ethics committees for the last decade, and the transformation in public and professional attitudes has been striking indeed. Contrary to Hill's suggestion ([1991a] 1992a: 220), patients, families, and physicians who support an assisted death for the terminally ill do not seem to have a weakened sense of the dignity of humanity.

19. See Hill (1974) and ([1991a] 1992a): 220, n. 17.

20. I discuss Kant's account of revolution and develop this thesis in "Kantian Revolutions" (manuscript).

8

THE SACRIFICES OF THE INNOCENT

Consistent rational action is constrained by the objective moral value of rational agents and their ends. As we saw in chapters 4 and 5, since all actions presuppose the objective value of persons, an action that does not treat persons as ends fail to give due recognition to the very value it presupposes. Immoral actions are inconsistent because they presuppose the objective value of agents and their ends, yet at the same time, they deny the reason-giving force of these values. Since immoral actions are internally inconsistent, they are also rationally indefensible.

We have already seen that this type of Kantian internalist foundational theory provides a fairly straightforward justification of a consequentialist principle of right action. It will surely be objected, however, that the consequentialist categorical imperative cannot be the whole story. We may have a duty to promote the good, but this duty is surely limited to the appropriate and acceptable means of doing so. After all, in promoting the good we must give due recognition to the status of other persons as ends-in-themselves. In principle, if not in practice, a consequentialist may be required to sacrifice an innocent person for the sake of some greater good. Clearly, it will be objected, the Kantian injunction to treat persons as ends rules out the sacrifice of the innocent as a means of promoting the good.

Although there are many possible variations, the basic idea behind this objection is as follows: As we have seen, a human being is an end-in-itself because rational nature has the capacity to set itself ends—that is, to act according to a conception of a law. Kant, of course, refers to this capacity as the autonomy of the will. For Kant, autonomy was tied to the notion of free and equal rational beings pursuing their legitimate ends in what he called a kingdom of ends. To respect the autonomy of persons is to "act in such a way that you treat humanity, whether in your own person or in the person of another, always at the same time as an end and never simply as a means" (GMM 429; CPrR 87, 131). The moral law cannot require us to sacrifice others, or ourselves, because to do so would be to treat persons as a means only, rather than as a free and equal member of a kingdom of ends.

It is a basic structural feature of consequentialism that it may sometimes (at least in principle) require us to sacrifice some persons in order to save others. The issue we must now settle is whether or not such sacrifices fail to adequately treat persons as ends-in-themselves. As I have emphasized, Kant does not set out an argument against normative consequentialism and for agent-centered constraints. In order to see if Kant's normative theory supports such constraints, we must consider the structure of Kant's theory and see for ourselves what it does and does not show.

I have argued that Kant's foundational theory naturally leads to normative consequentialism (chapters 2 through 5). We have also discussed the relevance of Kant's distinction between perfect and imperfect duties, his distinction between dignity and price, and his formula of the kingdom of ends (chapter 6 and 7). We will now focus directly on the problem of conflicting grounds of obligations that arise when the only way to save some involves sacrificing others. In these types of tragic situations, a commitment to the unconditional equal value of all persons should lead individuals to accept the legitimacy of their own sacrifice when it is truly necessary to preserve others. If the sacrifice of the innocent is rationally defensible to the sacrificed, then it is also consistent with respect for individual human dignity.

I.   THE RESOLUTION OF CONFLICTING DUTIES

What must a Kantian do when faced with the horrible choice between killing some people or letting many more people die? What if, for example, the only way to end quickly an otherwise long and drawn-out war were be to attack a population center? Such an act surely constitutes aggression against many noncombatants (children, the elderly, citizens of the opposing country who oppose their war effort, etc.). If we assume that the act will greatly reduce human suffering and oppression and that it will save many lives, then it is not at all clear why a Kantian should not sacrifice some to save many.[1] The formula of the end-in-itself requires that one not use another solely as a means to a subjective end. But in this type of case, the ends of the action are objective, not subjective (GMM 427). The objective end in question is first to preserve the lives and liberty that would be lost by a prolonged conflict and, second, to promote, according to one's means, the fundamental and basic needs of others (MM 452).

According to Kant, the formula of humanity generates both negative and positive duties (GMM 430; MM 221–22, 448–51).[2] In the negative sense, we treat persons as ends when we do not interfere with their pursuit of their (legitimate) ends. In the positive sense, we treat persons as ends when we endeavor to help them realize their (legitimate) ends. Kant describes the positive interpretation of the second formulation of the categorical imperative as a duty to make others' ends my own. Given that, if one wills an end, one also wills the necessary means (GMM 417), it follows that the positive interpretation requires that we do those acts that are necessary to further the permissible ends of others (chapter 5). In addition to any constraints on action that Kant's principle might generate, it also provides a rationale for a moral goal that we are obliged to pursue (GMM 398, 430, 430; MM 384–87; see chapter 6).

Since Kant maintains that his principle generates both positive and negative duties, and since there are many situations that involve at least prima facie conflicts of these duties, we need a rationale for giving priority to one duty rather than the other.[3] More specifically, the Kantian deontologist needs a non-consequentialist rationale for the intuitive priority of negative duties over positive duties, which prohibits the sacrifice of the innocent.[4]

In cases of conflicting duties, how can we determine which duties take priority? Kant's own account of the resolution of apparent conflict is not very helpful. On the one hand, he often simply assumes that negative duties are "perfect" duties, which take priority over "imperfect" positive duties. This unhelpful distinction was discussed and rejected in chapter 6. On the other hand, Kant's conception of the kingdom of ends and his teleology of nature do help explain his lack of concern with conflicting grounds of duty. According to Kant, the ends of fully rational beings will not conflict but will form a harmonious kingdom of ends. It is part of the very idea of lawful ends and rational beings that they coexist in a state of harmony, because fully rational beings would will ends that all other rational beings could endorse. Of course, as finite, imperfect rational beings (beings guided by both reason and natural inclination), we need some guide to the proper ends of rational beings. Kant seems to suggest that the teleological ends of natural law are our guide in identifying the proper and legitimate ends of a rational being. As imperfectly rational beings, we can act in accordance with the teleological laws of nature to assure that our ends are rational and thus worthy of being realized. As Bruce Aune explains, "if by treating an imperfectly rational being in a certain way, we promote a kingdom of nature, we can infer, by analogy, that we are acting in accordance with requirements of the pure moral law, which directly applies to an inaccessible domain of purely rational, intelligible beings."[5] Essentially, Aune's suggestion is that a kingdom of nature represents a kingdom of ends and natural law represents a universal practical law. Natural law is thus our analogue for universal practical law.

Most Kantians do not defend these parts of Kant's theory. If we reject (as I assume we do) the view of nature as a system of teleological laws that prescribes the natural and lawful ends to rational beings, then we must rely on the concept of rational nature as an end-in-itself to determine the obligatory ends of rational beings. The telos of rational action must replace the telos of nature. Thus, to discover which ground of obligation is stronger and thereby resolve prima facie conflicts of duty, we must appeal directly to the conception of rational nature as an end-in-itself.[6] Quite simply, one should decide which of two conflicting grounds of obligation is stronger by appealing to the ends or values that generate obligations in the first place.

The formula of the end-in-itself articulates the objective end of all justified actions, the matter or purpose of the supreme practical principle, and thus the objective determining ground of the good will. Kant writes, "Now I say that man, and in general every rational being, *exists* as an end in himself and *not merely as a means to be* arbitrarily used by this or that will" (GMM 428). As such, rational nature provides the basis for a constraint on all merely subjective action (chapter 4).

As we have seen, however, such a constraint is not necessarily an agent-centered constraint; while it does constrain the kinds of ends we may pursue, it does not in itself constrain the methods that we use to pursue them—including the sacrifice of the innocent. All nonegoistic consequentialist normative principles are constraints in this sense. Kant's main argument has only shown that the pursuit of non-moral, subjective ends or goals must be constrained by an equal concern for all (chapter 5). Rational nature is not to be arbitrarily used as a mere means to the personal goals of this or that individual. In addition, the maintenance of the conditions necessary for the development and exercise of rational nature constrain the pursuit of happiness. In this sense, the pursuit of subjective ends is constrained by the principle of respect for the dignity of rational beings (chapter 7).

So far so good for the consequentialist, but now we are concerned with a different type of objection: that the sacrifice of the few is an unacceptable means *because one cannot justify that means of promoting the good to them; it is not a choice that they can endorse while viewing themselves as autonomous beings with dignity.*[7] If this is right, it would be impermissible to sacrifice an innocent person for the sake of a beneficent end. Nonetheless, we have also seen that Kantian beneficence requires that we save or aid as many people as possible. We thus seem to have a conflict between these two different "grounds of obligation."

II.   THE LIMITS OF BENEFICENCE

Kant is correct to insist that we have a duty to promote the happiness of others. We can add that we have an additional and lexically prior duty to save lives and promote liberty. The duty to promote happiness is lexically constrained by the duty to maximally promote the conditions necessary for the flourishing of rational nature. The Kantian deontologist, however, objects to this unconstrained consequentialist principle: Kantian beneficence has two important limitations: We have an obligation to preserve the life and liberty or to promote the happiness of others (1) so long as doing so does not involve acting immorally and (2) so long as doing so does not involve unreasonable sacrifice on our part.[8] Now, there is a sense in which this objection is simply question-begging. A Kantian duty to sacrifice some to save many would not require one to act immorally or to take on unreasonable sacrifice. If it is a duty, then it is not immoral to obey and the sacrifice is not unreasonable; indeed, the sacrifice is required by reason. Consider limitation 1. According to the consequentialist interpretation, a Kantian may be duty-bound to sacrifice some to save many. If this suggestion is correct, then sacrificing some to save many does not involve acting immorally. As an objection to the consequentialist interpretation, limitation (1) requires a rationale that gives it a non-consequentialist content. Thus, if one justifies the first limitation by arguing that Kant's formula of the end-in-itself clearly entails the principle that evil is not to be done so that good may come of it,[9] then one cannot conclude that the sacrifice of some for the sake of others involves doing *evil* so that good may come. The issue in question is the Kantian basis for the assertion that such an act does not treat persons as ends-in-themselves and thus involves doing evil (i.e., the basis for claiming that the act is impermissible). Since we have a duty to maximally promote the necessary conditions of rational beings, we need a positive rationale for ruling out the sacrifice of some as a means to this end. Similar considerations apply to limitation 2. The issue in question is simply which sacrifices are unreasonable from the perspective of an agent whose conduct is determined by the objective end of treating all persons as ends-in-themselves.

Now, one non-question-begging way to develop limitation (1) is to defend a particular interpretation of limitation (2). If an action is required, then it would seem that the action should be rationally acceptable to all persons affected. If, for example, I am required to tax your land, then one would assume that the tax is rationally acceptable to you and that it is impermissible for you to resist paying the tax. Conversely, if you are not rationally required to pay the tax, then one would assume that it is not permissible for someone else to demand the tax. In general, if an agent is not morally required to take on a sacrifice, then how can it be permissible for someone else to sacrifice that agent as a means to an objective end? Indeed, as we shall see, Kant argues that it is permissible to coerce persons only in ways that they are rationally required to endorse. Limitation (2) may thus be used to provide a non-consequentialist content for limitation 1.

Kant's position on the extent of the demands of beneficence is not entirely clear. He clearly states that the duty of beneficence does require sacrifices, but he does not explicitly discuss how much sacrifice is required (MM 451–53). He says, for example, that we must provide ourselves with the essentials of life and not give away so much that we require the charity of others (MM 454). This would suggest that our duty to aid is limited only by our ability to continue to supply our own basic needs. It also suggests that the basis of this limitation involves the best means of promoting the charitable end: One should not sacrifice so much for the sake of some that one comes to need the charity of others. More generally, one might infer from these passages that Kant would endorse Peter Singer's principle of beneficence: If it is in our power to prevent something bad from happening, without thereby sacrificing anything of comparable moral significance, we ought to do it.[10] Given Kant's theory of value, this would imply that we should promote the happiness of others so long as we do not comparably sacrifice our own happiness and that we should sacrifice our freedom or life if doing so sufficiently promotes the necessary conditions of other rational beings.

In the next section, I will defend this interpretation of the duty of beneficence. For the sake of argument, however, let us first simply assume that beneficence does not require significant self-sacrifice and see what follows. Although Kant is unclear on this point, we will assume that significant self-sacrifices are supererogatory.[11] Thus, if I must harm one in order to save many, the individual whom I will harm by my action is not morally required to affirm the action. On the other hand, I have a duty to do all that I can for those in need. As a consequence I am faced with a dilemma: If I act, I harm a person in a way that a rational being need not consent to; if I fail to act, then I do not do my duty to those in need and thereby fail to promote an objective end. Faced with such a choice, which horn of the dilemma is more consistent with the formula of the end-in-itself?

We must not obscure the issue by characterizing this type of case as the sacrifice of individuals for some abstract "social entity." It is not a question of some persons having to bear the cost for some elusive "overall social good." Instead, the question is whether some persons must bear the inescapable cost for the sake of other persons. Robert Nozick, for example, argues that "to use a person in this way does not sufficiently respect and take account of the fact that he is a separate person, that his is the only life he has."[12] But why is this not equally true of all those whom we do not save through our failure to act? By emphasizing solely the one who must bear the cost if we act, we fail to sufficiently respect and take account of the many other separate persons, each with only one life, who will bear the cost of our inaction.

In such a situation, what would a conscientious Kantian agent, an agent motivated by the unconditional value of rational beings, choose? A morally good agent recognizes that the basis of all particular duties is the principle that "rational nature exists as an end in itself" (GMM 429). Rational nature as such is the supreme objective end of all conduct. If one truly believes that all rational beings have an equal value, then the rational solution to such a dilemma involves maximally promoting the lives and liberties of as many rational beings as possible (chapter 5).

In order to avoid this conclusion, the non-consequentialist Kantian needs to justify agent-centered constraints. As we saw in chapter 1, however, even most Kantian deontologists recognize that agent-centered constraints require a non-value-based rationale. But we have seen that Kant's normative theory is based on an unconditionally valuable end. How can a concern for the value of rational beings lead to a refusal to sacrifice rational beings even when this would prevent other more extensive losses of rational beings? If the moral law is based on the value of rational beings and their ends, then what is the rationale for prohibiting a moral agent from maximally promoting these two tiers of value?

If I sacrifice some for the sake of others, I do not use them arbitrarily, and I do not deny the unconditional value of rational beings. Persons may have "dignity, that is, an unconditional and incomparable worth" that transcends any market value (GMM 436), but persons also have a fundamental equality that dictates that some must sometimes give way for the sake of others (chapters 5 and 7). The concept of the end-in-itself does not support the view that we may never force another to bear some cost in order to benefit others. If one focuses on the equal value of all rational beings, then equal consideration suggests that one may have to sacrifice some to save many.

Nonetheless, since we assumed above that extreme self-sacrifice is not morally required, we have two theses—(1) I have a duty to sacrifice an individual for the sake of others, but (2) the individual to be sacrificed has no duty to take on the sacrifice in question—which are clearly in tension with a third Kantian thesis. From a Kantian perspective, (3) it would seem to be impermissible to coerce people to act in ways that they are not rationally required to act. Indeed, the formula of the kingdom of ends implies that the maxims a rational individual wills would be in harmony with the maxims that every other rational will would will, such that in a world of rational beings, all would coexist in a state of lawful freedom. Thus, if one interprets the formula of the end-in-itself as involving the harmony of rational maxims in a kingdom of ends, then sacrifices that are not rationally required should not be coercible.

Since all three theses cannot be true, we must abandon one of them. Since thesis 3 is a corollary of the kingdom of ends and is also an essential part of the Kantian conception of practical reason, and since I have already derived thesis 1, thesis 2 must go. Although thesis 2 may reflect deeply felt intuitions, no Kantian argument for it has been provided. In addition, any other solution will not cohere with Kant's vision of a harmonious kingdom of ends. To avoid the unharmonious solution, we must challenge the assumption that generates the dilemma.

The dilemma resulted from the assumption that beneficence does not require significant sacrifices. If, however, the objective ends of rational action are rational nature and happiness, then the Kantian duty of beneficence requires sacrifices that will sufficiently promote the lives, freedom, or happiness of others. According to this more Spartan interpretation of our positive duties, the legitimate ends of rational beings would not conflict. Indeed, if one maintains that the Kantian duty of beneficence requires significant sacrifices, then the resulting normative theory can readily include the Kantian idea of a harmonious kingdom of ends.

III.   SPARTAN KANTIANISM

In the standard cases, where the innocent must be sacrificed in order to promote freedom and flourishing, the Spartan Kantian would recognize that her sacrifice is required by the moral principles she accepts. Thus, as a conscientious moral agent she would either voluntarily take on the burden in question or, if voluntary action is impossible, would recognize that others' actions against her life, liberty, or property were a necessary means to an obligatory end. According to this interpretation, one may be morally required, in order to further a moral goal, to sacrifice one's innocent self or to accept one's sacrifice by others.

The law that conscientious moral agents would give themselves would require sacrifices that sufficiently promote the legitimate ends of others. Such a position coheres well with Kant's view that we are "rational beings with needs, united by nature in one dwelling place so that [we] can help one another" (MM 453). Of course, Nozick and others can correctly point out that the sacrificed individual "does not get some overbalancing good from his sacrifice"[13] but is Kant not right in emphasizing that every person's duty to be beneficent is to be performed "without hoping for something in return" (MM 453)?

One might object, however, that because the Spartan interpretation requires *self-sacrifice*, it violates the Kantian injunction not to treat humanity, whether *in oneself* or in others, as a means only, and the interpretation thus violates the second formulation of the categorical imperative. This objection fails. If a sacrifice is required by the moral law, then it does not involve using others, or oneself, as a means only. Indeed, if we were not permitted to put others' interests before our own, then all acts of disinterested aid to others would be categorically prohibited. If we were not sometimes required to put others' interests before our own, then Kantians would not recognize any positive moral duties. Indeed, the indirect proof, in chapter 5, suggests that if self-sacrifice were never required, "Kantians" would not even recognize any negative duties.

The Spartan Kantian position is distinct from other interpretations only because it recognizes no absolute limit on the sacrifices that, in principle, are obligatory. Although Kant does not discuss the issue at length, it clearly follows from Kant's arguments that such acts are *permissible*. To sacrifice oneself for the greater good of all is not "to dispose of oneself as a mere means to some arbitrary end" and does not presuppose that one is authorized "to withdraw from all obligation" (MM 422). The end is not arbitrary or based on mere inclination; on the contrary, it is an obligatory end for all rational beings. The motive is not self-interest; on the contrary, "To be beneficent, that is, to promote according to one's means the happiness of others in need, without hoping for something in return, is every man's duty . . . the maxim of common interest, of beneficence toward those in need, is a universal duty of men" (MM 453). Acts of self-sacrifice for a moral goal are permissible; the question is whether they are obligatory.

The most plausible response to the Spartan Kantian interpretation grants that duty may require significant beneficence but maintains that others cannot legitimately coerce one's beneficence. According to this response, beneficence is a duty, but it is not a coercible duty. Since, according to Kant, only duties of justice, not duties of virtue, are coercible, this response would have to maintain that beneficence is a requirement of virtue but not of justice. Indeed, to coerce beneficence is itself a violation of justice; as Donagan would put it, to coerce beneficence involves "doing evil so that good may come of it."

Much of Kant's discussion of beneficence supports this response to the Spartan interpretation. In the *Metaphysics of Morals*, Kant distinguishes coercible duties of justice and noncoercible duties of virtue, and he classifies beneficence as a duty of virtue. In addition, the basic view is an accurate reflection of common sense morality. Indeed, the conclusion that we should not coerce general beneficence has been defended by many consequentialists, even utilitarians. The issue is whether there is a non-consequentialist Kantian basis for this commonsense position.

The duty of beneficence is a universal duty of persons; beneficent acts are rationally required. Since negative duties are subject to coercion, it would seem that positive duties can also be subject to coercion. Thus, if one maintains that beneficence should not be coerced, then one must provide a reason for treating the requirements of beneficence differently from other duties, like prohibitions on force, theft, fraud, and promise-breaking. The most likely basis for maintaining that the duty of beneficence is not coercible would involve the nature of the justification of coercion. One would assume that the justification of coercion also provides an explanation for the limits of coercion. Kant's account of the justification and legitimate scope of coercion, however, provides no basis for such limitation and differentiation.

According to Kant, coercive activity is consistent with respect for the moral autonomy of persons. To be a Kantian autonomous agent is to act on the basis of moral reasons. To respect this capacity of persons does not exclude coercing those who fail to act as they morally ought. Kant explains as follows:

> If a certain use of freedom is itself a hindrance to freedom in accordance with universal laws (i.e., wrong [unjust]), coercion that is opposed to this (as a

hindering of a hindrance to freedom) is consistent with freedom in accordance
with universal laws, that is, it is right [just]. . . . one can locate the concept of
Right [justice] directly in the possibility of connecting universal reciprocal
coercion with the freedom of everyone. (MM 231–32)

The possibility of the universal reciprocal use of coercion exists in the kingdom
of ends. If some fail to act morally, then they may be coerced to act in accordance with their duty. If this were not so, all punishment and self-defense would
be impermissible.

Kant does argue that we can only coerce others to act in accordance with
duty and not from a motive of duty. He thus divides duties into those of external
legislation and those of internal legislation. He calls the former "duties of Right"
or "duties of justice" and the latter "duties of virtue" (MM 218–20). Kant also
claims that the "duties of benevolence, even though they are external duties
(obligations to external actions), are still assigned to ethics [virtue] because their
lawgiving can be only be internal" (MM 220). This point is misleading, however. The point is that genuine concern for others cannot be legislated, not that
the actions of aid themselves cannot be legislated. Since benevolence presupposes a particular motive, if aid is coerced, then the act of assistance is not an act
of benevolence. *Benevolence* thus cannot be externally legislated. The external
action of providing assistance can, however, be legislated and coerced. The
following quotation helps clarify this point:

All duties are either *duties of Right* [justice], that is, duties for which external
lawgiving is possible, or *duties of virtue*, for which external lawgiving is not
possible. Duties of virtue cannot be the subject matter of external lawgiving
simply because they have to do with an end which (or the having of which) is
also a duty. No external lawgiving can bring about someone's setting an end for
himself (because this is an internal act of the mind), *although it may prescribe
external actions that lead to an end without the subject making it his end*. (MM
239, emphasis added)

It is the motive, the internal set of mind, of the agent that cannot in principle be
externally legislated, not the corresponding external action. Indeed, Kant
clearly states that external actions may be prescribed that promote the ends that
we are morally required to adopt. It is clearly possible to externally legislate
positive acts of aid. As Kant draws the distinction, there is no reason why
beneficence, not benevolence, should not be considered a duty of justice.
Whatever Kant may elsewhere assume about coercion and positive duties, he
presents no argument limiting the use of coercion to the enforcement of (what
are normally called) negative duties.

On the other hand, Kant does claim that government is "authorized
to constrain the wealthy to provide the means of sustenance to those who
are unable to provide for even their most necessary natural needs." In addi-

tion to providing for the poor, Kant defends public taxation to provide hospitals, health care services, foundling homes, and the general administration of "the state's economy, finances, and police" (MM 325–26). Kant thus recognizes that beneficence can be a demand of justice and sometimes should be required by law. Kant does not discuss the more extreme measures that, in principle, the consequentialist interpretation would authorize. But whatever our common sense convictions may be, Kant's arguments simply do not rule out the types of the sacrifices that allegedly plague only the house of consequentialists.

On the other hand, in practice, consequentialists do not defend the sacrifice of the innocent as a principle of public policy! In practice, of course, a Kantian consequentialist can and should appeal to good consequentialist reasons for limiting the use of coercion and maintaining a sphere of personal liberty. There are good consequentialist reasons for secondary principles that constrain a direct appeal to the more basic consequentialist principle.[14] Just as honesty is typically the best policy, protecting individual rights really does advance the common good. In addition, the demands of duty are such that, as Kant would say, finite rational beings cannot be expected to fully satisfy them. We must distinguish what one should do if one can from what we should expect or demand of ourselves and others. Although consequentialists reject moral complacency and self-satisfaction, they also provide a justification for a distinction between extraordinary and ordinary compliance with duty. Thus, the Kantian consequentialist should follow the tradition, going back at least to Aquinas,[15] that recognizes that "human law" should externally legislate only the more harmful vices and should set its demands at a level a normally virtuous person can satisfy. Full virtue is indeed best left to the internal legislation of finite rational beings.

Consequentialism thus provides an *indirect* justification for our intuitive conviction that we should not demand that the innocent sacrifice themselves, and also that we should not sacrifice the innocent. Kant's moral theory, however, simply does not provide a more direct and indefeasible justification for deontological constraints. In principle, a conscientious Kantian moral agent may be required to kill one in order to save two. Nonetheless, if someone is unable to do so, this may well not be grounds for reproach. Similarly, if I cannot amputate a leg to save a life—either my own or that of another—I may not be blameworthy for my failure, although it is true that I should have done the nasty deed. Still, in such a situation I must try to force my attention on the good I am doing and thereby enable myself to act. Similarly, in the highly unusual case where it would truly be best to kill some to save others, a good person should also try to focus on the lives to be saved rather than becoming fixated exclusively on those who will be killed.[16] Nonetheless, even though sacrificing some to save others is sometimes the right thing to do, one should still feel regret and mourn the people who are lost. After all, the goal is to save each and every person; thus, one should indeed feel the loss of even one.

According to Kant, the objective end of moral action is the existence of rational beings. Respect for rational beings requires that in deciding what to do, one must give appropriate practical consideration to the unconditional value of rational beings and to the conditional value of happiness. Since agent-centered constraints require a non-value-based rationale, the most natural interpretation of the demand that one give equal respect to all rational beings leads to a consequentialist normative theory. We have seen that there is no sound Kantian reason for abandoning this natural consequentialist interpretation.

In particular, a consequentialist interpretation does not require sacrifices that a Kantian ought to consider unreasonable, and it does not involve doing evil so that good may come of it. It simply requires an uncompromising commitment to the equal value and equal claims of all rational beings and a recognition that in the moral consideration of conduct, one's own subjective concerns do not have overriding importance.

Nonetheless, as I have tried to emphasize, although Kantian consequentialism does not rule out the sacrifice of the innocent, it does rule out most of the counter-intuitive implications of utilitarianism. Indeed, as we shall see in the next chapter, a two-tiered principle justifies a reasonable degree of distribution-sensitivity in the allocation of primary social goods. As a result, the major motivation for Rawls's Kantian theory of justice is sufficiently accommodated by Kantian consequentialism.

NOTES

1. To state the obvious, I do not think that, even given the right circumstance, one should calmly and without any qualms kill innocent people. I have reluctantly come to see that in principle I may be morally required to kill the innocent. Nonetheless, as I have said, I believe that consequentialists have convincing explanations and justifications of our intuitive judgments about hard cases that involve conflicting moral demands. My conclusion is that the Kantian must also rely on these indirect consequentialist accounts. The Kantian simply has no better justification and is thus, like other consequentialists, stuck with the counter-intuitive actions that, at least in principle, may be morally required.

2. It is generally agreed that Kant's formula of the end-in-itself does generate both positive and negative duties. See, e.g., H. J. Paton, (1947): 152, 156–57, 165–74; Wolff (1973): 157–77; Nell (1975): 23–101; Donagan (1977): 57–111, 229–39; Alan Gewirth (1978): 226–27, 329–32, 58–66; Bruce Aune (1979): 181–88.

3. Of course, according to Kant, there cannot be unresolvable conflicts of duty. The concept of duty involves the objective practical necessity of an action, and since two

conflicting actions cannot both be necessary, a conflict of duties is conceptually impossible. Kant does, however, does grant that "grounds of obligation" can conflict, even if
obligations cannot. He is thus left with the priority problem at this level. Kant argues that
in cases of conflict, "the stronger *ground of obligation* prevails" (MEJ 224). Although
such a response is intuitively plausible, without an account of how one ground of
obligation can be stronger than another, it does not provide any practical guidance.

4. Notice that this rationale must justify an agent-centered account of negative
duties. It is not enough to show that, other things being equal, it is worse to kill someone
than it is to let someone die. This still leaves open the possibility that it is permissible, or
perhaps required, to kill one person in order to prevent even more killings. This is the
"utilitarianism of minimizing killings" problem discussed in the introduction (chapter
1., sect. III). The concept of an agent-centered requirement is meant to capture the
distinctive element necessary to exclude the sacrifice of the innocent.

Nonetheless, since I do not believe that the Kantian can establish any *basic* priority
of negative over positive duties—that is, can reach the conclusion that it is worse to kill
one than to allow two others to die—I usually focus on the more common (but still
uncommon) type of case of killing one to save two. Of course, if the Kantian were to
justify the simpler prohibition, this would still leave in doubt the rationale for a more
extreme prohibition against killing even to prevent more killings.

5. Aune (1979): 111.

6. Aune has also pointed out that it is not sufficient to view nature as if it were a
teleological system of laws, for to view nature as if it were governed by the teleological
laws would provide no rational ground for settling disputes about nature's purposes.
Suppose we disagree about what function a natural phenomenon is supposed to serve:
e.g., I argue that self-love serves the function of stimulating the furtherance of life, and
you argue that self-love serves the function of stimulating the furtherance of life where
pleasure outweighs pain. In such a dispute we are left with no criterion by which to
decide. As Aune puts it, "if we are merely viewing nature as if it operated according to
purpose there seems to be no limit on the variety of purposes we could credit it with"
(1979: 60).

7. This is similar to Hill's objection that one cannot intentionally kill the innocent
and continue "honestly to affirm an untarnished respect for human dignity" ([1991a]
1992a: 220), which we discussed in the last chapter. However, as Andrews Reath has
pointed out, the focus here is on what the agent could consistently consent to, while still
thinking of herself as an autonomous being with dignity.

8. Larry Temkin has prompted me to make my response to this objection more
explicit.

9. Donagan at times seems to argue in this way; see his discussion of the "Pauline
principle" (1977: 155). For Donagan's specific account of the impossibility of conflicts of
perfect and imperfect duties, see chapter 6.

10. This is the principle Peter Singer uses in arguing for a duty to relieve world
hunger (1979).

11. When Kant called an act "meritorious" he did not mean supererogatory; he
simply meant that the act was in accordance with duty but beyond what we are
compelled to do by justice or law (MM 227–28, 447). In the next section, I will discuss

whether beneficence can legitimately be a legally enforced demand of justice. On supererogation see chapter 6, section III. See also chapter 5, section III.

12. Nozick (1974): 33.

13. Ibid.

14. See, for example, J. S. Mill ([1861] 1962): chs. 2, 5, ([1859, 1879] 1989); R. M. Hare (1981); John Rawls (1955); David Lyons (1976a), (1977); R. G. Frey, (1984); and Peter Railton (1984).

15. Thomas Aquinas ([1252] 1945): vol. 2, pp. 791–92.

16. Frey (1978).

9

CONCLUSION

I.   KANTIAN CONSEQUENTIALISM

Kantian consequentialism combines a Kantian conception of the nature of moral principles with a consequentialist principle of right actions. Moral requirements tell us what we ought to do, but these are not external requirements that we can rationally reject if we are so inclined. The basis of morality is our own rational nature—our capacity to critically reflect on our lives and ourselves and decide how we ought to live and the kind of character we ought to nourish. Kant makes essentially the same point, in his own distinctive way, when he says that rational nature sets itself apart from the rest of nature because it can set itself ends and act on principle and according to its conception of a law. This distinguishing capacity of persons is the familiar ability to step back, so to speak, from our day-to-day concerns and evaluate ourselves and perhaps rethink the kind of person we wish to be. In a very important sense, morality presupposes the complex capacity of critical self-evaluation, novel self-definition, and effective self-determination. In this relatively uncontroversial sense, persons are self-determining or autonomous beings. Rational nature, in this sense, is the only true source of values or reasons for action. If there are any reason-giving values at all, then rational choice, or autonomy, has "value-conferring" status.

For rather complex reasons, if rational nature is going to confer value on ends, it must have a special kind of value; specifically, it must depend on no other thing for its value, and it must have a value that is higher than and incommensurable with the value it confers. The basis for this thesis is not as clear as it might be, but it does seem clear that in some significant sense the conditions necessary for the flourishing of rational agency take priority over all other values.

Rational action—that is, any action that has a purpose that the agent believes justifies the action—requires that the agent conceive of himself or herself as a source of value and thus also as an end-in-itself, the final and complete justifying basis for the action. (This is Kant's notion of intrinsic value, or the unconditioned condition of value, and of the final objective determining ground of the will). Since my status as a self-originating source of reasons for action is no different from the status of all other rational beings, I must think of all rational beings as ends-in-themselves.

According to the consequentialist interpretation of this conclusion, insofar as we are able, we are obligated to promote the conditions necessary for the exercise of rational nature (unconditional, intrinsic value), and, second and subordinately, we are obligated to promote the ordered set of ends or happiness of rational beings (conditional, extrinsic, value). Clearly, given this interpretation, a Kantian may have to sacrifice some rational beings, or be sacrificed, in order to promote the existence of other rational beings; or a Kantian may have to sacrifice the happiness of a few, including his or her own happiness, in order to sufficiently promote the happiness of other persons.

Let us review the argument. In chapters 2 and 3, we saw that consequentialism is consistent with Kant's account of the motive of duty and with his thesis that the supreme moral principle must be a "formal" principle, not a "material" principle. In chapters 4 and 5, the main Kantian argument for consequentialism, which is based on Kant's conception of rational nature as an end in itself, was presented. In chapter 6, we focused on Kant's normative theory and saw that it includes a robust principle of beneficence. If one concedes that consequentialism is consistent with Kant's conception of duty and his account of formal principles, then it is hard to see how there could be any constraints on the robust principle of beneficence. We explored several alternative sources of constraints in chapters 7 and 8: respect for persons, the dignity principle, the formula of the kingdom of ends, and the distinction between justice and virtue. Together these two chapters show that Kant's normative theory provides no rationale for basic constraints on the Kantian consequentialist normative principle. Although we may be required to sacrifice the innocent, this structural feature of consequentialism is consistent with Kantian internalism and is also grounded in the most important aspect of Kantianism. The defense of Kantian consequentialism is thus complete.

Before concluding, however, it is worth emphasizing some of the more intuitively compelling consequences of the theory. At the heart of Kantian consequentialism is the idea that in addition to our capacity to experience pleasure and pain, our rational nature has a special practical significance. As we have seen, our rational nature—our capacity to set ourselves ends—both provides the basis of morality and accounts for much of the normative content of morality. In particular, the two tiers of Kantian value provide significant constraints on the kinds of permissible sacrifices and trade-offs to which we can be subject, and they also generate a distribution-sensitive principle of social justice.

II.   THE SIGNIFICANCE OF THE TWO TIERS OF VALUE

I have suggested that when it comes to *deciding* what to do, a Kantian consequentialist would accept standard consequentialist justifications of character traits (virtues and vices), secondary principles (negative and positive duties), the priority of negative duties, and the importance of individual commitments and responsibilities. These aspects of the view are clearly important, but it is equally clear that they do not significantly differentiate the normative content of Kantian consequentialism from its more familiar utilitarian relative.

Unlike utilitarianism, however, Kantian consequentialism requires a two-tiered theory of value. The justificatory priority of rational nature generates a normative hierarchy in the theory of the good. In deciding what to do, the existence of rational beings and the development and free exercise of their capacities for rational choice are more important than the maximization of happiness. There are two tiers of value, and rational nature is (for all practical purposes) lexically prior to happiness. The two tiers of value generate a requirement maximally to promote the conditions necessary for rational agency before we concern ourselves with maximizing happiness.

This priority rules out many of the counter-intuitive cases that have plagued utilitarian consequentialism. For example, Kantian consequentialism would not accept a standard utilitarian justification of slavery or of the gladiators. The conditions necessary for the existence of rational beings and for the realization of their capacities for rational choice take priority over other preferences and projects that each individual person may affirm and pursue. The luxurious benefits of a life aided by the toils of slavery cannot compensate for the slave's loss of liberty to develop his or her rational capacities and to form and to pursue a conception of a good life. For the same reason, the pleasure of watching gladiators fight to the death or of watching Christians getting devoured by lions cannot override the individual's claims to life and to liberty.

Since a rational agent must recognize the priority of rational nature as such over the particular content of a rationally chosen set of ends, each agent should strive to choose ends that are maximally compatible with the ends of all others. The content of our preferences is to a greater or lesser degree malleable. If I have chosen ends that conflict unnecessarily with the status of other rational beings as self-originating sources of value, then my particular ends are not even internally justified, and I am thus required to change them accordingly. We are thus individually responsible for forming and affirming, insofar as possible, harmonious and sociable preferences.

III. DISTRIBUTION SENSITIVITY

For similar reasons, two-tiered consequentialism generates an extremely plausible distribution-sensitive principle of justice. Utilitarianism has been criticized, most famously by John Rawls, for its lack of distribution sensitivity.[1] In maximizing utility, the interests of all count equally, so the least well-off individuals, at least in principle, may have to bear burdens that benefit those better off than themselves. Indeed, if the optimal social policy greatly increases the happiness of the well-off at a lesser cost to the worse off, then, other things being equal, a utilitarian is obliged to implement the policy. Rawls has argued that such distribution insensitivity reveals the inability of utilitarianism to capture the notions of fairness and reciprocity that are essential to social justice.

Rawls's own principle of distribution, however, is implausibly strong. He suggests that social inequalities are justified only if they benefit the least well-off members of society. So, even the slightest loss to the less well-off cannot be compensated by any amount of gain to those who are better off. Rawls is driven to this principle of distribution, which he calls the difference principle, in his attempt to avoid the distribution insensitivity of utilitarianism. In particular, his goal is to guarantee each member of society, when possible, a satisfactory minimum share of the basic goods necessary to live a worthwhile life. Rather than defining what counts as a satisfactory minimum, he offers this difference principle, which simply maximizes the size of the minimum share.

Kantian consequentialism generates an alternative to the distribution insensitivity of utilitarianism and the extreme bottom-only sensitivity of Rawls's theory. The priority of the maintenance and flourishing of rational nature over happiness provides a more objective basis for determining the satisfactory minimum that must be guaranteed before happiness is maximized. (It would also support and supplement Rawls's account of the priority of liberty, although the Kantian consequentialist may focus more on the worth of liberty.) The main point, as Thomas Scanlon has argued, is that from a moral point of view, some preferences are more urgent than others.[2] Indeed, from a moral point of view, an individual's own ranking of his or her preferences does not determine the demand the preferences present to others. For example, I may be duty-bound to provide you with nutritional food and yet not be duty-bound to provide you with your favorite dessert (or your cigarettes), even though you rank the dessert (or cigarettes) much more highly than nutritional food. Whatever *your* preferences may be, *others* are primarily bound to recognize claims to subsistence, education, security, and liberty. We should not simply distribute social goods—like rights and liberties, education, health care, powers and opportunities, and income and wealth—so as to maximize the average happiness of the society. Until everyone has a satisfactory minimum of these primary goods, demands based on all other preferences are secondary. Since these social goods provide the necessary conditions for the growth and exercise of our rational capacities, the priority of rational nature justifies their moral primacy.

For the same reason, the content of a satisfactory minimum is not determined by the contents of diverse particular conceptions of the good; for example, it is not that these goods are neutral values, or all-purpose means, or things we all equally want (no matter what else we might happen to want). On the contrary, these goods are primary because they are the necessary social preconditions of rational agency, and the demands of rational agency take priority over happiness. Kantian consequentialism thus provides a justification for what seem to be the basic demands of social justice.

IV.   KANT, KANTIANS, AND CONSEQUENTIALISM

Despite the widespread assumption that Kant's normative theory generates agent-centered constraints, we have found no Kantian justification for such constraints. Perhaps the anti-consequentialist emphasis of Kant's foundational theory encourages this widespread assumption. Perhaps Kant's own rigorously deontological application of his theory makes it seem obvious that Kantian normative theory must be fundamentally deontological. Perhaps Kant's distinction between justice and virtue, or perfect and imperfect duties, appears to generate agent-centered constraints and thus leads to that widespread assumption. Indeed, perhaps these distinctions even led Kant to wrongly assume that his theory generates agent-centered constraints. Whatever the explanation for the assumption, the Kantian demand to treat persons as ends-in-themselves, and not means only, does not generate a normative theory with a fundamentally deontological structure.

Indeed, despite Kant's deontological intuitions about particular moral cases, his basic normative principle is best interpreted as having a fundamentally consequentialist structure. In order to justify agent-centered constraints, one needs a non-value-based rationale. Many Kantians attempt to provide such a rationale by appealing to the Kantian principle of treating persons as ends. The Kantians' strategy is clear: Treating persons as ends involves respecting persons, and respecting persons involves recognizing agent-centered constraints on action. We have seen, however, that this strategy is problematic. The Kantian principle itself generates a duty to advance a moral goal: The duty to strive as much as one can to promote the flourishing of rational beings, and to make others' ends one's own, is the very essence of treating humanity as an end. Morality thus constrains and shapes the pursuit of individual well-being or happiness. We have seen, however, that Kant's moral theory does not provide a rationale for basic agent-centered constraints that limit what we can do in the pursuit of this complex moral goal. The imperative to respect persons thus does indeed generate a consequentialist normative theory, rather than the desired deontological alternative.

It certainly seems that a Kantian ought to be a normative consequentialist. Conscientious Kantian agents have a basic duty to strive, as much as possible, to promote the freedom and happiness of all rational beings. In the pursuit of this moral goal, it may be necessary for the interests of some to give way for the sake of others. If we are sacrificed, we are not treated simply as a means to another's goal; on the contrary, our sacrifice is required by a principle we endorse. Our non-moral interests and inclinations may cause us to feel reluctant, but since our sacrifice furthers a moral goal that we endorse and that we are required to pursue, our sacrifice does not violate our moral autonomy or our rights.

Of course, many deontologists would abandon the Kantian conception of justification and of value rather than accept consequentialism. This sort of unrevisable hostility to consequentialism is more likely to be evidence of some form of deontological intuitionism than of the true normative force of a Kantian approach to ethics. For many, commonsense intuitions are the final court of appeal on all normative questions. We have not focused on this non-Kantian alternative, but one surely should pause in light of all the practices, policies, and duties that others have found intuitively obvious. Nonetheless, whatever the merits of other forms of deontology, it is unhelpful to hide these other positions under a shroud of Kantian rhetoric. What if one is uncomfortable with intuitionism, though? What are we then to make of the intuition that our negative duties are more stringent than our positive duties? Kantian deontologists object to consequentialist justifications of the priority thesis by arguing that because of the indirect and defeasible nature of a consequentialist account, such an account fails to adequately capture the justification of our intuitive moral judgments. We have seen, however, that a more direct Kantian justification of our intuitive moral judgments is not easily forthcoming. Indeed, it would seem that the only plausible account of these intuitions will be consequentialist.

Of course, Kantian deontologists will construct new arguments that provide the long-promised refutation of consequentialism and rationale for deontological constraints, and they may wish to call the position Kantian. It should be clear, however, that these new Kantian positions must stand or fall on their own merits. Indeed, I would be pleased if our arguments prompted a clear explication of the Kantian derivation of deontological constraints.

The consequentialism that we have defended is aptly called "Kantian" for two reasons. First, it is based on Kantian internalism, and second, its theory of value is distinctively Kantian. Of course, any consequentialist normative theory may require actions that Kant would find unacceptable, but it is hardly a prerequisite of being a Kantian that one agree with Kant's rather extreme and inflexible moral judgments. On the one hand, consequentialism requires actions to which Kant would clearly object—indeed, from which he would recoil. On the other hand, consequentialism is itself a rather extreme and uncompromising position. Although (again) this is not part of its justification, Kantian consequentialism strikes me as more Kantian than the moderate, morally undemanding, deontological, or rights-based theories that now claim the name "Kantian."

The two-tiered system of value clearly distinguishes Kantian consequentialism from utilitarianism, and it provides a principled response to many of the intuitive objections to utilitarianism. Thus, in addition to having Kantian foundations, Kantian consequentialism comes as close as a consequentialist theory can come to capturing our commonsense deontological intuitions.

Finally, even if one still insists that Kant and consequentialism are incompatible, I would still insist that Kantian consequentialism is an independently plausible moral theory. Call the view non-Kantian if you must, but it is still a new form of consequentialism.

NOTES

1. John Rawls (1971).
2. Thomas M. Scanlon (1973), (1975): 655–69, and (1988). See also Scheffler (1982a): 26–32.

APPENDIX:
KANTIAN INTERNALISM

The Kantian maintains that morality is a system of unconditional and universal principles, or categorical imperatives. Categorical imperatives are supposed to have some form of rational necessity. The Kantian claim that there is a necessary connection between morality, rationality, and motivation, however, has generated a good deal of controversy and skepticism. Indeed, as a system of categorical imperatives, the Kantian conception of morality strikes many consequentialists as quaint but confused. Properly understood, however, the Kantian position, which we will call "Kantian internalism," is both quite plausible and clearly compatible with consequentialism.

Much of the rejection of the Kantian internalist approach is based either on a misunderstanding of the Kantian thesis about rationality and morality or on the common opinion that it leads to an unacceptably rigid deontological view. Now, Kant does tend to run together two distinct theses, which adds to the confusion over these issues. The first thesis is that the basic principle of morality is a categorical imperative and that morality is a system of such imperatives. The second is that morality is made up of specific categories of duties that admit of no exceptions. Whether or in what form Kant held the second thesis is a controversial issue. The first thesis, however, is our concern. Clearly, if the Kantian approach does indeed support consequentialism, then it is not unacceptably rigid. In this appendix, we develop and explain the first thesis. The main goal is to clarify the Kantian conception of the rational necessity of morality. Although I do not attempt to prove that morality presupposes categorical imperatives, I do hope to undermine the most important objections to this conception of morality and thereby to encourage even those who have previously dismissed Kant's moral theory to reconsider their skepticism about the necessity of categorical imperatives. In addition, and more important for the main thesis of the book, we will see why and in what sense Kant's theory is agent-centered, and that consequentialism can also be agent-centered (in the requisite sense).

I.   INTERNAL AND EXTERNAL REASONS

Moral principles provide unconditional reasons for action. Morality is about what one ought to do, and this ought does not presuppose that I want to do that which I ought to do. Moral principles are also universally valid principles. In some sense, morality is the same for all agents and applies equally to all agents. Moral principles are unconditional and universal. This is a familiar and ordinary conception of morality, but it is also a controversial conception of morality. How is it possible for moral principles to be unconditional and universal? What must the relationship between moral principles and reasons be, if moral principles are to provide unconditional and universally valid reasons for action?

One possibility, which Kantians reject, is that moral reasons are "external reasons"—that is, reasons that need not motivate a rational agent. For example, one might argue that moral reasons involve an optional "moral point of view." More specifically, one might argue that moral reasons are reasons from an ideal, impartial point of view. Since the reasons that move an ideal observer will not necessarily move a partial observer, a fully rational agent may remain unmoved by these "reasons." According to this external view of reasons, if one does not care about the moral point of view, one need not care about moral reasons. Nonetheless, even if one does not care, the moral rules and principles still apply. If I am a rogue, then I am not properly moved by moral reasons; but far from releasing me from moral criticism, this fact probably explains why I am a rogue.

It has been argued that in this type of externalist view, morality is unconditional only in the same sense that etiquette or the rules of a club are unconditional, and it thus does not necessarily provide any directly *motivating* reason for a rational agent to act.[1] Moral rules will still have wider scope than club rules or etiquette; they may even apply to all rational agents and thus have the requisite universality. But in this external sense, morality is not rationally binding and thus does not necessarily provide a rational agent with any motivating reason for action. Moral principles are universal and unconditional, but this does not imply that they have any rational necessity. These external "reasons" are not really practical reasons at all. According to this view, moral principles are *categorical norms*, but not really categorical reasons. In an important sense, externalist views see morality as optional.

Although much may be said in defense of such a view, Kantians find this type of externalist view dissatisfying for many reasons.[2] Most important, moral principles and the moral point of view have a peculiar grip on us. If morality is just one point of view among many, then its significance is diminished. The personal importance placed on morality becomes simply a contingent consequence of moral education. Although this issue remains controversial, we will set this controversy aside and focus instead on the Kantian alternative.

We want to know if it is possible for morality to provide "internal reasons" that are unconditional and universal. Since internal reasons are motivating reasons, an internal reason must, in some sense to be determined, depend on the contingent desires of the agent. How is it possible to provide a conclusive and objective justification of a principle of action? There are actually two distinct but related questions here. First, there is the question of the nature of the reason-giving force or "rational necessity" of moral principles. Second, there is the question of the rational status of moral motivation: Will a rational agent necessarily be motivated to do the right thing? Do moral principles have a "motivational necessity"?

Although these two questions are rarely distinguished, they are, as we shall see, distinct. Of course, given some theories of reasons for action, one may legitimately conflate reason and motivation. But such theories must be the conclusion of an argument and not simply question-begging assumptions. From a Kantian perspective, one can defend the overriding rational necessity of moral reasons for actions and yet claim that a rational agent will do the moral act, for the moral reason, only insofar as reason has *decisive* influence on the will—that is, on the agent's practical deliberation (GMM 413).[3] The Kantian does not claim that reason will necessarily determine the choice of a finite rational agent. Reason tells us what we ought to do, but it does not guarantee that we will be decisively moved to do what is right. So on the Kantian view, one will be motivated by moral reasons insofar as reason determines one's actions. A rational agent who is not moved by moral considerations is thus ignoring reasons for action. If one willfully ignores the dictates of reason, then one is unreasonable and one's actions are not justified.

It is misleading, however, to conclude that an immoral agent is thus irrational. Rationality typically denotes the capacity to consciously take effective means to one's ends. Even if one's ends are not morally justified, one can still pursue the ends in a clearly rational fashion. The claim that morality involves rational necessity is a claim about the status of moral ends and principles; it is not a claim about instrumental rationality. The idea is not that immoral action somehow necessarily defeats the agent's own purposes or ends.[4] Immoral action is not supposed to be irrational in this sense. The idea, however, is that there are principles and ends that a rational agent must accept as authoritative and binding. Immoral action is inconsistent with these principles and ends; thus, in the final analysis, it is not rationally defensible. So although there is a clear sense in which rational evil is possible, there is also a clear sense in which immoral action may be contrary to reason. When it is said that morality has "rational necessity," the idea is that moral principles have a conclusive rational justification and provide decisive and motivating reason for a fully rational agent.

II. MORAL INTERNALISM

The position that moral judgments necessarily provide all rational agents with internal reasons for action is called moral internalism (and its denial is called externalism). In its most familiar guise, internalism is the view that there is a conceptual connection between moral judgments of obligation and motivation. The idea, very roughly, is that obligations provide reasons for action, but reasons for action must be capable of guiding actions, so reasons for action necessarily involve motivating considerations. The conceptual link between moral obligation and motivation presupposes a conceptual relation between obligations, reasons, and motives. Clearly, however, this presupposition calls for additional clarification and discussion. We need to first differentiate distinct but related uses of 'reason' and then use these distinctions to articulate a philosophically favored conception of moral internalism.

There are at least three notions of 'reason' that we should distinguish: justificatory reasons, a person's motivating reasons, and explanatory reasons.[5] Some reasons justify actions; these reasons are normative in the sense that they provide rational guidance or advice and a basis for rational choice. Such justificatory reasons are distinct both from explanatory reasons and from a person's reason for action. A person's reasons often reflect what the person believes to be a justificatory reason, but, of course, such a belief may or may not be accurate. A person's reason also provides a possible causal explanation of the "reason why" the action happened. The three kinds of reasons are thus related. We are especially interested in the relationship between justificatory reasons and the reasons that move a person to action.[6]

First, there is a conceptual connection between a person's reason for an action and her having some motivation to do the action. We cannot, however, simply identify a person's reasons with her motives, because a person's reason for action may not provide the only factor that moves her. In cases of self-deception and unconscious motivation, for example, the explanation of the action may not involve the agent's reason. In addition, fear and anger, rather than reason, often move a person to action. So one can have a motive that is not reason-based, but if a person has a reason, then she has a motive.

The connection between justificatory reasons for actions and motives is less straightforward. Clearly, a particular action can be justified without the agent's knowing of the justification, so justification does not entail actual motivation. Nonetheless, there (probably) is a *counter-factual* conceptual connection between justification and motivation. For example, one might insist that justification presupposes that if the agent were *appropriately aware* of the justificatory reasons, then he would be motivated to do the action. There is no need for us to flesh out the details yet, but there will surely be questions about the nature of the awareness constraint. In particular, one needs to provide a non-circular account of what it is to be "appropriately aware" of the reason, such that it necessarily motivates.

Building on this distinction between justificatory reasons and a person's motivating reasons, we can distinguish different theses that a moral internalist might wish to defend. Much of the rejection of Kantian internalism is the result of confusion and misinterpretation of these distinct theses.[7]

First, we need to distinguish two kinds of *moral internalism*: reason internalism and motive internalism. *Reason internalism* claims that there is a necessary connection between moral judgment and justifying reasons for action. *Motive internalism* claims that there is a necessary connection between moral judgment and a person's motivating reasons for action.

Reason internalism is not about the agent's own judgment and appraisal of reasons; it is about the justificatory reasons that ought to move an agent who is deciding what to do. Reason internalism claims that the moral judgment (that an action is required) entails that there is an all-things-considered justificatory reason for the agent to do the required action. Reason internalism is about justificatory reasons.

Motive internalism, on the other hand, is about a person's reasons—in particular, about a person's moral judgment that one of her actions is required by moral reasons. According to motive internalism, an agent appraising her own actions necessarily has a motive to act in accordance with her moral judgment. Motive internalism maintains that there is a necessary connection between making a moral judgment and having a corresponding motive to act on the basis of that judgment.

In the term 'judgment,' however, there is an ambiguity between the proposition judged and the mental act of judging. Reason internalism is about the former: If one has a moral obligation to do A, then necessarily, there is a justificatory reason for one to do A. Motive internalism is about the latter: If one judges that one has a moral obligation to do A, then necessarily, one has a motivating reason to do A.

One might also say that reason internalism is objective because it links the reasons for an agent to moral requirements, independently of the agent's particular moral judgments. Motive internalism is subjective because it links an agent's motives to her own moral judgments about what she ought to do.

If one accepts both positions (that is, reason internalism and motive internalism), then one believes that all agents have *reason to do what is right* and *motivation to do what they recognize is right*. Of course, the plausibility of both of these positions ultimately depends on the nature of practical reason and moral obligation. Both forms of moral internalism are part of a larger conception of the nature and point of morality.

One last point, however: We need to clarify whether the reason or motive is overriding or not. We shall call the overriding position "strong" internalism and all the many other possible positions "weak" internalism. When these two positions are combined with reason internalism and motive internalism, we get four possible positions. Each possibility has had its defenders, but I am interested in only two positions: strong-reason internalism and weak-motive internalism. It is most plausible to maintain that a moral requirement is (or provides) an overriding reason for action and that the judgment that one is morally required to do an action includes (or provides) some motivation to do the action.

III.   KANTIAN INTERNALISM

Kant was a strong-reason internalist and a weak-motive internalist: Moral principles provide an agent with conclusive reasons for action. In addition, if an agent concludes that an action is morally required, then the agent will have a motive for doing the action. The motive may or may not be sufficient for action. The strength of the moral motive depends both on the significance of reason in the deliberation of the agent and on the competing influences on the agent's will (GMM 412–13). For the Kantian, it is important that the agent not simply believe that the action is justified and thus required but also *see why* the action is required. The motivation is the result of the person's practical reasoning; it is not a passive belief. The thesis that obligation entails motivation is thus a substantial claim based on a particular account of the nature of practical reason.

'Kantian internalism,' and 'internalism' unless otherwise indicated, will refer to this complex dual position. In addition, 'reason,' unless otherwise indicated, will stand in for 'overriding justificatory reason, the awareness of which would provide some corresponding motivation to act accordingly; the reason would provide overriding motivation, if the agent were decisively moved by practical reason.'

So with a sharpened conception of Kantian internalism in mind, we need to return to the first question of Kantian ethics: What is the nature and source of the reason-giving force of moral principles? To answer this question we must look more closely at the idea of a moral obligation or a moral requirement.

According to the Kantian internalist, there are two aspects to the idea of a moral requirement. In addition to providing a reason for action for any rational agent, a moral requirement is also unconditionally binding. Moral judgment tells us what we are *required to do*, and at the same time, it provides all rational agents with *motivating reason for doing* the required action.[8] The central problem of moral theory, I believe, involves developing a theory that captures both these aspects. How can an unconditional requirement provide a motivating reason for all rational agents?

Many contemporary philosophers (and political scientists and economists) assume that only contingent desires or subjective preferences can provide a person with reasons for action. Since a person's reasons can explain actions and since desires cause actions, they argue, reasons for action must depend on the contingent desires of a particular agent. If this view of the nature of a person's reasons is correct, *and* if moral judgments must provide reasons for action, then moral reasons must be relative to the individual. Different individuals have different desires and preferences, so different individuals will be governed by different moral reasons. But this subjectivist, relativist view fails to capture the universally and unconditionally binding nature of moral requirements.

According to this view, we are required to do what we most want to do; if an action does not advance my desires, then I am not required to do it. This simply does not capture the idea of a moral requirement. Rather than providing an explication of the concept of moral judgment, it is more properly viewed as a rejection of the very idea of moral judgment.[9]

Alternatively, if one accepts the desire-based account of reasons for action, one might retain the concept of a moral requirement but abandon the idea that such requirements necessarily provide motivating reasons for action. Whether or not one has a reason to do that which one is required to do will depend on one's subjective preferences. Reasons are then individual-relative, but moral requirements remain universally and unconditionally binding. (This would be a form of moral externalism. Familiar examples of this type of externalist theory include versions of moral realism that claim that there are objective moral facts that are part of the fabric of the universe and some versions of divine command theory.)[10] According to positions of this type, morality is a set of external standards that apply to us; but since reason is desire-dependent, these standards do not necessarily provide us with any motivating reason to do what is required. As a consequence, externalist views conflict with (what Kantians and others believe to be) the conceptual internalism of moral judgments.

In short, if one believes that all reasons depend on individual desire or preference, the alternatives are either some version of individual relativism, which accepts the action-guiding aspect of morality but fails to capture (or rejects) the universally and unconditionally binding nature of obligations, or some version of externalism, which rejects the idea that moral judgment necessarily provides all agents with reasons for action but retains the idea that requirements are universal and unconditional principles.[11]

What is the Kantian alternative? How can the Kantian endorse motive internalism and reject a desire-based, and thus conditional, account of practical reason? The non-Kantian internalist seems to have the upper hand: Reasons will provide motives if and only if there is a *connection* between an agent's reasons for action and the agent's passions, desires, or subjective preferences. Since desires and passions vary from individual to individual, reasons for action will also vary.

This argument from motivation moves too fast. Of course, it is not exactly clear what types of inner states should be included as sources of motivation. Nonetheless, the point is that an agent's reasons must be derived from, or relative to, an agent's "subjective motivational set," to use Bernard Williams's generic phrase.[12] Williams and others take this to imply that all practical reasons must take a conditional, or instrumental, or means/end form: Practical reason is a system of hypothetical, not categorical, imperatives. It would then follow that either morality involves external reasons (categorical norms) or the principles of morality must be based on the individual's particular contingent ends (individually relative norms). Such arguments thus suggest a "motivational skepticism" about categorical imperatives, as Christine Korsgaard calls it, which seems to limit the scope or content of practical reason and thereby seems to exclude the possibility of unconditional practical reason and thus also Kantian internalism.

However, Korsgaard has shown that Williams's internalism about reasons for action actually does not exclude the possibility of Kant's unconditional reasons or categorical imperatives—and thus does not undermine Kantian internalism. She writes,

> If one accepts the internalist requirement, it follows that pure practical reason will exist if and only if we are capable of being motivated by the conclusions of the operations of pure practical reason as such. Something in us must make us capable of being motivated by them, and this something will be part of the subjective motivational set. . . . What sort of items can be found in the set does not limit, but rather depends on, what kinds of reasoning are possible.[13]

Contrary to initial appearances, all practical reasoning will be of the conditional means/end variety only if it is impossible to provide an unconditional justification of principles of action. On the other hand, if ends are also subject to rational justification, such that it is possible for a rational agent to be motivated by the recognition that a principle is unconditionally justified, then unconditional reasons satisfy the internalist requirement. The subjective motivational set of a rational agent would include the capacity to be moved by the recognition that a principle of action is rationally required. So internalism itself does not provide a motivational constraint on the scope or content of practical reason!

Korsgaard, following Thomas Nagel, concludes that skepticism about practical reason must be based on skepticism about the possibility of the unconditional justification of principles—what she calls "content skepticism." She maintains that if we can show that something is a practical reason, we have demonstrated that it can motivate a rational agent. It follows that if we show that something is an unconditional reason, we have demonstrated that pure practical reason is possible.

Nonetheless, Korsgaard recognizes that an account of how such unconditional reasons motivate still seems demanded by the internalist requirement. At this point, I believe, a form of motivational skepticism does indeed limit the content of practical reason. Williams and others, it would seem, are skeptical about the possibility of unconditional justifications because they do not see how a motivating reason can be unconditional and universal. The subjectivity of an agent's motivational set suggests that there will be no one item or principle that is necessarily shared by all rational agents as such. Furthermore, even if there is such a principle, why would it provide the *overriding* reason for action? If the capacity to be moved by morality is just part of the motivational set, why is it not simply one motivating reason among equals? So why would the conclusions of pure practical reason provide the requisite decisive and unconditional justifications? These skeptical questions about moral motivation suggest to many that an ultimate or unconditional justification of a principle can provide only an "external reason" to adopt the principle—which, for an internalist, is really no reason at all, since such a reason can motivate a rational agent only if the agent has an antecedent internal reason to accept the principle; but then the internal reason provides the only real reason for the agent to act.

IV.   CATEGORICAL MOTIVATING REASONS

The thesis that reasons for action must be related to an agent's subjective motivational set is clearly essential to any internalist position. This *internal source requirement* implies that any unconditional justification must be rooted in and related to the otherwise variable internal features that motivate particular agents. It does not imply, however, that the source must be a particular contingent desire of the agent. The subjective motivational set of a rational agent (that is, an agent decisively moved by reason) could contain ends and principles that are not contingent, such as ends and principles to which any rational agent must be committed. This is all that is necessary for there to be necessary ends and unconditional principles.

How can pure reason motivate? Here is an initial rough and schematic account: The idea is that my own evaluation of my desire-based reasons for action, say D *at* t, necessarily commits me to recognize "pure" reasons for action, say R *at* t, where R *at* t need not be antecedently included in my subjective motivational set of desires, D *at* $t-1$, either as an end or as a means to an end. The relationship between R and D is a relationship of condition and conditioned, not means and end; that is, D provides reasons for action only on the condition that R is also taken to be an end (in the sense spelled out in chapter 4). If D has motivational force, and if we are determined by reason, R will also have motivational force. Just as we experience a rational *transmission of motivation* from ends to means, so too we experience a rational transmission of motivation from our ends to the necessary conditions of their reason-giving force.

If there are ends that are presupposed by the value of any end whatsoever, then there are necessary or objectively justified ends of action. The rational motivational mechanism would then be no more mysterious in the case of categorical imperatives than it is in the case of hypothetical imperatives. In the one case we are moved to take the necessary and available means to an end (or abandon the end), and in the other case we are moved to perform the actions required by the principle we must accept, if we value anything at all.

The justification of necessary objective ends is itself, *in a sense*, based on individual subjective contingent ends. The motivation to adopt these ends is thus also derived, via practical reasoning, from individual desires. Rational motivation does not arise ex nihilo, there is a necessary relationship between an agent's contingent desires and objective reasons. Nonetheless, these reasons are not desire-dependent in the familiar Humean sense. The justification of objective ends and thus moral principles does not presuppose that there is an antecedent desire to do the right (or that doing the right is a necessary means to some other desired end). In short, for any internalist, the derivation of moral principles must start with the perspective of a particular agent and his or her contingent ends; but practical deliberation nonetheless justifies universal and unconditional moral principles.

Although much groundwork is necessary to clarify the structure of pure practical reason, the main conceptual idea is familiar and intuitive enough: I believe my freely and rationally chosen ends have value and thus provide reasons for action. The reason-giving force of my ends presupposes that rational choice is a source of value. The value of my ends thus presuppose that I am a source of value. But my capacity for free rational choice is no different from the capacity of other rational agents: If I am a source of value, then so too are all other rational agents. Since the reason-giving basis of the end is the same in each case, each also provides a reason for action that any agent must recognize. Just as my ends provide me with reasons for action, so too do others and their ends. There is an inconsistency or contradiction in the claim that the one is a reason but not the other. (These ideas are developed in chapter 4.)

Of course, much would have to be added to flesh out this line of thought and fortify it against the egoists, the amoralists, and the skeptics, but for our purposes let us focus on the motivational structure of the reasoning. The idea is that the initial motivation to perform an action because it will promote a rationally chosen end commits the agent to the reason-giving force of rationally chosen ends as such. The initial motivation thus provides additional motivation to consider other actions that are similarly justified. Just as there is a motivation to perform actions that are a necessary means to one's ends, so too there is motivation to consider ends that are presupposed by the ends one antecedently values. Of course, how this is possible remains somewhat of a mystery; but it is also a mystery how my desire to have good teeth in my old age now moves me to endure the drill of the dentist.[14]

The important point, however, is that the rejection of the Kantian internalist argument for moral obligations should be based on a skepticism about the soundness of the practical reasoning itself—and not about any problem with how this type of reasoning can possibly motivate a rational agent. If the reasoning is sound, then a fully rational agent will be motivated by the conclusion. A failure to be motivated by a rational argument would simply be evidence of a failure of practical rationality; it would show that one is not a being that is moved by good reasons. After all, one does not reject instrumental practical reasoning because some people have an inability to follow hypothetical imperatives.

So this is why Korsgaard claims that motivational skepticism presupposes content skepticism. Motivational skepticism simply does not provide an independent constraint on the content of practical reason. All reasons for action are indeed essentially related to the internal motivational capacities of a rational agent. We cannot simply assume, however, that the only rational practical inferences are from ends to means. The question is thus one about the nature of practical reason and the possibility of unconditional and universal reasons for action.

V.   KANTIAN INTERNALISM AND CONSEQUENTIALISM

Now our main concern is not the defense of Kantian internalism but the consequences of it. Like Kant, we ask what the supreme principle of morality would have to be for morality to provide unconditional and universally valid reasons. Clearly, internalism itself provides significant constraints on the normative content of morality. The concept of morality as universal and unconditional provides "formal" conditions or constraints on what can be a moral principle (chapters 2 through 4). Any moral principle must be universal and unconditional, so what normative principle can satisfy these conditions? Kantian internalism sets up the possibility, which is explained in chapter 2, of extracting the supreme principle of morality from the motives of a morally good agent. This is why Kant starts the *Groundwork* by focusing on an agent acting from duty. This is also the starting point for our derivation of Kantian consequentialism.

Internalism clearly implies that moral theory must take the perspective of the deliberating moral agent as its starting point. In this very important sense, moral principles are necessarily agent-centered. As I reconstruct and interpret Kant's internalist argument, we are *required* to promote the two tiers of Kantian value (chapter 5). Consequentialism, so understood, is a constraint on all subjective and "arbitrary" ends. So interpreted, morality constrains one's inclinations, or merely subjective projects, but it does not include agent-centered constraints on the maximization of value. The requirement to promote Kantian value is an agent-centered requirement, and it is even an agent-centered constraint on the maximization of one's *own good*. What distinguishes Kantian consequentialism from standard deontology is simply that it does not recognize any additional agent-centered constraints on the maximization of *the good*. If all the requirements have a consequentialist structure, there is no practical difference between agent-centered and agent-neutral requirements.[15]

Although Kantian internalism does reflect an agent-centered view of morality, consequentialism can be agent-centered in the sense required by internalism. Since a moral principle must be universal and unconditional, morality is clearly a constraint on subjective desires. Nonetheless, Kantian consequentialism is also supposed to be a constraint in this sense. Kantian internalism seems to provide absolutely no rationale for insisting that morality involves basic agent-centered constraints on the maximization of the good. Rather, Kantian internalism provides a plausible and important conception of the relationship between morality and rationality, and this conception of morality is fully compatible with normative consequentialism.

NOTES

1. Philippa Foot (1978), esp. pp. 160–64.

2. On this issue see, for example, Scheffler (1982b) and Darwall (1982).

3. The distinction between rational causality, or *Wille*, and the capacity to choose, or *Willkür*, is relevant here (MM 213, 226–27, 407). Kant's position is (must be) that *Wille* must be able to determine *Willkür*; but *Willkür* is also influenced by the counterweight of the inclinations; the agent, when deciding what to do, thus questions the validity of moral reasons and is inclined to make exceptions to the rationally authoritative demands of *Wille* (GMM 405).

4. Thus, objections to the Kantian position often miss the target. See Foot (1978): 161–62 and Peter Railton (1986).

Moral internalism also seems to fly in the face of the possibility of rational amoralism. David Brink, for example, argues that amoralism refutes internalism (1989). Whatever the merits of his argument against desire-based internalism, his argument does not undermine Kantian internalism as I understand it. As we will see, moral internalism involves a substantive thesis about the nature of practical reason itself. Motivational skepticism alone does not refute Kantian internalism.

5. See Darwall (1983): ch. 2 for a good discussion of the distinction between justificatory and explanatory reasons.

6. The following example may help clarify the difference and relationships between these three kinds of reasons. Imagine that, without reflection, I cross my legs and lean back on the sofa immediately after you cross your legs and lean back in your chair. There is a causal explanation, which provides a *reason why* I crossed my legs, but which may have nothing to do with *my reasons* at the time. Now, imagine that I notice that I have just unconsciously mimicked my associate's bodily behavior, so I uncross my legs and lean forward. This second action results from my reflection on what has just happened, and the causal explanation of this now-deliberate action thus will involve my reasons. We need not assume, however, that I have deliberated about this second action and concluded that I ought to return to my earlier posture. I may react with reflection but without any real deliberation. Often we act for a reason but without any sense that the action is truly justified. Indeed, on leaning forward, I may decide that the initial reflex was a good one because, say, it helps us both relax and does no harm. The explanation for this last action thus involves my conception of a *justificatory reason* for action. Of course, I may nonetheless be in error, and the action may not really be justified after all. We thus need to distinguish between these three distinct kinds of reasons.

I have benefited from Thomas Hill's discussion (1986: 604–19, esp. 605) of Darwall's position.

7. The distinction between internalism and externalism was first drawn by W. D. Falk (1947: 137). See William Frankena (1958) for a characterization of the history and nature of the internalist vs. externalist debate.

In an extremely useful discussion David Brink has set out the distinctions between kinds of moral internalism (1989: 37–43). In outline, but not in every detail, I follow Brink's account of the distinctions.

8. For now I use the all-purpose 'requirement.' In chapter 6, we discuss possible distinctions between strict requirements, recommendations (or things that it is good to do), and permissions. One begins, however, with the core notion of moral requirements in the broadest possible sense. The basic normative principle tells us how we ought to live our lives and thus supremely governs all conduct. This principle, however, may itself require some actions, recommend others, and judge yet others to be simply permissible. I am also not concerned with distinctions between a requirement, a duty, an obligation, and even a responsibility. Of course, in some contexts all distinctions are important; so I will draw attention to these distinctions when necessary.

9. Of course, there are also non-Kantian accounts of moral requirements. See, for example, David Gauthier (1985) for a desire-based argument for universal, but not unconditional, requirements. For an interesting example of the relativist approach, see Gilbert Harman (1975, 1978).

10. For a more compelling versions of externalist moral realism, see Brink (1989); Peter Railton (1986): 163–207; and Geoffrey Sayre-McCord, (1988). Also see Foot's position (1978). Of course, one can also try to be a moral realist and internalist. Whether such a view suffers from mere queerness or complete incoherence, I leave to others to decide.

11 For the relativist alternative, see Harman (1975, 1978). For the externalist alternative, see Brink (1989), Foot (1978), and Railton (1986).

12. Williams (1981): 101–13.

13. Korsgaard (1986b): 5–25, esp. p. 21. See also Paton (1951a).

14. So, as I understand these issues, unconditioned, pure practical reason does not have its source in a separate intelligible world, and we need not assume that it involves contra-causal freedom. It does, however, provide us with a "higher vocation" than the rest of nature in the fairly simple sense that we can be moved by a conception of a sufficient reason for action. Indeed, the human capacity to deliberate and critically evaluate desires clearly involves higher-order rational capacities. Even if this does not show that we are more important than the rest of nature, the autonomy of the human will does provide the basis for a special sense of responsibility and accountability for our actions.

15. As we see in chapter 5, agent-neutral reasons are inescapable, necessary requirements of agent-centered practical reason. Although all reasons are agent-centered, and thus objective reasons are derived from subjective concerns, objective practical reasons are not agent-relative in any significant sense.

REFERENCES

Allison, Henry (1990). *Kant's Theory of Freedom*. Cambridge University Press.

——(1991). "On a Presumed Gap in the Derivation of the Categorical Imperative," *Philosophical Topics* 19, pp. 1–15.

Anscombe, G. E. M. (1958). "Modern Moral Philosophy," *Philosophy* 33, pp. 1–19.

Aquinas, Thomas ([1252] 1945). *Summa Theologica: The Basic Writings of Saint Thomas Aquinas*, edited by Anton C. Pegis. Random House.

Aune, Bruce (1979). *Kant's Theory of Morals*. Princeton University Press.

Bales, R. E. (1971). "Act Utilitarianism: Account of Right-Making Characteristics or Decision-Making Procedures?" *American Philosophical Quarterly* 8, pp. 257–65.

Baron, Marcia (1984). "The Alleged Moral Repugnance of Acting from Duty," *The Journal of Philosophy* 81, pp. 197–220.

——(1987). "Kantian Ethics and Supererogation," *The Journal of Philosophy* 84, pp. 237–62.

Barry, Brian (1973). *The Liberal Theory of Justice*. Oxford University Press.

Bennett, Jonathan (1981). "Morality and Consequences," in *The Tanner Lectures on Human Values*, edited by Sterling McMurrin. University of Utah Press.

Benson, Paul (1987). "Moral Worth," *Philosophical Studies* 51, pp. 365–82.

Brandt, Richard (1979). *A Theory of the Good and the Right*. Oxford University Press.

Brink, David (1986). "Utilitarian Morality and the Personal Point of View," *The Journal of Philosophy* 83, pp. 417–38.

——(1989). *Moral Realism and the Foundations of Ethics*. Cambridge University Press.

Buchanan, Allen (1975). "Revisability and Rational Choice," *Canadian Journal of Philosophy* 85, pp. 395–408.

Byrd, Sharon (1989). "Kant's Theory of Punishment: Deterrence in Its Threat, Retributivist in Its Execution," *Law and Philosophy* 8, pp. 151–200.

Christman, John (1989). *The Inner Citadel: Essays on Individual Autonomy*. Oxford University Press.

Conly, Sarah (1983). "Utilitarianism and Integrity," *The Monist* 66, pp. 298–311.

——(1985). "The Objectivity of Morals and the Subjectivity of Agents," *American Philosophical Quarterly* 22, pp. 275–86.

——(1986). Review of Samuel Scheffler's *The Rejection of Consequentialism*, *Philosophical Review* 95, pp. 147–50.

Cummiskey, David (1987). "Desert and Entitlement: A Rawlsian Consequentialist Account," *Analysis* 47, pp. 15–19.

——(1989). "Consequentialism, Egoism, and the Moral Law," *Philosophical Studies* 57, pp. 111–34.

——(1990). "Kantian Consequentialism," *Ethics* 100, pp. 586–615.

——(1994). "Kantian Revolutions" (manuscript).

Darwall, Stephen (1977). "Two Kinds of Respect," *Ethics* 87, pp. 36–49.

——(1982). "Scheffler on Morality and Ideals of the Person" and "Reply to Scheffler" *Canadian Journal of Philosophy* 12, pp. 247–55, 263–64.

——(1983). *Impartial Reason.* Cornell University Press.

——(1986). "Agent-Centered Restrictions from the Inside Out," *Philosophical Studies* 50, pp. 291–319.

Donagan, Alan (1977). *The Theory of Morality.* University of Chicago Press.

Dworkin, Ronald (1978). *Taking Rights Seriously.* Harvard University Press.

Falk, W. D. (1948). " 'Ought' and Motivation," *Proceedings of the Aristotelian Society* 48, pp. 111–38.

——(1965). "Morality, Self, and Others," in *Morality and the Language of Conduct,* edited by H. N. Castaneda and G. Nakhnikian. Wayne State University Press.

Feinberg, Joel (1973). *Social Philosophy.* Prentice Hall.

Feldman, Fred (1978). *Introductory Ethics.* Prentice Hall.

Fishkin, James (1984). "Utilitarianism versus Human Rights," *Social Philosophy and Policy* 1, pp. 103–7.

Foot, Philippa (1978). "Morality as a System of Hypothetical Imperatives," in *Virtues and Vices.* University of California Press.

Frankena, William (1958). "Obligation and Motivation in Recent Moral Philosophy," in *Essays in Moral Philosophy,* edited by A. I. Melden. University of Washington Press.

——(1973). *Ethics.* Prentice Hall.

Frankfurt, Harry (1971). "Freedom of the Will and the Concept of a Person," *The Journal of Philosophy* 68, pp. 5–20.

Frey, R. G. (1978). "What a Good Man Can Bring Himself to Do," *Journal of Value Inquiry* 12, pp. 134–41.

——(1984). *Utility and Rights.* University of Minnesota Press.

Fried, Charles (1978). *Right and Wrong.* Harvard University Press.

Gauthier, David (1985). *Morals by Agreement.* Oxford University Press.

Gewirth, Alan (1978). *Reason and Morality.* University of Chicago Press.

——(1991). "Can Any Final Ends be Rational?" *Ethics* 102, pp. 66–95.

Gibbard, Allan (1982). "Inchoately Utilitarian Common Sense," in *The Limits of Utilitarianism,* edited by H. B. Miller and W. H. Williams. University of Minnesota Press.

——(1984). "Utilitarianism and Human Rights," *Social Philosophy and Policy* 1, pp. 92–102.

——(1991). *Wise Choices, Apt Feelings.* Harvard University Press.

Goldman, Holly Smith (1980). "Rawls and Utilitarianism" in *John Rawls's Theory of Social Justice,* edited by H. Gene Blocker and Elizabeth H. Smith. Ohio University Press.

Gomberg, Paul (1989). "Consequentialism and History," *Canadian Journal of Philosophy* 19, pp. 383–403.

Haber, J. G., ed. (1994). *Absolutism and Its Consequentialist Critics.* Rowman & Littlefield.

Hare, R. M. (1981). *Moral Thinking: Its Levels, Method, and Point.* Oxford University Press.

Harman, Gilbert (1975). "Moral Relativism Defended," *Philosophical Review* 84, pp. 3–22.

——(1978). "Relativistic Ethics: Morality as Politics," *Midwest Studies in Philosophy* 3, pp. 109–121.

Harsanyi, John (1975). "Can the Maximin Principle Serve as a Basis for Morality? A Critique of John Rawls's Theory," *American Political Science Review* 59, pp. 594–606.

——(1982). "Morality and the Theory of Rational Behavior," in *Utilitarianism and Beyond*, edited by A. K. Sen and Bernard Williams. Cambridge University Press.

Hart, H. L. A. (1976). "Rawls' Theory of Justice," in *Reading Rawls*, edited by Norman Daniels. Basic Books.

Herman, Barbara (1981). "On the Value of Acting on the Motive of Duty," *The Philosophical Review* 90, pp. 359–82. Reprinted in *The Practice of Moral Judgment.* Harvard University Press, 1993.

——(1985). "The Practice of Moral Judgement," *The Journal of Philosophy* 82, pp. 414–36. Reprinted in *The Practice of Moral Judgment.* Harvard University Press, 1993.

——(1989). "Murder and Mayhem," *The Monist* 72, pp. 411–20. Reprinted in *The Practice of Moral Judgment.* Harvard University Press, 1993.

——(1993a). *The Practice of Moral Judgment.* Harvard University Press.

——(1993b). "Leaving Deontology Behind," in *The Practice of Moral Judgment.* Harvard University Press.

Hill, Thomas Jr. (1971). "Kant on Imperfect Duty and Supererogation," *Kant-Studien* 61, pp. 55–76. Reprinted in *Dignity and Practical Reason.* Cornell University Press, 1992.

——(1972). "The Kingdom of Ends," in *Proceedings of the Third International Kant Conference*, edited by Lewis White Beck. Reidel. Reprinted in *Dignity and Practical Reason.* Cornell University Press, 1992.

——(1973). "The Hypothetical Imperative," *The Philosophical Review* 82, pp. 429–50. Reprinted in *Dignity and Practical Reason*, Cornell University Press, 1992.

——(1974). "Kant's Utopianism," *Akten des 4. International Kant-Kongresses, Mainz, 1974*, Teil II.2, pp. 918–24. Reprinted in *Dignity and Practical Reason.* Cornell University Press, 1992.

——(1978). "Kant's Anti-Moralistic Strain," *Theoria* 44, pp. 131–51.

——(1980). "Humanity as an End in Itself," *Ethics* 91, pp. 84–90. Reprinted in *Dignity and Practical Reason.* Cornell University Press, 1992.

——(1986). "Darwall on Practical Reason," *Ethics* 96, pp. 604–19.

——(1989a). "The Kantian Conception of Autonomy," in *The Inner Citadel: Essays on Individual Autonomy*, edited John Christman. Oxford University Press. Reprinted in *Dignity and Practical Reason.* Cornell University Press, 1992.

———(1989b). "Kant's Theory of Practical Reason," *The Monist* 72, pp. 363–83. Reprinted in *Dignity and Practical Reason*. Cornell University Press, 1992.

———(1991a). "Making Exceptions without Abandoning the Principle: How a Kantian Might Think about Terrorism," in *Violence, Terrorism, and Justice*, edited by Ray Frey and Christopher Morris. Cambridge University Press. Reprinted in *Dignity and Practical Reason*. Cornell University Press, 1992.

———(1991b). *Autonomy and Self Respect*. Cambridge University Press.

———(1992a) *Dignity and Practical Reason in Kant's Moral Theory*. Cornell University Press.

———(1992b). "A Kantian Perspective on Moral Rules," *Philosophical Perspectives, 6: Ethics*, edited by James E. Tomberlin. Ridgeview Press.

———(1993). "Donagan's Kant," *Ethics* 104, pp. 22–52.

Hospers, John (1982). *Human Conduct*. Harcourt Brace Jovanovich.

Irwin, Terence (1984). "Morality and Personality: Kant and Green," in *Self and Nature in Kant's Philosophy*, edited by Allen W. Wood. Cornell University Press.

Jackson, Frank (1991). "Decision Theoretic Consequentialism and the Nearest and Dearest Objection," *Ethics* 101, pp. 461–82.

Kagan, Shelly (1987). "Donagan on the Sins of Consequentialism," *Canadian Journal of Philosophy* 17, pp. 643–53.

———(1989). *The Limits of Morality*. Oxford University Press.

———(1992). "The Structure of Normative Ethics," *Philosophical Perspectives, 6: Ethics*, edited by James E. Tomberlin. Ridgeview Press.

Korsgaard Christine (1983). "Two Distinctions in Goodness," *Philosophical Review* 92, pp. 169–95.

———(1985). "Kant's Formula of Universal Law," *Pacific Philosophical Quarterly* 66, pp. 24–47.

———(1986a). "Kant's Formula of Humanity," *Kant-Studien* 77, pp. 183–202.

———(1986b). "Skepticism about Practical Reasoning," *The Journal of Philosophy* 83, pp. 5–25.

———(1986c). "Aristotle and Kant on the Source of Value," *Ethics* 96, pp. 486–505.

———(1989a). "Kant's Analysis of Obligation: The Argument of *Foundations I*," *The Monist* 72, pp. 311–40.

———(1989b). "Morality as Freedom," in *Kant's Practical Philosophy Reconsidered*, edited by Y. Yovel. Kluwer Academic Publishers.

———(1992). "The Sources of Normativity," in *The Tanner Lectures on Human Values*, edited by Sterling M. McMurrin. University of Utah Press.

———(1993). "The Reasons We Can Share: An Attack on the Distinction between Agent-Relative and Agent-Neutral Values," *Social Philosophy and Policy* 10, pp. 24–51.

———(1996). "From Duty and For the Sake of the Noble: Kant and Aristotle on Morally Good Action," in *Aristotle, Kant, and the Stoics: Rethinking Happiness and Duty*, edited by Stephen Engstrom and Jennifer Whiting. Cambridge University Press.

Kymlicka, Will (1989). *Liberalism, Community and Culture*. Oxford University Press.

Lyons, David (1976a). "Mill's Theory of Morality," *Noûs* 10, pp. 101–20.

——(1976b). "The Nature and Soundness of the Contract and Coherence Arguments," in *Reading Rawls*, edited by Norman Daniels. Basic Books.

——(1977). "Human Rights and the General Welfare," *Philosophy and Public Affairs* 6, pp. 113–29.

MacIntyre, Alaisdair (1981). *After Virtue*. University of Notre Dame Press.

MacKinnon, Catharine (1987). *Feminism Unmodified: Discourses on Life and Law*. Harvard University Press.

——(1989). *Toward a Feminist Theory of the State*. Harvard University Press.

McCarty, Richard (1992). "Is Kant's Formula of Humanity a Consequentialist Categorical Imperative?" Paper presented at the Pacific Division meeting of the American Philosophical Association, March.

Meyers, Diana T. (1987). "The Socialized Individual and Individual Autonomy: An Intersection between Philosophy and Psychology," in *Women and Moral Theory*, edited by Eva Feder Kittay and Diana T. Meyers. Rowman & Littlefield.

Mill, J. S. ([1861] 1962). *Utilitarianism and Other Writings*, edited by Mary Warnock. Meridian Books.

——(1989). *On Liberty* [1859] *with On the Subjection of Women* [1869] *and Chapters on Socialism* [1879], edited by Stefan Collini. Cambridge University Press.

Moore, G. E. (1903). *Principia Ethica*. Cambridge University Press.

Murphy, Jeffrie (1970). *Kant: The Philosophy of Right*. St. Martin's Press.

——(1987). "Does Kant Have a Theory of Punishment?" *Columbia Law Review* 87, pp. 509–32.

Nagel, Thomas (1970). *The Possibility of Altruism*. Princeton University Press.

——(1979a). "Subjective and Objective," in Thomas Nagel, *Mortal Questions*. Cambridge University Press.

——(1979b). "The Fragmentation of Value," in Thomas Nagel, *Mortal Questions*. Cambridge University Press.

——(1980). "The Limits of Objectivity," in *The Tanner Lectures on Human Values*, edited by Sterling S. McMurrin. University of Utah Press.

——(1986). *The View from Nowhere*. Oxford University Press.

——(1992). *Equality and Partiality*. Oxford University Press.

Narveson, Jan (1982). "Rawls and Utilitarianism," in *The Limits of Utilitarianism*, edited by Harlan B. Miller and William H. Williams. University of Minnesota Press.

Nell (O'Neill), Onora (1975). *Acting on Principle*. Columbia University Press.

Nielsen, Kai (1972). "Against Moral Conservatism," *Ethics* 82, pp. 219–31.

Nietzsche, Friedrich ([1887] 1967). *On the Genealogy of Morals*, translated by Walter Kaufman. Vintage Books.

Nozick, Robert (1974). *Anarchy, State, and Utopia*. Basic Books.

O'Neill, Onora (1989a). *Constructions of Reason*. Cambridge University Press.

——(1989b). "Consistency in Action," in *Constructions of Reason*. Cambridge University Press.

——(1989c). "Universal Laws and Ends-in-Themselves," in *Constructions of Reason*. Cambridge University Press.

Parfit, Derek (1984). *Reasons and Persons*. Oxford University Press.

Paton, H. J. ([1942] 1971). *The Categorical Imperative.* University of Pennsylvania Press.

——(1951a). "Can Reason Be Practical?," in *In Defense of Reason,* Hutchinson's University Library.

——(1951b). "Kant's Idea of the Good," in *In Defense of Reason,* Hutchinson's University Library.

——(1951c). "The Alleged Independence of Goodness," in *In Defense of Reason,* Hutchinson's University Library.

Pettit, Philip (1987). "Rights, Constraints, and Trumps," *Analysis* 47, pp. 8–14.

Railton, Peter (1984). "Alienation, Consequentialism, and the Demands of Morality," *Philosophy and Public Affairs* 13, pp. 134–71.

——(1986). "Moral Realism," *Philosophical Review* 95, pp. 163–207.

Rawls, John (1955). "Two Concepts of Rules," *Philosophical Review* 64, pp. 3–32.

——(1971). *A Theory of Justice.* Harvard University Press.

——(1975). "Fairness to Goodness," *Philosophical Review* 84, pp. 536–54.

——(1980). "Kantian Constructivism in Moral Theory," *The Journal of Philosophy* 77, pp. 515–72.

——(1982a). "The Basic Liberties and Their Priority," in *The Tanner Lectures on Human Values,* edited by Sterling M. McMurrin. University of Utah Press.

——(1982b). "Social Unity and Primary Goods," in *Utilitarianism and Beyond,* edited by A. K. Sen and Bernard Williams. Cambridge University Press.

——(1985). "Justice as Fairness: Political Not Metaphysical," *Philosophy and Public Affairs* 14, pp. 223–51.

Reath, Andrews (1989a). "Hedonism, Heteronomy and Kant's Principle of Happiness," *Pacific Philosophical Quarterly* 70, pp. 42–72.

——(1989b). "Kant's Theory of Moral Sensibility: Respect for the Moral Law and the Influence of Inclination," *Kant-Studien* 80, pp. 284–302.

——(1994). "Legislating the Moral Law," *Noûs* 28, pp. 435–64.

Richards, David A. J. (1981). "Rights and Autonomy," *Ethics* 91, pp. 3–20.

Rorty, Amelie (1976). *The Identities of Persons.* University of California Press.

Ross, W. D. (1930). *The Right and the Good.* Oxford University Press.

Sayre-McCord, Geoffrey (1988). *Essays on Moral Realism.* Cornell University Press.

Scanlon, Thomas M. (1973). "Rawls' Theory of Justice," in *Reading Rawls,* edited by Norman Daniels. Basic Books.

——(1975). "Preference and Urgency," *The Journal of Philosophy* 72, pp. 655–69.

——(1982). "Contractualism and Utilitarianism," in *Utilitarianism and Beyond,* edited by A. K. Sen and Bernard Williams. Cambridge University Press.

——(1988). "Rights, Goals, and Fairness," in *Consequentialism and Its Critics,* edited by Samuel Scheffler. Oxford University Press.

Scheffler, Samuel (1982a). *The Rejection of Consequentialism.* Oxford University Press.

——(1982b). "Ethics, Personal Identity, and Ideals of the Person" and "Reply to Darwall," *Canadian Journal of Philosophy* 12, pp. 229–46, 257–62.

——(1988). "Agent-Centered Restrictions, Rationality, and the Virtues," in *Consequentialism and Its Critics,* edited by Samuel Scheffler. Oxford University Press.

Scheid, Don (1983). "Kant's Retributivism," *Ethics* 93, pp. 262–82.

Schroeder, H. H. (1940). "Some Common Misinterpretations of the Kantian Ethics," *Philosophical Review* 49, pp. 424–46.

Sen, A. K. (1983). "Liberty and Social Choice," *The Journal of Philosophy* 80, pp. 5–28.

Sidgwick, Henry ([1907] 1981). *The Methods of Ethics*, 7th ed. Hackett Publishing.

Simmons, A. J. (1982). "Utilitarianism and Unconscious Utilitarianism," in *The Limits of Utilitarianism*, edited by H. B. Miller and W. H. Williams. University of Minnesota Press.

Singer, Peter (1979). *Practical Ethics*. Cambridge University Press.

Slote, Michael (1985). *Common Sense Morality and Consequentialism*. Routledge & Kegan Paul.

——(1989). *Beyond Optimizing*. Harvard University Press.

Stocker, Michael (1976). "The Schizophrenia of Modern Ethical Theories," *The Journal of Philosophy* 73, pp. 453–66.

——(1990). *Plural and Conflicting Values*. Oxford University Press.

Taurek, John (1977). "Should the Numbers Count?" *Philosophy and Public Affairs* 6, pp. 293–315.

Walzer, Michael (1977). *Just and Unjust Wars*. Basic Books.

——(1980). "The Moral Standing of States," *Philosophy and Public Affairs* 9, pp. 209–29.

——(1983). *Spheres of Justice*. Basic Books.

Williams, Bernard (1973). "A Critique of Utilitarianism" in *Utilitarianism: For and Against*, by J. J. C. Smart and Bernard Williams. Cambridge University Press.

——(1976). "Persons, Character, and Morality," in *The Identities of Persons*, edited by Amelie Rorty. University of California Press. Reprinted in *Moral Luck*, Cambridge University Press, 1981.

——(1981a). "Utilitarianism and Moral Self-Indulgence," in *Moral Luck*. Cambridge University Press.

——(1981b). "Internal and External Reasons," in *Moral Luck*. Cambridge University Press.

Wolf, Susan (1982). "Moral Saints," *The Journal of Philosophy* 79, pp. 419–39.

Wolff, Robert Paul (1973). *The Autonomy of Reason*. Harper & Row.

——(1977). *Understanding Rawls*. Princeton University Press.

Wood, Allen (1989). "The Emptiness of the Moral Will," *The Monist* 72, pp. 454–83.

INDEX

affirmation, defined, 72. *See also*
    rationality
agent-centered constraints
    agent-relative constraints and, 92–93
    characteristics of, 13
    consequentialism and, 26, 89–90
    defined, 12
    good and, 25, 26
    justification of, 13, 146
    Kantian consequentialism and, 11–15,
      26
    Kantianism and, 3, 14, 87–91, 172
    respect and, 125–26, 137n.1
    universalizability of, 59
    value and, 26
agent-centered prerogatives, defined, 14
agent-relative constraints, 20n.15, 92–93
agent's ends, defined, 89. *See also* ends
aid, duty to, 107–8
amoralism. *See* moral principles
appraisal respect, defined, 125. *See also*
    respect
autonomy, 79, 132, 148
autonomy of the will, 47, 81n.21, 140

Baron, Marcia, 38, 44n.35, 123nn.8, 9
beneficence
    coercion of, 148
    constraints on, 106, 123n.15, 143–47
    defined, 111, 120
    derivation of, 126
    as duty, 106–22, 144–45, 148
    laws and, 150
    moral principles and, 144–45
    as narrow duty, 119–21
    sacrifice of the innocent and, 143
    self-sacrifice and, 144–45
    two-tier structure of, 107–8
    universalizability of, 112-13, 148

    as virtue, 148
    as wide duty, 119–21
benevolence, 38, 126–27

capital punishment, 5–6, 19n.4
categorical imperative
    characteristics of, 90
    concept of the good, 47–48
    consequentialism and, 6, 10
    defined, 5
    determining ground of the will and, 85
    end-in-itself and, 47, 49
    formal principles and, 46
    free will and, 52
    hypothetical imperative and, 90–91
    interpretations of, 23
    as law, 55–56
    moral principles and, 27, 87–88
    self-love and, 54
    universalizability and, 23, 54, 56, 57
coercion, 148–49
consequentialism
    agent-centered constraints and, 26,
      89–90, 172
    categorical imperative and, 6, 10
    deliberative procedures and, 12,
      20n.10, 36–38, 44n.35, 74, 98–99
    derivation of, 84–101
    distribution sensitivity and, 157
    duty and, 12, 89, 105–6
    egoism and, 14
    end-in-itself and, 84, 89–90, 93
    equivalence argument for, 85–95
    as formal principle, 46, 48
    good and, 3, 4, 35, 84, 93
    good will and, 29, 41n.16
    harm to others and, 5
    humanity and, 114
    indirect proof of, 95–97